# Stages of History

WILLIAM BARRETT has had a long and distinguished career at New York University, where he served as chairman of the Department of Philosophy. He is widely known as one of the first philosophers to introduce existentialism to America. Barrett has been editor of *Partisan Review* and the literary critic for *Atlantic Monthly*. He is the author of *Irrational Man*, *The Illusion of Technique*, and *The Truants*, among other books. He is now Distinguished Professor of Philosophy at Pace University.

# STAGES
## *of*
# HISTORY

*Shakespeare's English Chronicles*

Phyllis Rackin

**CORNELL UNIVERSITY PRESS**
*Ithaca, New York*

*PR
2982
.R34
1990*

First published 1990 by Cornell University Press.

Printed in the United States of America

*Librarians: Library of Congress cataloging information
appears on the last page of the book.*

⊛ The paper used in the text of this publication meets the minimum requirements of American National Standard for Information Sciences—Permanence of Paper for Printed Library Materials, ANSI Z39.48-1984.

*For Ethel Rackin*

# Contents

# Preface

This book represents an attempt to historicize Shakespeare's historical practice—to situate his English history plays in the context of Tudor historiography, in his theater, and in his world. It has seemed especially important to me to construe the plays as playscripts to be performed in a theater rather than as "literature" to be read, both because that is the way they were written and also because theatrical performance by its very nature constitutes a critical point of interaction between words and the world. The theater of a world in transition, Shakespeare's playhouse constituted an arena where cultural change was not simply represented but rehearsed and enacted. It was, in short, a place where history was made.

Despite my efforts to locate Shakespeare's history plays in their own historical setting, my project is compromised by a circularity that resists the move to historicize. There is a disquieting sense in which my representations of Shakespeare's representations are *mise en abîme*, trapped in the infinite regress that appears at present inseparable from the practice of historiography. The questions I ask are the products of my own historically specific concerns; the answers I recover, even when couched in the words of sixteenth-century texts, are the products of my own selection and arrangement. The history I write, like the Renaissance history-making it describes, takes its shape from the pressures of a world where rapid cultural change has given the study of history a new urgency and an academic setting where the practice of historiography has become a subject of intense controversy and radical transformation. Chapter

1 discovers a similar urgency and describes a similar process of contestation and transformation in late sixteenth-century England. The problematics I identify as defining the Renaissance historiographic project—of causality, of anachronism and nostalgia, of historiographic representation—prefigure the issues that shape my own.

This prefiguring is also a postfiguring, a construction of the past determined by present interests and driven by the need to authorize present practice. Chapter 2 discovers in the Renaissance transition from providential to Machiavellian accounts of historical causation an anticipation of the twentieth-century movement from providential to Machiavellian interpretations of Shakespeare's history plays. The product of a time when the possibility of postulating historical causality has come into question, my analysis attributes a similar crisis to the Renaissance conflict between theological and secular explanations of historical events. The chapter ends by describing Shakespeare's emplotment of history as an obsessive circling around a lost and irrecoverable center. In so doing it also describes the structure of my own narrative. The paradoxical union of anachronism and nostalgia that Chapter 3 finds in the Renaissance sense of history constitutes a similar pre/postfiguration of a historiographic project driven and finally disappointed by an intensified sense of the distance and difference that separate the history-writing present from the historical past it seeks to recover. Struggling to represent an absent past, my narrative finds that past engaged in a similar struggle, one that anticipates my efforts in the last two chapters to recover the voices of the women and common people who were marginalized or excluded in previous historical writing.

In the light of the contemporary revolution in historiography, the old positivist claims about an objectively "true" history beyond the reach of ideology seem impossible to sustain. Because the production of history must take place within a particular historical situation, there is no ahistorical vantage point from which history can be written. This lack, however, does not mean that the only alternative is solipsism or an aestheticization of history as a kind of fiction beyond the reach of ethical judgment. If the history I write is the product of my own fabrication, it is not fabricated out of whole cloth. Moreover, I who write am the product of historical fabrication, and so is the language I use. The same historical embeddedness that prevents any history from being written under the aspect of eternity also provides the medium that connects past and present, the matrix of the often obscure process of cultural generation. The words I use and the categories of my thought are not only the medium that imposes contemporary designs on the history I describe; they are also my inheritance from that history, the medium by which it imposes its designs on me.

The discursive exclusions of an elitist, patriarchal culture that marginalized the roles of women and of common men in Shakespeare's historical sources helped to transmit a legacy of oppression that can still be seen in the writing of contemporary historians (and of scholars of Shakespeare's plays) and also in the material world I inhabit. To oppose those exclusions, I turn to an oppositional history—to the recent scholarship on the place of Shakespeare's stage in the changing world of early modern England and to the contemporary social history that looks beyond customary sources to discover the traces of the daily experience of ordinary people. In such a history, Shakespearean texts are reconstituted as playscripts designed for performance in a volatile theatrical setting where the erasures in the official historical record could be restored and the voices silenced by the repressions of the dominant discourse could speak and be heard.

Resituating Shakespeare's history plays in terms of these oppositional histories and representing them as a series of negotiations between separate, and often opposed, discursive fields, my text itself attempts to perform such a negotiation. To write it, I had to venture beyond the disciplinary boundaries in which I was trained. I did so with considerable uneasiness, but I was fortunate in the help I received. Cornell University Press provided me with the best of readers, Scott McMillin and Mary Beth Rose. The staffs of the General Honors Program at the University of Pennsylvania and the Folger and Furness Shakespeare libraries were unfailingly generous with their time; Linda Wiedmann and Georgianna Ziegler deserve special mention. My graduate students at the University of Pennsylvania provided challenging questions, bright insights, and helpful bibliographic citations; I especially thank Greg Bredbeck, Gwynne

Kennedy, Gerry O'Sullivan, and Jean Peterson. My colleagues Roger Abrahams, Nina Auerbach, Rebecca Bushnell, Lucienne Frappier-Mazur, Maureen Quilligan, Peter Stallybrass and Robert Y. Turner all read portions of the manuscript, as did Alvia Golden, David Scott Kastan, Leah Marcus, Gabrielle Spiegel, and Barbara Traister; I am much indebted to their generosity, their critical acumen, and their erudition. Cary Mazer was an infallible source of information about theater history. Jean Howard, with her characteristic generosity, read the manuscript twice; her incisive criticisms helped me to understand what I was doing. Carroll Smith-Rosenberg and Donald Rackin read and reread it more times than I can remember; from beginning to end the project was sustained by their emotional support and shaped by their intellectual challenge. To all these good teachers and magnanimous friends, I am indebted for encouragement, for careful readings and incisive criticisms, and for many helpful suggestions, large and small.

I am also indebted to the Mellon Foundation for a grant during the summer of 1984 which enabled me to begin the project, to the ACLS for a fellowship during the academic year 1988–89 which enabled me to complete it, and to the journals and publishers that gave me permission to use material from articles I had earlier published: to *Shakespeare Quarterly* for portions of "The Role of the Audience in Shakespeare's *Richard II*," 36 (Autumn 1985), 262–81, and to Northwestern University Press for portions of "Temporality, Anachronism, and Presence in Shakespeare's English Histories," *Renaissance Drama* n.s. 17 (May 1987), 140–75, both of which were incorporated in Chapter 3; to The Johns Hopkins University Press for portions of "Anti-Historians: Women's Roles in Shakespeare's Histories," *Theatre Journal* 37 (October 1985), 329–44, to the University of Delaware Press for portions of "Patriarchal History and Female Subversion in *King John*," from *King John: New Perspectives*, ed. Deborah T. Curren-Aquino, and to Wayne State University Press for portions of "Genealogical Anxiety and Female Authority: The Return of the Repressed in Shakespeare's Histories," from *Contending Kingdoms*, ed. Peter L. Rudnytsky and Marie-Rose Logan, all of which were incorporated in Chapter 4.

PHYLLIS RACKIN

*Philadelphia, Pennsylvania*

# Stages of History

Scene from *Titus Andronicus*, drawing. Longleat Portland Papers I f.159ᵛ. Reproduced by permission of the Marquess of Bath, Longleat House, Warminster, Wiltshire, Great Britain.

# 1

## Making History

The earliest Shakespearean illustration we have (ca. 1595) depicts characters from *Titus Andronicus*. With its anachronistic mixture of contemporary English and ancient Roman costume, the drawing can stand as an emblem for Shakespeare's peculiar situation in the history of historical consciousness. Despite the ancient Roman setting of the play, the two figures at the left, soldiers, wear Elizabethan military costume and carry halberds. In this they follow the standard practice of medieval artists, who depicted biblical personages wearing the costumes of medieval Europe, and medieval writers, who depicted pre-Christian Romans as knights and ladies going to mass in church.[1] Titus, by contrast, is dressed in a costume that might have been copied from a Roman statue, a "classical"-looking, draped garment that, regardless of its source or authenticity, clearly manifests an effort at historical re-creation. In this, he looks forward to the practice of the age to come, when a new historical consciousness would transform the images of the past on canvas and stage alike.[2]

In the scene from *Titus Andronicus*, the two modes coexist:

[1] Peter Burke, *The Renaissance Sense of the Past* (London: Edward Arnold, 1969), pp. 1–2. See also Thomas Greene, *The Light in Troy: Imitation and Discovery in Renaissance Poetry* (New Haven: Yale University Press, 1982), pp. 242–47.

[2] In addition to the books cited in note 1, see F. J. Levy, *Tudor Historical Thought* (San Marino, Calif.: The Huntington Library, 1967); F. Smith Fussner, *The Historical Revolution: English Historical Writing and Thought 1580–1640* (London: Routledge and Kegan Paul, 1962); and Arthur B. Ferguson, *Clio Unbound: Perception of the Social and Cultural Past in Renaissance England* (Durham, N.C.: Duke University Press, 1979).

the Elizabethan soldiers attend their Roman general on a stage where past and present confront each other as, perhaps, at no other time in history. The very term "Renaissance" indicates how thoroughly Shakespeare's world was conditioned by its relationship to the past. The study of history was highly esteemed throughout the period. In rediscovering the world of antiquity, the Renaissance humanists gave shape to their own. Cicero's tribute to history as *"the light of trueth, the witnesse of tymes, the Mistresse of lyfe, the Messenger of antiquitie, and the lyfe of memorye, preservinge from oblivion deedes worthye of memorye,* atchieved thorough longe processe of tymes" was endlessly quoted.[3] The English humanist Sir Thomas Elyot made history the center of his educational program: "Surely if a noble man do thus seriously and diligently rede histories," he declared, "I dare affirme there is no study or science for him of equal commoditie and pleasure, havynge regarde to every tyme and age."[4] When Roger Ascham, who had been tutor to Princess Elizabeth, came to write his own treatise on education, he also commended the study of history, which, he wrote, "could bring excellent learning and breed staid judgment in taking any like matter in hand."[5] Matthew Coignet emphasized history's power to provide vicarious experience: "We do gaine more by reading [histories] in our youth; then by whatsoever is either attributed to sence, or experience of old men, or to suche as have beene in farre voyages." Moreover, the lessons of history, better than those of life, were taught "without hasarde, expense, or daunger." History taught "the preceptes eyther of politicke lawes, or of the art of warre." Its examples "inflame us to vertue"; and the fear of its testimony could act as a deterrent from wickedness: "There is no doubt but manye tyrauntes have refrayned the executing of a number of mischiefes they have determined, for feare of the spotte which a historie would staine them with."[6]

---

[3]Matthieu Coignet, *Politique Discourses upon trueth and Lying*, trans. Sir Edward Hoby (London, 1586), STC 5486, p. 71, translating Cicero. Cf. Leonard Dean, "Tudor Theories of History Writing," *University of Michigan Contributions in Modern Philology* 1 (1947), 2.

[4]*The Boke Named the Governour*, edited from the edition of 1531 by Henry H. S. Croft (London: Kegan, Paul, Trench, 1883), 1:91.

[5]Roger Ascham, *The Schoolmaster* (1570), ed. Lawrence V. Ryan (Ithaca: Cornell University Press, 1967), p. 129.

[6]Coignet, pp. 70–72.

The power and scope of history seemed boundless. For Elyot, history comprehended "all thinge that is necessarie to be put in memorie"—Pliny's *Natural History*, holy scriptures, Homer's epics, and the fables of Aesop all included.[7] For Sir Walter Ralegh (1614), it began with the creation, giving "so fair and piercing eyes to our mind, that we plainly behold . . . that great world as it was then, when but new to itself." The best of human knowledge, history could triumph over mortality itself: "among many other benefits, for which it hath been honoured, in this one it triumpheth over all human knowledge, that it hath . . . triumphed over time, which, besides it, nothing but eternity hath triumphed over. . . . it hath made us acquainted with our dead ancestors; and, out of the depth and darkness of the earth, delivered us their memory and fame."[8] History, it seemed, could raise the dead, inspire the living, reveal the secrets of statecraft, teach the details of military tactics, expose the deceits of fortune, and illuminate the ways of providence. It could even cure the sick: Coignet reports that "*Alphonus* sayd of *Qu. Cursius*, that he was soner healed by his history, then his Phisitions."[9]

Nowhere was this interest in recovering the past and shaping the present by its models more lively than in England. There were obvious local reasons for the Elizabethan preoccupation with history. The Wars of the Roses, which had occupied much of the preceding century, destroying families, devastating the land, and disrupting ancient allegiances, made the study of recent English history a pressing concern for a nation that wished to preserve the peace and political stability of the present and to avoid the mistakes that had led to the insecurity of the past. As Edward Hall reminded his readers, "What noble man liveth at this daie, or what gentleman of any auncient stocke or progeny is clere, whose linage hath not ben infested and plaged with this unnaturall devision."[10] Moreover, the Tudors, a new

---

[7]*Governour*, 2:387–400.

[8]Sir Walter Ralegh, *The History of the World* in *The Works of Sir Walter Ralegh, Kt., now first collected* (1829; rpt. New York: Burt Franklin, 1966), Preface, 2:v-vi.

[9]Coignet, p. 70.

[10]*The Union of the Two Noble and Illustre Famelies of Lancastre & Yorke* (1548), B1ʳ, (rpt. London: J. Johnson et al., 1809), p. 1. Cf., however, Paul Murray Kendall, *The Yorkist Age: Daily Life during the Wars of the Roses* (New York: Doubleday, 1962), pp. 8 and passim, for an argument that Tudor historians

dynasty whose founder had won his crown in battle, sponsored official histories that constructed a myth of ancient descent and providential purpose in order to authenticate their questionable claim to the throne.[11]

For subjects as well as sovereigns, the emergent nation-state made the study of English history a matter of pride and interest as well as an essential source of self-definition. Living in a time of rapid social, economic, and political change, Renaissance readers looked to the past for the roots that would stabilize and legitimate their new identities.[12] The ideology of the "Ancient Constitution," for instance, emerged during this period to assert the antiquity of English liberties in order to legitimate a new political consciousness.[13] Individual social status was also rationalized historically: having a history, in fact, was exactly equivalent to having a place in the status system, a connection that was implicit in the rage to acquire coats of arms (i.e., historical genealogies) and explicit in the prefatory letter to Hall's *Union*, in the rhetorical question, "What diversitie is betwene a

---

exaggerated the unsettling effects of the civil wars in order to emphasize the benefits of strong Tudor government.

[11]See Hall's original title, "The Union of the Two Noble and Illustre Famelies of Lancastre & Yorke, beeyng long in continual discension for the croune of this noble realme, with all the actes done in bothe the tymes of the princes, bothe of the one linage and of the other, beginnyng at the tyme of Kyng Henry the fowerth, the first aucthor of this devision, and so successively proceadyng to the reigne of the high and prudent prince, Kyng Henry the Eight, the undubitate flower and very heire of both the sayd linages." See also his emphasis that the genealogical authority of the Tudor dynasty is indisputable, resulting as it does from the union between "Kyng Henry the seventh and the lady Elizabeth his moste worthy Quene, the one beeyng indubitate heire of the hous of Lancastre, and the other of Yorke..." (*Union*, p. 1).

[12]This mechanism is vividly figured in Walter Benjamin's image of the angel of history: "His face is turned toward the past.... The angel would like to stay, awaken the dead, and make whole what has been smashed. But a storm is blowing from Paradise: it has got caught in his wings with such violence that the angel can no longer close them. This storm irresistibly propels him into the future to which his back is turned, while the pile of debris before him grows skyward. This storm is what we call progress." "Theses on the Philosophy of History," in *Illuminations*, trans. Harry Zohn, ed. Hannah Arendt (New York: Schocken Books, 1969), pp. 257–58.

[13]See J. G. A. Pocock, *The Ancient Constitution and the Feudal Law: English Historical Thought in the Seventeenth Century* (New York: W. W. Norton, 1967), chaps. 2 and 3, and *The Machiavellian Moment: Florentine Political Thought and the Atlantic Republican Tradition* (Princeton: Princeton University Press, 1975), pp. 340–41.

noble prince & a poore begger . . . if after their death there be left of theim no remembrance or token."[14]

Many factors, ranging from an individual need to assert an identifiable continuum after a period of political chaos to official court constructions of the past, encouraged an intense popular interest in English history. Warner's *Albion's England* (1586) had seven editions in a period of twenty years.[15] John Stow's *Summarie of Englyshe Chronicles*, published in 1565, had ten by 1611.[16] Other historical works, ranging from verse narratives like the *Mirror for Magistrates* to Raphael Holinshed's massive prose *Chronicles of England, Scotland and Ireland* to Shakespeare's English history plays, enjoyed comparable popularity among a large and varied audience.[17]

— II —

Despite the widespread interest in history and the overwhelming chorus of praise for the benefits its study could confer, there was no clear consensus about its nature and purpose; for this was a period of transition, when radically different conceptions of history and historiography were endorsed, often by the same writer. Three great innovations, all originating in Italy, were changing English historiography during the second half of the sixteenth century—a new interest in causation, a recognition of anachronism, and a questioning of textual authority.[18] Like all great ideological shifts, however, these were gradual, affecting different writers at different times and with different degrees of intensity and self-consciousness. Thus, the adoption of newer ideas and methods did not always mean the immediate

[14]For an extended discussion of this point, see Chapter 5.

[15]Levy, p. 220.

[16]Irving Ribner, *The English History Play in the Age of Shakespeare* (Princeton: Princeton University Press, 1957), p. 6.

[17]Levy, chap. 6: "The Popularization of History," in *Tudor Historical Thought*, pp. 202–36. Cf. Alfred Harbage, *Shakespeare's Audience* (New York: Columbia University Press, 1941), pp. 48–49. Harbage points out that the gallery receipts for the opening performance of *1 Henry VI* "set the all-time record of 1,840d" and that its overall receipts during the first season were "surpassed by only one other play mentioned in Henslowe's *Diary*."

[18]Peter Burke (p. 1) characterizes these as "the interest in causation," "the sense of anachronism," and "the awareness of evidence."

6

aband[ ]                    [ ]hen the two were logically
oppos[ ]                     [ ]d many of the older ideas
persist[ ]                        [ ]:entury.[19]

The [ ]                    es was the gradual separation [ ]                    xplanations of events in
terms [ ]                       providence were giving
way to Machiavellian analyses of second causes—the effects
of political situations and the impact of human will and ca-
pabilities. Medieval chronicles, often written in monasteries,
were informed by the religious perspective that viewed all
human actions under the aspect of eternity. The first cause
of all things was the will of God, the alpha and omega who
contained past, present, and future in one eternal, unchanging presence. The secular events recorded in the chronicles
were simply set down in the order of their occurrence, usually with little or no attempt to discover or supply the causal
links that might have transformed them into a connected
story unfolding in human time. Living in a universe governed by the absolute, unchanging, but finally inscrutable
will of God where the sacred history revealed in the Bible
was the only sure truth, medieval chroniclers had little impetus to probe the material, human causes of secular historical change. The medieval model for describing the progress
of human [ ]                    fortune, an endlessly
recurrent [ ]                    designed to show the
transience [ ]                    the hub, the still center that r[ ]                    nd the intersection of
time with [ ]                    be found.

The ne[ ]                    Renaissance still made
reference [ ]                    cause behind historical
change; [ ]                    rn with the life of this
world, they described historical causation primarily in terms of
"second causes," that is, of human actions and their consequences; and they evaluated actions more in terms of their ex-

[19]As S. K. Heninger has argued (in "The Problematics of Reality in the English
Renaissance") an older "epistemology of faith" coexisted throughout the period
with an emergent "epistemology of empiricism," but "neither was privileged
above the other." I am grateful to Professor Heninger for giving me a copy of
this excellent unpublished paper.

pediency, less in terms of their morality. Sir Walter Ralegh mul-
tiplies examples of royal misfortunes to demonstrate that "ill
doing hath always been attended with ill success," for "the
judgments of God are for ever unchangeable": Henry VI suffered a "great storm" of misfortunes in punishment for "his
grandfather's grievous faults," and so did Richard II for the
crimes of *his* grandfather, Edward III.[20] But Ralegh could still
write, "To say that GOD was pleased to have it so, were a true,
but an idle answer (for his secret will is the cause of all things)."[21]
In more extreme versions, the new doctrine meant that "all
things roll and run at a venture, and . . . there is no other cause
of good and evill accidents of this life, but either fortune or els
the will of man";[22] but for the most part the histories cheerfully
mingled providential and Machiavellian explanations, with no
apparent sense of contradiction.

Holinshed's *Chronicle*, for instance, in describing the defeat
of the Earl of Huntington's rebellion against Henry IV, starts
with a detailed, circumstantial account of the tactical errors that
caused the defeat. It relates that the earl "set fire on diverse
houses in the towne, thinking that the assailants would leave
the assault and rescue their goods" and describes the failure of
the ruse when the earl's own men, "hearing noise, and seeing
this fire in the towne, thought verelie that King Henrie had béene
come thither with his puissance, and thereupon fled without
measure, everie man making shift to save himselfe." Thus, Holinshed explains, "that which the lords devised for their helpe
wrought their destruction; for if the armie that laie without the
towne had not mistaken the matter, when they saw the houses
on fire, they might easilie have succoured their chéefeteins in
the towne." His explanation is detailed and circumstantial: the
chieftains in town "were assailed but with a few of the townes-
men ["the bailiffe of the towne with fourescore archers"], in
comparison of the great multitude ["twentie thousand men"]
that laie abroad in the fields." But it is also providential: "But

[20]Ralegh, pp. viii–xi.
[21]Quoted by Levy, p. 290.
[22]Plutarch, *The Morals*, trans. Philemon Holland, 1603, p. 538, quoted by
Michael Quinn in "Providence in Shakespeare's Yorkist Plays," *Shakespeare
Quarterly* 10 (1959), 45.

such was the ordinance of the mightie Lord of hostes, who disposeth althings at his pleasure."[23]

E. M. W. Tillyard cites Hall's *Union* as the chief source of the providentialism he finds in Shakespeare,[24] but even Hall was capable of mingling first and second causes in his accounts of historical causation. The misfortunes of Henry VI, he writes, were attributed by some to Henry's lack of wit and "coward stommack," by others to "the stroke & punishment of God" because "the kingedome, whiche Henry the .iiii. hys grandfather wrongfully gat . . . could not by very divyne iustice, longe contynew in that iniurious stocke."[25] Hall clearly seems to favor the providential view that "God by his divine prouidence, punished the offence of the grandfather in the sonnes sonne." He attributes the charge of cowardice to Henry's enemies and associates the charge of foolishness with the "vulgare opinion" and "wisdom of this world" that is "folishenes before God." Nonetheless, it is significant that even Hall is able to entertain rationalistic explanations of historical causality along with the providential ones he prefers. Despite the far-reaching implications of the conflict between the two views of historical causation, Renaissance historians often resolved it by the simple expedient of explaining the same course of events on both levels, often without even going so far as Hall does to acknowledge that they conflicted.

Another major innovation in English Renaissance historiography, also introduced from Italy, was awareness of anachronism. Like the new interest in second causes, this new conception of temporality was implicated in the process of secularization, in the movement from a vision centered on the timeless province of God to the humanistic consciousness that assigned new importance to the transitory material life of this

---

[23]Raphael Holinshed, *Chronicles of England, Scotland and Ireland* (1587; rpt. London: J. Johnson et al., 1808), 3:11.

[24]*Shakespeare's History Plays* (New York: Collier Books, 1962), first published 1944, pp. 11, 51–67, and passim.

[25]*Union*, pp. 285–86. This point is made by David Scott Kastan, *Shakespeare and the Shapes of Time* (Hanover, N.H.: University Press of New England, 1982), pp. 15–16. Kastan also cites the author of John Tiptoft's tragedy in *The Mirror for Magistrates*, who criticizes Hall's practice of providing alternative explanations for the same event: "For this or that (sayeth he) [i.e., Hall] he felt the whip."

world. Even the words that distinguish the profane from the holy—"secular" and "temporal"—indicate how thoroughly that distinction is involved in the distinction between the timeless and the historical. In the Middle Ages, a person who entered a monastery was said to leave time behind (*relinquere saeculum*).[26] The Renaissance experience of *secularization* was, quite literally, a movement into time. Regarded under the aspect of eternity, the changing pageant of earthly human life is illusory because events are seen from a perspective that transcends time. Collapsing time into space, a medieval tapestry could represent various stages of the same event, and a medieval painting could bring together images of biblical personages or saints with those of contemporary donors. Renaissance painters continued the practice of bringing the living and the dead or two temporally separate representations of the same person together in one picture, but their settings became increasingly specific in place and time. As Wylie Sypher explains, they learned to use light as "a local and secular effect, changing with the hour and cast from a given source."[27]

Typically, medieval writers of history display no sense of anachronism: for them, all history is present history: Theseus and Alexander the Great are knights, and the customs, clothing, and manners of the historians' own times are uncritically ascribed to other times and places. Caxton refers to Vergil as a "grete clerke," and Gavin Douglas speaks of "Sir Diomed" and the "nuns of Bacchus."[28] It was not until the Renaissance, with the new recognition that the past was genuinely different from the present, that historians questioned the authenticity of venerable records that had been accepted for centuries despite their use of a vocabulary and references to objects that were unknown at the time of their supposed origin.

The Donation of Constantine, for example, had been accepted for centuries when it suddenly came under attack from a number of scholars working independently in the fifteenth century. Purportedly written in the fourth century for Pope Sylvester I, this document gave him and his successors temporal power over

---

[26]Burke, p. 19.

[27]Wylie Sypher, *The Ethic of Time: Structures of Experience in Shakespeare* (New York: Seabury Press, 1976), p. 42.

[28]Greene, pp. 242–43.

Italy. Of the various arguments that exposed the document as a crude forgery, Lorenzo Valla's was the most extensive, citing the many anachronisms in language and details that showed it was a later fabrication. Some of Valla's arguments are purely philological ("Who ever heard 'tiara' [*phrygium*] used in Latin?"); but most often they combine philological with antiquarian evidence to provide an elaborate demonstration that the writer of the document was unfamiliar with Constantine and the world in which he lived:

> He says, "of purest gold and precious gems". The ignorant fellow did not know that a diadem was made of coarse cloth or perhaps of silk. . . . [but] imagines that it is of gold, with a gold band and gems such as kings now usually add. But Constantine was not a king, nor would he have dared to call himself king, nor to adorn himself with royal ceremony. He was Emperor of the Romans, not king. Where there is a king, there is no republic. But in the republic there were many, even at the same time, who were *imperatores* [generals]; for Cicero frequently writes thus, "Marcus Cicero, imperator, to some other imperator, greeting": though, later on, the Roman ruler, as the highest of all, is called by way of distinctive title the Emperor.[29]

As Valla's biting rhetoric reveals, his interest in exposing the anachronisms in the Donation was more than academic. Marshaling evidence of historical change to discredit papal authority, he anticipates a crucial strategy of Reformation polemic. Luther used Valla's arguments in his struggle with the pope, and John Foxe used them in his *Actes and Monuments*.[30] The recognition of anachronism, in fact, was a basic premise of Reformation thought. No longer seen as an institution unchanged from its beginnings, the contemporary church was contrasted with the church as it had been before centuries of Roman Catholic corruption had polluted it.[31] A great impetus for the close scrutiny of historical records was the reformers' desire to purge the church of those corruptions and restore Christianity to its original pure form. In so doing, however, they helped to render

[29]Burke, pp. 56–58; cf. Levy, pp. 36, 77.
[30]Denys Hay, *Annalists and Historians: Western Historiography from the Eighth to the Eighteenth Centuries* (London: Methuen, 1977), pp. 92–93; Fussner, *Historical Revolution*, p. 18; Levy, p. 102.
[31]Levy, p. x.

all textual authority problematic. Once biblical interpretation became a subject of passionate dispute, the Bible was no longer taken as simply "given" as the eternally present word of God; rather, it came to be seen as a historical document, the product of a particular time and place.[32] Translated into the vernacular, subjected to different interpretations from rival Christian sects, the Bible became an object of contestation in which alternative words contended to translate the meaning of the original text and alternative interpretations contended to explicate it. In "a situation where Catholics and Protestants each worked to undermine the foundations of the other,"[33] philology "complicated the authority of the sacred text, shook its absolute status by calling attention to the specific circumstances of its production."[34] In such a context, the writings of secular authorities could hardly escape the same skeptical questioning that formed the basis of theological debate.

A major impetus for the Elizabethan interest in history was the often-reiterated faith of the humanists that the past could provide lessons for the present and models for the future. Looking to the past to understand the present, Tudor historians focused on historical figures and situations that provided instructive analogues for contemporary persons and predicaments.[35] Elyot advised that English princes should "studiously" read Caesar because "thereof may be taken necessary instructions concernynge the wars against Irisshe men or Scottes, who be of the same rudenes and wilde disposition that the Suises and Britons were in the time of Cesar."[36] The history of King John, the theme of the first English history play (John Bale's *Kynge Johan*, ca. 1539), was a popular subject in the sixteenth century, but the story of Magna Carta was usually omitted (as it is in Shakespeare's play on John). Instead, sixteenth-century accounts emphasized John's quarrel with Rome, celebrating his defiance of the pope and depicting him as a prototype of Henry VIII. It was not until the seventeenth century, when royal au-

[32]Burke, pp. 3, 60–62.
[33]Burke, p. 149.
[34]Greene, p. 47.
[35]M. M. Reese, *The Cease of Majesty: A Study of Shakespeare's History Plays* (London: Edward Arnold, 1961), pp. 12–14.
[36]Pp. 87–89.

thority was once more subject to question and attack, that the story of Magna Carta became historically significant.

As long as humanist historians retained their faith that human experience was always and everywhere the same, they could look to the past for sure guides to the conduct of present affairs.[37] But the progress of Renaissance historiography and theory of history was characterized by an increasing sense of alienation from the past, of its ineluctable otherness, even while the desire to know and recover that past remained intense, lending a deep poignancy to the entire historiographic enterprise.[38] Historical fact was now open to question, and historical truth was now debatable. Records were subject to loss or distortion, witnesses could be biased, and all things were vulnerable to the ravages of time.

—— III ——

On his way to the Tower, where he will be murdered, the little Prince Edward in *Richard III* initiates a curious bit of dialogue, for which there is no precedent in Shakespeare's sources: "Did Julius Caesar build that place?" he asks. "He did, my gracious lord, begin that place," Buckingham answers, "which since, succeeding ages have re-edified." But this answer is not enough for the prince, who continues his inquiry:

> *Prince.* Is it upon record, or else reported
>           Successively from age to age, he built it?
> *Buck.* Upon record, my gracious lord.
> *Prince.* But say, my lord, it were not regist'red,
>           Methinks the truth should live from age to age,
>           As 'twere retail'd to all posterity,
>           Even to the general all-ending day.[39]
>
> (III.i. 69–78)

[37]Levy, p. 290.

[38]See Greene, p. 57 and passim, on "the humanist pathos" of the Renaissance.

[39]*The Riverside Shakespeare*, ed. G. Blakemore Evans et al. (Boston: Houghton Mifflin, 1974). Unless otherwise indicated, all citations to Shakespeare's plays will be from this edition.

The little Prince's historical sophistication is strikingly precocious, as his uncle Richard is quick to observe ("So wise so young, they say do never live long" [III.i. 79].) It is also anachronistic—historically as well as biographically premature. For it was not until the sixteenth century that Englishmen subjected the records and monuments of the past to the kind of critical scrutiny that the doomed prince brings to bear upon his final prison. The difficulty of recovering the past, the need to check written records against physical relics and to compare both with oral tradition, were not likely to have occurred to historians in Prince Edward's time, let alone to a child.

Buckingham's pun on "edify" associates the building with the oral historical report, both constructed "successively from age to age," and both serving as a present record of past glory; but the word probably did not take on its metaphorical meaning until the sixteenth century (the first instance listed in the *OED* is dated 1534), and the use of physical remains as historical evidence was virtually unknown in Buckingham's time. The monuments of the past were simply "there": marvels to be wondered at, but not historically meaningful evidence. The edifices did not become "edifying" until the Renaissance, when the recognition that history was not necessarily identical with historiography led to an increased reliance on physical remains to correct or corroborate the written accounts of the past, which were no longer accepted as authentic simply because they existed.

Historiographic writing no longer had a direct, unequivocal relation with historical truth. Alternative accounts of historical events and opposed interpretations of their causes and significance now threatened each other's credibility, a process intensified by the development of the printing industry and the spread of literacy. With the invention of movable type and the proliferation of written texts, variant versions of the same event could coexist in the same libraries to challenge each other's authority. Lowering the price of texts, the new technology also diminished their value. The historian became a problematic figure: no longer an authority simply by virtue of his authorship, he came to be seen as a fallible human being, located in a particular time and place, limited by ignorance, subject to bias and blindness, struggling to recover a past in which he had not lived.

Like Shakespeare's precocious little prince, the historian had to compare written record with oral tradition and both with physical relics and, when they did not agree, struggle in his own mind to discover the truth that lay behind them.

One response to this disillusionment was the development of antiquarianism. Physical evidence became more important as verbal accounts no longer convinced by the mere fact of their existence. In the Middle Ages, authors were by definition "authorities," and their accounts were ipso facto "authentic." Bede's description of Hadrian's Wall, for instance, is based on a text by Vegetius, even though Bede himself lived near the wall and could easily have observed it. Gregory of Tours displays the same preference for authority over observation when he recounts a miracle he never saw even though he was present on the occasion when it supposedly occurred. He accepts the written testimony that contradicted his own experience, believing that he was simply unworthy to see the miracle (*haec videre non merui*).[40] Living in a world where authority and faith often contradicted the evidence of the physical senses, these historians were ready to accept a reality that did not meet their eyes. Bede's observation of the wall or Gregory's failure to observe the miracle could no more challenge the written accounts they relied on than a worshiper's physical experience of eating the consecrated Host could challenge the doctrine of transubstantiation.

During the sixteenth century, all this was to change. Historians became antiquarians, using material remains—Roman roads, monuments, inscriptions, coins—to judge the accuracy of written records. Unlike the earlier humanists, who looked to the past for moral and political guidance in the conduct of present life, the antiquarians, replacing rhetoric with archaeology, were motivated by a curiosity about the actual details of past life rather than by a desire to discover large, significant patterns.[41] "The classical world," as Felix Gilbert notes, "was no longer what classical writers reported, but what a scholar re-

[40]Burke, p. 7.
[41]J. G. A. Pocock, "The Sense of History in Renaissance England," in *William Shakespeare: His World, His Work, His Influence*, ed. John Andrews (New York: Charles Scribner's Sons, 1987), 1:156.

constructed after having evaluated all relevant material."[42] Although the Elizabethan Society of Antiquaries had no official standing, it held regular meetings, beginning in about 1586, where members presented the results of their research as well as evidence for their findings.[43] Explicitly discouraged by King James, the society stopped meeting around 1608,[44] at about the same time the vogue of the history play on the English stage came to an end; but the scholarly scrutiny of historical records was to continue and improve during the coming years.

By the end of the Elizabethan period, popular interest in history probably owed at least as much to its exotic otherness as to its present relevance. Steven Mullaney has pointed out that

> the late sixteenth and early seventeenth centuries collected and exhibited not only the trappings but also the customs, languages, and even the members of other cultures on a scale that was unprecedented. In forums ranging from wonder-cabinets to court masques and popular romances, from royal entries and traveller's narratives to the popular playhouses of Elizabethan London, the pleasures of the strange are invoked to solicit our attention as spectators, auditors, or readers.[45]

Like a geographically remote culture, a temporally remote historical era could appeal to a growing appetite for experience of what Mullaney calls "cultural Others," a taste that marks the final stage in the Renaissance experience of alienation from the past.

[42]Felix Gilbert, "The Renaissance Interest in History," in *Art, Science, and History in the Renaissance*, ed. Charles S. Singleton (Baltimore: Johns Hopkins University Press, 1967), p. 384; see also Ferguson, p. 81: "By mid-century, tombs, coins, artifacts of all sorts, ruins of ancient walls, inscriptions—to say nothing of the bones of prehistoric animals taken for those of legendary giants— were all coming to be recognized as the 'footprints' (the word was a favorite) of early societies."

[43]Fussner, *Historical Revolution*, pp. 92–94; May McKisack, *Medieval History in the Tudor Age* (Oxford: Clarendon Press, 1971), pp. 155–69.

[44]Richard Helgerson, "The Land Speaks: Cartography, Chorography, and Subversion in Renaissance England," in *Representing the English Renaissance*, ed. Stephen Greenblatt (Berkeley: University of California Press, 1988; originally published in *Representations* 16 [1986]), p. 344; Fussner, p. 101. See Helgerson, *passim*, for a subtle and persuasive analysis of the ways the antiquarian movement was implicated in subversion and cultural change.

[45]"Strange Things, Gross Terms, Curious Customs: The Rehearsal of Cultures in the Late Renaissance," *Representations* 3 (1983), 43.

That experience of alienation, locked in a conflicted relationship with a continuing desire to appropriate or colonize the past,
constituted the problematic of Renaissance historiography. In a
time of rapid and profound cultural change, the study of history—the study of change itself—took on a new urgency, as did
the desire to recover and preserve a rapidly receding past. The
emergence of the Renaissance city and the growth of commerce
and capitalism both contributed to the experiences of loss and
of temporal isolation that conditioned the development of Renaissance historiography. The invention and proliferation of
mechanical clocks is a good case in point. They were, as David
Landes points out, both "sign and consequence of . . . a new,
urban social order."[46] As such, they literally reconstituted the
nature of time. Medieval Europe told time by the sun and the
canonical hours. Time was measured in "natural, equal fractions
of day and night": as days lengthened and shortened, the daylight hours followed suit. In this agrarian society, the length of
the hours varied with the seasons, increasing in summer, decreasing as the daylight decreased in winter. With the rise of
the urban system of wage labor and the proliferation of mechanical clocks, the workday was defined in equal hours, me-
chanically determined and invariant.[47] No longer following the
rhythms of nature, time became an abstract system to measure
human work in monetary terms. Metaphors expressing this link-
age exhorted the wise "spending" of time and warned against
its "waste."[48]

[46]David Landes, "Clocks: Revolution in Time," *History Today* (1984), 23. Cf.
Lewis Mumford's argument—quoted by Carlo Cipolla, *Clocks and Culture, 1300–
1700* (New York: Walker, 1967), p. 60—that it is not the steam engine but the
clock that constitutes "the key machine of the modern industrial world." The
date of their invention is unknown, but there are many references to clocks in
late thirteenth-century texts. See David Landes, *Revolution in Time: Clocks and
the Making of the Modern World* (Cambridge: Harvard University Press, 1984),
pp. 55–56. Spring-driven clock mechanisms were probably invented in the
beginning of the fifteenth century, allowing the construction of portable clocks.
By the sixteenth century domestic clocks and watches had become relatively
common, and pocket watches had appeared. In the development of clock-
making as in the development of modern historiography, England lagged behind the continent, but by the last two decades of the sixteenth century, both
the new technology and the new historiography had become established there
(Cipolla, pp. 48–49, 126, 66–67).

[47]Landes, "Clocks: Revolution in Time," pp. 23, 22, 24.

[48]Russell Fraser, *The War against Poetry* (Princeton: Princeton University Press,
1970), chap. 3: "The Thief of Time," pp. 52–76.

The inexorable, mechanical progression of time is the subject of Jacques's pessimimistic description in *As You Like It* of the seven ages of man, an ineluctable process that ends in second childhood and mere oblivion, "sans everything." A fifteenth- or sixteenth-century timepiece often served as a *memento mori*, taking the form of a skull and inscribed, Landes notes, with a "motto reminding the user that every . . . tick brought him closer to death."[49] Time becomes the implacable enemy in countless Renaissance sonnets, destroying youth and beauty, obliterating the best of human achievements. The only defense was writing, but writing itself was now seen as subject to the universal process of mutability. The little prince in *Richard III* thinks that even without a historical record the truth of Julius Caesar's achievement should "live from age to age . . . even to the general all-ending day"; but Shakespeare's King John sees history in much more pessimistic terms when he describes himself as "a scribbled form, drawn with a pen upon a parchment" that "shrink[s] up" in the fire that will destroy it (V.vii.32–34).

To Dante, the voice of Vergil was "hoarse from long silence." To Lorenzo Valla, "not only has no one been able to speak Latin for many centuries, but no one has even known how to read it."[50] Even the language of Chaucer had already become archaic to his countrymen living a mere two centuries after he wrote.[51] The heroic ambition of Renaissance historiography to recover the noble names and glorious deeds of past heroes from the universal grave of oblivion was threatened by the very power that made it necessary. Time, the universal enemy of all human achievements, also threatened the works of history that attempted to preserve them. Thomas Nashe describes the heroic Talbot as "buried" in "rustie brass and worme-eaten books"[52] (the historiographic text itself becomes a kind of grave) and, as Thomas Greene points out, the Renaissance humanists repeatedly used metaphors of "disinterment, rebirth, and resuscitation" to describe their transactions with the classics.[53]

[49]Landes, *Revolution in Time*, p. 91.

[50]Greene, pp. 17, 8–9.

[51]See, e.g., George Puttenham, *The Arte of English Poesie* (1589), in *Elizabethan Critical Essays*, ed. G. Gregory Smith (London: Oxford University Press, 1904), 2:150.

[52]*Pierce Penilesse his Supplication to the Diuell* (1592), reprinted in E. K. Chambers, *The Elizabethan Stage* (Oxford: Clarendon Press, 1923), 4:238–39.

[53]Pp. 32–33.

Shakespeare expresses the same kind of ambivalence in his sixty-fifth sonnet. Time, the universal destroyer, has defaced all that remains of "outworn buried age"—lofty towers, steel gates, monuments of brass and stone. Contemplating the universal ravages of time, the poet asks,

> where, alack
> Shall Time's best jewel from Time's chest lie hid?
> Or what strong hand can hold his swift foot back
> Or who his spoil of beauty can forbid?

The punning answer—

> O none, unless this miracle have might,
> That in black ink my love may still shine bright—

at once asserts the power of writing and exposes its limitations. The only "strong hand" that can hold back the ravages of Time is the black ink of the poet's words. But the image of the brightly shining love preserved in black ink recapitulates the imagery of the jewel immured in Time's chest. For Shakespeare as for Nashe, the text preserves the past but only in the sense that a grave preserves the body it entombs.

— IV —

Shakespeare's Sonnet 65 describes the power and the limitations of his poetry in terms that apply equally well to the work of the historian, but Shakespeare wrote at a time when history and poetry were increasingly contrasted. Dating back at least to the time of Aristotle, a long tradition defined poetry in opposition to history. Nonetheless, at the beginning of the sixteenth century in England, there was no clear demarcation. *Historia* was still "story," and the term *history*, like the modern French word *histoire*, could mean either "history" or "story." Edmund Spenser's prefatory letter to *The Faerie Queene* (1590), while insisting upon the difference between his work as a "Poet historical" and that of a "Historiographer," still refers to his

allegorical romance as a "History."[54] Even at the end of the
century, texts as obviously unhistorical as *Clyomon and Clamydes*
(1599) and *The Merchant of Venice* (1600) were still described as
"histories."[55] There were no chairs in history at the English
universities before the seventeenth century, and at the beginning of the sixteenth century, English writers made no clear
distinction between poetry and history, either of which could
be written in prose or verse, both of which freely mingled fact
and legend, event and interpretation, and endowed characters
from the past with the customs and manners of the present. By
the seventeenth century, all this had changed: history had become an autonomous discipline with its own purposes and
methods, clearly distinct from myth and literature, and account-
able to different formal requirements and different truth criteria.
Rhyme gave way to reason, verse to prose, as the new historians
banished the legendary material and invented speeches that had
adorned their predecessors' work to the newly distinct province
of poetry. Even the arrangement of incidents was strictly regulated. Thomas Blundeville's *The true order and Methode of wryting
and reading Hystories* (1574) flatly stated, "An Hystorye ought to
declare the thynges in suche order, as they were done";[56] and
Spenser distinguished between the poet historical and the historiographer on that same basis: "An Historiographer discour-
seth of affayres orderly as they were donne, accounting as well
the times as the actions, but a Poet thrusteth into the middest,
even where it most concerneth him, and there recoursing to the
thinges forepaste, and divining of things to come, maketh a
pleasing Analysis of all."[57]

The same distinctions were made on both sides of the rising
barrier between poetry and history. Blundeville's *True Order*, an
adaptation and abridgement of two Italian texts, was the first
book on the writing of history published in English. To Blundeville, although poets can "make much of nothing [or of] naught"
when they "faine" their "fables," historians must "tell things

---

[54]*Edmund Spenser's Poetry*, Norton Critical Edition, ed. Hugh Maclean (New
York: W. W. Norton, 1968), pp. 3, 4.
[55]Kastan, *Shakespeare and the Shapes of Time*, p. 39.
[56]Hugh G. Dick, "Thomas Blundeville's *The true order and Methode of wryting
and reading Hystories*," *Huntington Library Quarterly* 3 (1940), 155.
[57]Letter to Sir Walter Ralegh, Maclean, p. 3.

as they were done without either augmenting or diminishing them or swarving one iote from the truth." In the interests of strict accuracy, even the historian's traditional practice of inventing orations—a license with classical precedent—was now prohibited: "Hystoriographers ought not to fayne anye Orations nor any other thing, but truely to report every such speach, and deede, even as it was spoken, or done" (E4$^r$).[58]

The earliest elaboration of the distinction from the other side came from Sir Philip Sidney (1583). Defending poetry against the growing reverence for fact that threatened to assign its traditional educational and inspirational functions to history, Sidney makes the same sharp distinctions that Blundeville makes, even though he uses them to argue the superior worth of poetry. For Sidney, the historian is "tied . . . to the particular truth of things" and "captived to the truth of a foolish world," while the poet can depict ideal—and therefore morally instructive— images of virtue and vice. For Sidney as for Blundeville, any invention on the part of the historian inevitably involves him in the activity of the poet:

> The historian, bound to tell things as things were, cannot be liberal (without he will be poetical) of a perfect pattern but, as in Alexander or Scipio himself, show doings, some to be liked, some to be misliked. . . . the historian in his bare *was* hath many times that which we call fortune to overrule the best wisdom. Many times he must tell events whereof he can yield no cause, or, if he do, it must be poetically.[59]

Michael Drayton's gigantic and never-completed historical poem *Poly-Olbion* was twenty years in the making, and in 1612, when he finally published the first installment, he began with

---

[58]Dick, pp. 149–50, 164.

[59]*Sir Philip Sidney's Defense of Poesy*, ed. Lewis Soens (Lincoln: University of Nebraska Press, 1970), pp. 15–23. Cf. Sidney's letter to his brother Robert dated 18 October 1580, which, although it highly commends the study of history, makes essentially the same distinction between poetic fiction and historical fact: "the Historian makes himselfe . . . a Poet sometimes for ornament . . . in painting forth the effects, the motions, the whisperings of the people which though in disputation one might say were true, yet who will marke them well shall find them taste of a poeticall vaine . . . for though perchance they were not so, yet it is enough they might be so." *The Prose Works of Sir Philip Sidney*, ed. Albert Feuillerat (Cambridge: Cambridge University Press, 1912; rpt. 1968), 3:131.

the story of Brut, the mythical great-grandson of Aeneas. Standard practice among earlier Tudor historians, the inclusion of the legendary account of Britain's founding by the Trojan Brut had been exploited by Henry VII to justify his claim to the throne (since he claimed descent from Brut) and by Henry VIII to justify his break with Rome (since with Brut as its founder England would be an *imperium* as ancient as Rome).[60] But by the time Drayton published his *Poly-Olbion*, the serviceable old story required John Selden's learned historical commentary to defend it against the skeptical scrutiny of "this critique age." More flexible, Drayton's contemporary Samuel Daniel modified his practice to suit the times. In 1592, he published *The Complaint of Rosamund*, a traditional blending of history and fiction. In 1595, the first four books of his *Civil Wars between Lancaster and York* appeared, still written in verse, but now with the explicit disclaimer of any fictional contamination other than the invention of speeches, a license he justified by citing Sallust and Livy as precedents. Finally, in 1612, when he published the *Collections of the Historie of England*, he wrote in prose and restricted himself to a factual account of the past.[61]

— V —

Written at the end of the sixteenth century, Shakespeare's history plays occupy various sites of contention between older and newer conceptions of history and between the emergent distinctions that defined history and poetry in terms of mutual opposition. They show the pressures of the cultural changes that made the representation of historical truth a difficult—and dramatically appealing—enterprise at the time. The very act of adapting historical texts for theatrical performance, however, complicated the problems of historical representation: if history and poetry were defined as mutually opposed, the theater belonged to a radically different discursive field, in many ways the direct antithesis of historical writing.

[60]Lawrence Manley, ed., *London in the Age of Shakespeare* (University Park: Pennsylvania State University Press, 1986), p. 212.

[61]William Nelson, *Fact or Fiction: The Dilemma of the Renaissance Storyteller* (Cambridge: Harvard University Press, 1973), pp. 105–6.

The public commercial theater, in fact, was deeply implicated in the many changes that made history problematic for Shakespeare's contemporaries. Like the historical project itself, the theater was a focus for political, religious, and philosophical anxieties. Nevertheless, although both historical writing and theatrical performance were sites of instability—history in the process of change and the public commercial theater in the process of creation—and although both revealed the pressures of a rapidly changing culture, there were also profound cultural oppositions between the regulated domain of historical writing and the volatile scene of theatrical performance. A major impetus for the Tudor fascination with history was to defend against the forces of modernity, to deny change, and to rationalize a bewildering world in fictions of hereditary privilege. The public commercial theater, by contrast, was a totally new phenomenon, a disreputable place where common players draped in the discarded clothes of aristocrats impersonated their betters for the entertainment (and the pennies) of a disorderly, socially heterogeneous audience. As such, it was deeply involved in the same destabilizing social transformations that produced the nostalgic desire for a stable, historical past.

The generic differences between historical writing and dramatic performance combined with the opposed cultural locations of the two discourses to reconfigure the project of historical recuperation. Played out in the theater, the problems of historiographic representation were redefined and intensified. A new sense of anachronism emphasized the absence of the historical past and its alienation from the history-writing present. In the theater, the physical presence of modern audiences and modern actors transformed the theoretical problems of temporal distance and mediation into the visible material conditions of performance. The traditional union of history and poetry was breaking up, but Shakespeare's hybrid genre transgressed the emergent boundary between historical fact and fictional artifact. History represented the objects of present desire and loathing in the form of past heroes and their enemies, the objects of present contention in the form of ancient quarrels. In the theater, those objects of anxiety were actually present. Recording the heroic struggles of medieval kings and noblemen, Shakespeare's historical sources told the story of the elite. The players who took

their parts on Shakespeare's stage were upwardly mobile en-
trepreneurs, the products of a new commercial economy. Marginalized in the historical record, both women and common
men were visibly present in the theater audience. The exclusive
protocols of historical writing reproduced the divisions of the
traditional social hierarchy. The disorderly, socially heterogeneous audiences in the theater presented an indiscriminate
mingling. With their places determined only by the amount
of money they paid for admission, they constituted an ever-
present reminder of the new economy that was disrupting the
traditional system of hereditary status.[62] Authoritative and univocal, historical writing mystified and obscured cultural contradictions. Theatrical performance exposed them in a cacophony
of contending voices.

Although historical texts were the products of collaborative
effort, the conventions of historical writing tended to obscure
the plurality of voices that went into their production. It is
customary to speak of Shakespeare's sources by the names of
individual authors (Hall, Holinshed, etc.), even though the
chronicles included the work of many writers—predecessors
whose work was incorporated, successors who augmented the
narratives after their authors' deaths, and collaborators at the
time of their production. In the case of "Holinshed," for instance, the original plan was conceived by a printer named
Reyner Wolfe; the first edition included William Harrison's
descriptions of Britain, England, and Scotland and Richard
Stanyhurst's description and history of Ireland, as well as Holinshed's histories of England and Scotland, themselves compiled from a variety of sources ranging from Caesar's account
of his invasion of Britain to sixteenth-century chronicles of London life. The second edition, published after Holinshed's death,
greatly expanded the text with additions by John Hooker (Vowell), Francis Thynne, Abraham Fleming, and others.[63] The title
page attributed the initial collection to "Raphaell Holinshed,
William Harrison, and others" and the continuation to "John

[62]Jean E. Howard, "Crossdressing, the Theatre, and Gender Struggle in Early
Modern England," *Shakespeare Quarterly* 39 (1988), 440.
[63]Levy, 182–86. See also Vernon F. Snow, "The Printing History of Holinshed's *Chronicles*—an introduction to the reprint edition," in *Holinshed's
Chronicles* (New York: AMS Press, 1976), 1:i-x.

Hooker alias Vowell Gent. and others"; there was a three-page list of "names of the authors from whome this historie of England is collected"; and marginal notations marked the names of sources and augmenters. Nonetheless, the history came to its readers mediated by a single authorial voice, the plurality of its contributors obscured by the conventions of historical narrative.

The 1587 edition of the *Chronicles,* the one Shakespeare used, was augmented by Abraham Fleming's insistently moralistic commentary. Fleming's providentialist interpretations of historical events, "set forth," as Guy Hamel points out, "in the most commonplace . . . expressions and confirmed by absurd tags of second-rate Latin," thus become part of "Holinshed's" text.[64] William Harrison's *Description of England,* included in the *Chronicles* from the beginning, actually belonged to a different genre of representation, the new discourse of chorography, closely related to the antiquarian movement and in many ways the antithesis of a historical chronicle.[65] Organized by temporal sequence and divided into units that represented the reigns of successive kings, chronicles told the histories of royal dynasties. Each page in a chronicle like Holinshed's or Hall's is identified by the name of the reigning king and the regnal year. Substituting the spatial organization of a map moving from one part of the land to another for the temporal sequence that structured chronicle accounts of royal dynasties, chorography, as Richard Helgerson has pointed out, implicitly "defines itself in opposition to chronicle." In a chronicle, the story of England is the story of its kings. Patriotic loyalty means loyalty to the crown.

[64]"Holinshed and the 'History' of *Richard II,*" a paper presented at the seminar on Shakespeare's history plays at the 1988 annual meeting of the Shakespeare Association of America. Hamel also points out that Holinshed's own historical method, in contrast to Fleming's, "is marked by caution and general good sense."

[65]As did Drayton's *Poly-Olbion,* subtitled *A Chorographicall Description of Tracts, Rivers, Mountaines, Forests, and other Parts of this renowned Isle of Great Britaine.* Burke, p. 29, defines chorography as "the study of geo-history, or a study of local history with special reference to surviving physical remains" and describes it as the "offspring of traditional local history and the new antiquarianism." He points out that chorography was practiced in classical times, revived in fifteenth-century Italy, and spread to England during the latter part of the sixteenth century. On the complicated relationships between the antiquarian movement, the practice of chorography, and the changing political climate in England, see Helgerson.

In the chorographies, by contrast, it "means loyalty to the land; to its counties, cities, towns, villages, manors, and wards," and ultimately to the gentry that owned them and the parliament that represented them. Like the metaphor of the king's two bodies, chronicles told the story of England in the persons of its monarchs.[66] Like Parliament, chorography represented an assembly of places as "the body of all England."[67] Despite these profound differences, however, Harrison's chorography, like Fleming's moralistic interventions, is assimilated into the text we call "Holinshed."

The univocal form of historical writing conflated providential moralizing with pragmatic skepticism, the dynastic ideology implicit in Holinshed's chronicle structure with the new conception of the nation implicit in Harrison's chorography, the heroic legends that expressed the ideals of feudal aristocracy with the city chronicles whose contents were dictated by the interests of London merchants. Monologic, it obscured the differences between the disparate authorial voices, opposed discursive positions, divergent accounts, and contradictory interpretations that were incorporated into the historiographic text. The polyphonic form of theatrical performance enacted them. Moreover, the social construction of writing for the public theater, the material conditions of theatrical production, and the generic requirements of drama all militated against the conception of playwrights as authors.[68] The writers were hirelings of the players, the scripts they produced the ephemeral equipment for a not entirely reputable trade. Unlike the printed books in which the chronicles were published in multiple copies, the handwritten text of a playscript was likely to be altered as it was acted in different places, by different players, or for different audiences. Transported from one place to another, the history book remained unchanged; the playtext was subject to

[66]Helgerson, pp. 347–49. On the metaphor of the king's two bodies and its ideological work, see Ernst Kantorowicz, *The King's Two Bodies: A Study in Mediaeval Political Theology* (Princeton: Princeton University Press, 1957).

[67]"The Land Speaks," pp. 348–56.

[68]On the status of dramatists, see Gerald Eades Bentley, *The Profession of Dramatist in Shakespeare's Time 1590–1642* (Princeton: Princeton University Press, 1971), pp. 38–61. On Ben Jonson's innovation in redefining the playwright as author, see Peter Stallybrass and Allon White, *The Politics and Poetics of Transgression* (Ithaca: Cornell University Press, 1986), pp. 59–61, 66–79.

variation at every performance.[69] Both plays and histories were often produced in collaboration and incorporated the work of preceding writers, but unlike the historical texts that obscured their multiple authorship in the guise of univocal narrative, playscripts were designed for polyphonic performance, even when all the parts were composed by a single writer. These differences can be seen in the material differences between the two kinds of texts: the histories were published in printed books, while the playscripts were written out on narrow strips of paper, each containing the speeches and cues for a single part.[70] For the sequence of the entire play, the actors relied on a "Plot," also written out by hand, mounted on a board that probably hung backstage during the performance; but many details of performance were left to the discretion of individual players.[71]

Moreover, although printed history books and performed history plays were both commercial commodities, their intended consumers were different, as were the conditions of their consumption. History was designed for the privileged minority who could read. Theatrical performance was accessible to anyone who had the price of admission, the illiterate as well as the learned. Like the actors on stage, theater audiences were multiple: like the characters those actors portrayed, they came from a variety of social locations and responded differently to the same events. Historical texts were written for solitary reading, to engage one reader at a time. Theatrical performance had to appeal simultaneously to a variety of spectators, a requirement emphasized by the physical structure of the theater. Because the theater was open-roofed and the plays were performed in daylight, the members of the audience were as visible to each other as the players were to them. Because the apron stage was surrounded on at least three sides by that audience, no single

[69]William B. Long, "*John a Kent and John a Cumber*: An Elizabethan Playbook and Its Implications," in *Shakespeare and Dramatic Tradition: Essays in Honor of S. F. Johnson*, ed. W. R. Elton and William B. Long (Newark: University of Delaware Press, 1989), pp. 125–43.

[70]A facsimile of the only extant "part," that of Orlando in Greene's *Orlando Furioso*, can be found in W. W. Greg, *Dramatic Documents from the Elizabethan Playhouses: Stage Plots: Actors' Parts: Prompt Books* (Oxford: Clarendon Press, 1931), vol. 2.

[71]Long, pp. 125–43; Bernard Beckerman, "Theatrical Plots and Elizabethan Stage Practice," in *Shakespeare and Dramatic Tradition*, pp. 109–24.

place afforded a privileged perspective on the action. Although the members of the audience would see the action, literally as well as figuratively, from multiple angles, a successful play would have to please as many of them as possible, and please them simultaneously.

Although the commercial theatrical setting tended in general to subvert historical tradition, the heterogeneity of the audience and the discursive instability of the new institution produced a polyvalent discourse that resisted the imposition of one single meaning. Addressed from a univocal narrator to a solitary reader, historical writing obscured contradictions. The heterogeneity of theater audiences required them, and the polyphonic form of playscripts projected them as dramatic conflicts. Drama thrives on every form of conflict, on conflicts between ideas as well as conflicts between persons. The products of a time when changing conceptions of historiography made history a focus for conflict between ideologies in transition, Shakespeare's English histories play out those conflicts in the form of dramatic action and dramatic structure. Ranging from the Saturnalian comedy of the *Henry IV* plays, to the different forms of tragedy exemplified in *Richard III* and *Richard II*, to a variety of structures that elude traditional generic classification, the history play in Shakespeare's hands was clearly an experimental genre.

Contradictory notions of historical truth and changing conceptions of historiography inform those experiments, but it is impossible to derive a single, coherent theory of history from the plays. The first tetralogy begins with a loose chronicle structure that depicts a confused and confusing world where force and fortune are the only arbiters of events. It ends with an insistently moralized tragedy that depicts historical process as the working out of a clear, providential plan. Henry VI believes in divine providence, but his simple faith is repeatedly confronted with wickedness he cannot understand and disasters he cannot prevent. Insofar as events are explained in the *Henry VI* plays, they are explained in the Machiavellian terms of politic history; but the episodic plots, the large casts of characters, and the rapid whirl of events all work to frustrate any attempt by the audience to discover a clear principle of causality. In *Richard III*, by contrast, Shakespeare constructs a Marlovian tragedy centered on the rise and fall of a single, strong character; here the principle of historical causation is clearly providential. In this play, as in the three parts of *Henry VI*, the king's vision of historical causation is subjected to a powerful dramatic irony, but this time, the king is a Machiavel, and it is providence that asserts its power in the end. Pious and well-intentioned, Henry VI is confronted by a world ruled by Machiavellian *Realpolitik*. Ruthlessly clever, Richard III is subjected to the power of providential justice.

*Richard III* resolves the problems of historical causation and dramatic structure in a conventional providential moral and a conventional dramatic plot, but Shakespeare returns to both those problems in later plays. In *King John* he returns to a diffuse, episodic structure to depict a world where no principle of historical causation can be discovered. Here, as in the Henry VI plays, no one has an undisputed right to the English throne, and no conflict is fully resolved. Battles end in stalemates, alliances are no sooner made than broken, and the conflict between John's power and Arthur's right is never really resolved but only rendered moot by Arthur's accidental death and John's fatal illness. The second tetralogy moves in the opposite direction from the first. It begins in *Richard II* with a tightly constructed tragedy centered on a single character whose personal weakness incapacitates him for his role as king, moves through a comedy of expiation in the two parts of *Henry IV*, and ends in *Henry V* with a unique and disquieting dramatic structure that sets the historical narrative of the chorus against the dramatic action on stage and suggests the impossibility of ever discovering the full truth about the past.

Taken as a whole, Shakespeare's history plays cannot be said to argue the superiority of either theory of historical causation. Instead, they cast their audiences in the roles of historians, viewing the events from a variety of perspectives, struggling to make sense of conflicting reports and evidence, and uncomfortably reminded of the anachronistic distance that separated them from the objects of their nostalgic yearning. Taken in the order of their composition, the plays can be read as a long meditation on the difficulty of retrieving the past.[72] Henry V,

---

[72] The exact order of composition—and indeed the authorship—of the three

the most heroic of England's kings, lies dead at the beginning of Shakespeare's first tetralogy, and he is not brought to life until the last play in the second tetralogy. Shakespeare's order of composition thus fails to follow the order in which the historical events took place. It takes instead the order in which history is known, the order of memory or archaeological excavation, which moves from the present backward, rather than the order of living or historical narrative, which moves forward in time. The progress Shakespeare traces in his history plays is not simply the progress of historical events but the progress of historiography. The order of the plays' composition follows the progress of Renaissance historiography, as history becomes increasingly problematic and truth more and more difficult to determine.

At the same time, the plays become increasingly self-reflexive, encouraging their audiences to meditate on the process of historical representation rather than attempting to beguile them into an uncritical acceptance of the represented action as a true mimesis of past events. In the second tetralogy a proliferation of metadramatic allusions, an unruly crowd of anachronistically modern fictional clowns, and the overt commentary of the prologue and epilogue in 2 *Henry IV* and the choruses in *Henry V* disrupt, parody, and interrupt the historical action to undermine the authority of historical representation. They direct the audience's attention to the present reality of actors and audience in the theater, to the barriers of historical time and theatrical mediation that separate them from the desired objects of historical recuperation.

The image of Henry V, the mirror of all Christian kings, hovers just beyond the frame of both tetralogies. Henry is the lost heroic

---

parts of *Henry VI* has long been a subject of scholarly debate, and some editors consider that *Part One* was written last. See, e.g., Stanley Wells and Gary Taylor, *William Shakespeare: A Textual Companion* (Oxford: Clarendon Press, 1987), pp. 111–13. There is no doubt, however, that the plays designated in the First Folio as the three parts of *Henry VI* were composed before *Richard III* and the second tetralogy; and although even the term "tetralogy" is a post-Shakespearean invention, the plays are closely linked. *Part One* ends with the introduction of Margaret and the plan to marry her to Henry, *Part Two* with Clifford's promise to revenge himself upon the house of York, even including its children (V.i.51–60), and *Part Three* with Richard of Gloucester's resolution to get the crown.

presence that the entire historical project is designed to recover. *1 Henry VI* begins with his funeral, and the entire play can be seen as a struggle on the part of the English to preserve his rapidly disappearing legacy of national unity and French conquests. He hovers behind the second tetralogy as well. Always elusive, he is first mentioned in *Richard II* when his newly crowned father demands, "Can no man tell me of my unthrifty son? 'Tis full three months since I did see him last" (V.iii.1–2); but the audience does not see him either until the *Henry IV* plays, and even there he plays a series of roles designed, he tells the audience from the beginning, to conceal his true nature (I.ii.195–217).

Just as the first tetralogy looks back to Henry V as an emblem of lost glory that shows up the inadequacy of his son's troubled reign, the second looks forward to his glorious accession, the anticipated reward that will make up for his father's troubled reign and justify his own indecorous conduct as Prince Hal. But in *Henry V*, the last play in the second tetralogy, when he finally appears as king, all that longingly remembered and eagerly anticipated glory evaporates in ambiguity, as the historically authorized, heroic words of the chorus are repeatedly contradicted by the events enacted on stage and challenged by the irreverent voices of vulgar theatrical clowns. Even in the play that bears his name, Henry V eludes representation. The progress of the two tetralogies, then, is a progress back in time to a dead hero and a lost heroic age that evaporate in ambiguity as soon as we reach them.

After the turn of the seventeenth century, Shakespeare stopped writing English history plays. In *Macbeth* and *King Lear*, he returned to material from Holinshed's *Chronicles*, but his concerns in those plays center on the tragic errors and sufferings of his protagonists and their metaphysical implications rather than on the ambiguities of historical process and the difficulties of historical representation. The First Folio placement of these later plays among the tragedies has been ratified by a long tradition of critical commentary. *Henry VIII*, although classified as a history in the Folio, is markedly different from Shakespeare's earlier plays on the English kings, and recent commentators have pointed to the many ways in which it resembles the late romances that were written during the same period.

The English history play ceased to be a popular genre soon after Shakespeare abandoned it, and there is good evidence that the genre itself is largely Shakespeare's creation. Both F. P. Wilson and Robert Ornstein point out that "there is no certain evidence that any popular dramatist before Shakespeare wrote a play based on English history." Ornstein argues convincingly that Shakespeare was responsible for the history-play vogue, and that it was his plays that shaped the tradition.[73] The vogue of the history play was intense but remarkably brief. Beginning in the 1580s, the taste for historical drama reached its peak around the end of the sixteenth century and declined soon after the accession of James I. Irving Ribner's comprehensive survey, *The English History Play in the Age of Shakespeare*, lists nearly fifty history plays composed during the years 1579–1606, and only seventeen more from then until the middle of the seventeenth century. Moreover, many of those later plays were historical romances rather than history plays per se, and two were never printed.[74] As F. J. Levy has noted, "only one play of any importance, Ford's *Chronicle History of Perkin Warbeck*, came out of the years after the middle of James's reign."[75] As Ford's prologue acknowledged, English history was by then (ca. 1634) "out of fashion'" as a dramatic subject.

Shakespeare turned to other dramatic genres at the turn of the seventeenth century, when the theoretical contradictions that complicated the nature of history and its relationship to drama were sufficiently resolved that the shape of modern historiography—factual and positivistic—and the sphere of modern drama—personal and ahistorical—had already become apparent. In the seventeenth century, private and public theaters catered to increasingly specialized audiences, and historiography emerged as a specialized discourse with a distinctive purpose and methodology that defined it in opposition to fic-

[73]F. P. Wilson, *Marlowe and the Early Shakespeare* (Oxford: Clarendon Press, 1953), p. 106, quoted by Robert Ornstein in *A Kingdom for a Stage: The Achievement of Shakespeare's History Plays* (Cambridge: Harvard University Press, 1972), p. 6.

[74]Appendix B, pp. 319–27.

[75]*Tudor Historical Thought*, p. 233.

tion. The conflicting conceptions of historical causation and historical truth and the ambiguous relationship between historical representations of past stability and a volatile theatrical present that had provided the matrix for Shakespeare's English history plays gave way to a new scientific faith that was to shape the modern world and to increasingly restricted scenes of dramatic representation and sites of theatrical performance.[76]

Based on the premise that "facts could reveal laws, as in the natural sciences, with which Bacon had identified" it, the new historiography left little room for the work of the dramatist. As Matthew Wikander points out, "the story of post-Shakespearean historical drama in England" is one of "redefining the proper sphere of drama as ahistorical, private, outside time." Historians studied facts, dramatists invented fictions; history dealt with politics, drama probed "the private secrets of the heart." In the post-Shakespearean English history play, "distaste for historical fact . . . combines with a total relinquishment to historical discipline of authority over the past." The complicated interplay between history and theater that animates Shakespeare's history plays was no longer possible because a "wide gulf had opened up, early in the seventeenth century, between historian and playwright." The resulting division between historical fact and literary truth foreclosed the possibility of writing historical drama as Shakespeare had conceived it.[77]

[76]On changes in theaters, audiences, and the subjects of dramatic representation, see Andrew Gurr, *Playgoing in Shakespeare's London* (Cambridge: Cambridge University Press, 1987), pp. 115–90. On their embeddedness in cultural change, see Walter Cohen, *Drama of a Nation: Public Theater in Renaissance England and Spain* (Ithaca: Cornell University Press, 1985), pp. 255–406. See also Raymond Williams, "Theatre as a Political Forum," in *The Politics of Modernism: Against the New Conformists*, ed. Tony Pinkney (London: Verso, 1989), especially pp. 83–84.

[77]Matthew H. Wikander, *The Play of Truth and State: Historical Drama from Shakespeare to Brecht* (Baltimore: Johns Hopkins University Press, 1986), pp. 6, 8–9, 1, 4, 5, 1. See J. G. A. Pocock, "The Sense of History in Renaissance England," p. 156, for a similar suggestion that history in Shakespeare's time was beginning to "point away from the theater: away from poetry and toward prose, away from rhetoric and toward criticism, away from the court and toward parliament and the printing press. If history was moving away from its immediate relevance to the drama, this may be yet another reason why Shakespeare raised the English stage to heights that it found such difficulty in sustaining."

— VI —

The new sense of history as a distinct discipline was manifested in Shakespeare's time, not only in the practice of historians and the discourse of theorists, but also in the invention of those newly necessary terms "historiographer" (1494) and "historiography"(1569). The word "history" is ambiguous, referring equally to the signifying text and what the text signifies, to the present record and to the absent, and in fact dead, life the text attempts to resurrect. Strictly speaking, what is written is not history but "historiography," and what historiography writes about is history. Nonetheless, we continue to use "history" in both senses, a verbal conflation that points to and at the same time evades a persistent problem.

The conflation is evasive because it assumes a simple and unproblematic identity between the historical text and the historical past. In recent years, historians have again turned their attention to the inevitable gap that separates the historiographic text from the history it purports to describe. Theorists of history like Hayden White have pointed out that the "facts" of history, "in their unprocessed form, make no sense at all." Historical texts themselves, White argues, are literary artifacts, making stories out of chronicles by a process he calls "emplotment" to emphasize that the writer of history uses "all of the techniques that we would normally expect to find in the emplotment of a novel or a play."[78]

This new concern with representation and the nature of historical evidence and analysis coincides and increasingly collaborates with another revolution in contemporary historiography: the concern of modern historians with all those traditionally excluded from "historia." Contemporary historians are learning to supplement traditional sources with material that adumbrates the lives of all those nonheroic and often illiterate people who had no place in traditional history. The interest of modern historians in women, in social history, in unwritten history, reinforces a growing skepticism concerning the adequacy of

[78]"The Historical Text as Literary Artifact," *Tropics of Discourse: Essays in Cultural Criticism* (Baltimore: Johns Hopkins University Press, 1978), pp. 83–84.

traditional historiography to represent the past. The elusive objects of our own efforts at historical recuperation, the unrecorded lives of ordinary people constitute the focus for our own historical nostalgia, our own discontent with the methods and materials of a historiography that was developed to serve interests that are increasingly perceived as outmoded.[79]

Historians today, working at the end of the modern period, like their predecessors, working at its beginning, are impelled by a cultural and intellectual revolution that forces us to reevaluate the nature of history and the relationship between history and fiction. Just as the two became differentiated during the Renaissance, their differentiation is now beginning to seem more and more illusory. With the growing recognition that a history, no less than an avowedly fictional story, is a construct, as much the product of the sensibility that narrates it as a reflection of the "facts" it describes, the two genres once again meet and merge; we have, for example, "nonfiction novels" and "documentary dramas." New historicism has taught literary scholars to reconceive literary texts as constituents in a larger cultural discourse, and social historians increasingly turn to literary fictions to hear the voices that were silenced and recapture the details of ordinary life that were erased by traditional historiographic sources.[80]

Once again, the privileged position of historiography as a record of the "truth" about the past is undermined. Poststructuralist theory, as Jonathan Culler observes, deconstructs "the history invoked as ultimate reality and source of truth," exposing it as "narrative constructs, stories designed to yield meaning through narrative ordering."[81] Increasingly conceived in fictional terms, history is once again synonymous with "story,"

[79]Cf. Walter Benjamin's often-quoted aphorism: "Not man or men but the struggling oppressed class itself is the depository of historical knowledge." "Theses on the Philosophy of History," in *Illuminations*, p. 260.

[80]For an early formulation of the argument that literature can reflect the sensibility of an age better than history can, even though it fails to recount its "facts," see Murray Krieger, "The 'Frail China Jar' and the Rude Hand of Chaos" in *The Play and the Place of Criticism* (Baltimore: Johns Hopkins University Press, 1967).

[81]Jonathan Culler, *On Deconstruction: Theory and Criticism after Structuralism*, (Ithaca: Cornell University Press, 1982), p. 129. Cf. Roland Barthes, *Le discours de l'histoire, Social Science Information 6, Studies in Semiotics/Recherches Semiotiques* (1967), pp. 65–75.

no longer set apart by the positivistic assumptions that distinguished historical "truth" or "facts" from the often pleasant and sometimes edifying but always lying narratives that were trivialized by the name of fictions.

No longer the "authoritative monolith" it appeared in the eighteenth and nineteenth centuries, history once again inspires "radical questioning of the relationship between historical and dramatic ways of portraying the past." The historian Hayden White sees the origins of history, and its "greatest source of strength and renewal" in "the literary imagination."[82] The playwright Bertolt Brecht declares that theater is "history itself."[83] No longer privileged by the authority of fact, the historical text is once again subject to radical questioning under the impetus of a growing conviction that history, no less than theater, is "essentially fictive."[84]

Given these resemblances between the contemporary revolution in historiography and the unstable status of historiography in Shakespeare's time, it is not surprising that Shakespeare's history plays have proved increasingly attractive to modern scholars or that recent discussions of the plays have emphasized their skeptical attitude toward historical truth.[85] Fictionalized histories, the plays anticipate the blurred genres of contemporary discourse, produced as the long separation between fact and fiction again comes into question. Using historiographic sources to produce scripts for dramatic performance, Shakespeare's history plays straddle the boundary between the

[82]*Tropics of Discourse*, p. 99.

[83]*Gesammelte Werke* (Frankfurt: Suhrkamp, 1967), 15:302.

[84]These words as well as the quotations from White and Brecht and the translation of Brecht's words come from Wikander, p. 9, and my argument at this point is heavily indebted to the thoughtful introduction to Wikander's book.

[85]This emphasis was especially apparent during the 1986 Ohio Shakespeare Conference on the history plays, where virtually every paper advanced a skeptical thesis, regardless of the play or the issue under consideration. For an especially persuasive example of those arguments, see David Scott Kastan's "Proud Majesty Made a Subject: Shakespeare and the Spectacle of Rule," *Shakespeare Quarterly* 37 (1986), 459–75, an expanded version of the paper he presented there. Some recent books that exemplify this perspective are James L. Calderwood's *Metadrama in Shakespeare's Henriad: Richard II to Henry V* (Berkeley: University of California Press, 1979), John W. Blanpied's *Time and the Artist in Shakespeare's English Histories* (Newark: University of Delaware Press, 1983), and Wikander's *Play of Truth and State*.

written and the oral, anticipating our own post-Derridean grapplings with that problematic dichotomy.

Inevitably, what we see in those plays, like what we see in the past, reflects our own concerns. The products of our own discursive framework, our interpretations of the plays inevitably become mirrors for our own situations, even as we attempt to use them for windows into the past. Nonetheless, there is an important sense in which our own newly critical attitude toward historical constructions of the past provides a good vantage point for the study of Renaissance historiography and the place of Shakespeare's plays within it. In the Renaissance, both history and drama were conceived as mirrors. For Hamlet, the purpose of playing is to hold up a mirror "to show the very age and body of the time his form and pressure" (III.ii.20–24). One of the most popular books in Tudor England was the collection of versified histories entitled *A Mirror for Magistrates*. Reread in the light of our own historical revolution, the familiar Elizabethan trope seems to deny the illusion of transparency that conditioned the post-Shakespearean ideals of objective history and dramatic verisimilitude and effaced the disquieting realities of historiographic anachronism and discursive mediation.

The danger, of course, is that we will overestimate the resemblances, dehistoricizing the plays in order to appropriate them as texts for our own sermons. To some extent, that danger is unavoidable. In the final analysis, I do not believe we can read the plays from the vantage point of the sixteenth century any more than Shakespeare could write them from the perspectives of the fifteenth-century characters he attempted to represent. His versions of the history of medieval England were inevitably shaped by the concerns of the Renaissance audience for which he wrote, and they tell us more about his world than they do about the world of the Plantagenets. My versions of Shakespeare's plays, and his world, are inevitably shaped by my social and temporal location, my own interests and anxieties.

In this sense, it seems to me that all historical narratives are ideologically motivated—my own, no less than the ones I attribute to the Tudor historians and to Shakespeare—and that it is therefore necessary to historicize historical practice, to focus more on the temporal and social site in which a historical narrative is constructed than upon the historical facts it purports to represent. In the chapters that follow, I have attempted to situate Shakespeare's representations of medieval history not only in the discourse of Tudor historians but also in the contexts of the rapidly changing world of early modern England and the conditions of his theater and to situate my own arguments in the contexts of contemporary critical debates. Each of the chapters focuses on a feature of Renaissance historiography which is also a site of contention or a focus of concern in contemporary critical discourse, and each attempts to demonstrate the ways in which the performance of history in Shakespeare's theater participate(d) in the contentions between opposed theories of history and between the different ideological interests and historiographic practices they authorize(d). Chapters 2 and 3 center on issues that defined the problematics of Renaissance historiography—Chapter 2 on the conflict between Providential and Machiavellian views of historical causation, Chapter 3 on the problems of anachronism and nostalgia. Chapters 4 and 5 turn to the margins of Renaissance historiography to examine Shakespeare's theatrical representations of the women and plebeian men who were marginalized or excluded by a historiographic tradition that rationalized present privilege in the structures of patriarchal genealogy.

Because the chapters are organized by subject rather than by the order of Shakespeare's composition or the order of the history he represented, they circle back over the same plays. And because the subjects themselves are connected in intricate ways, the discussions often overlap, returning to the same territory to map it in other terms. Each chapter emphasizes a different discursive opposition, but many of those oppositions are encoded in the same passages, and all of them are involved in the material difference between the literal physical presence of theatrical performance and the imagined objects of historical representation.

A good case in point is the speech that ends the first tetralogy. Prefiguring Tudor peace and prosperity, Richmond invites the audience to join him in a prayer for a future that will be theirs as well as his own:

> O now let Richmond and Elizabeth,
> The true succeeders of each royal house,

By God's fair ordinance conjoin together!
And let their heirs (God, if thy will be so)
Enrich the time to come with smooth-fac'd peace,
With smiling plenty, and fair prosperous days!
Abate the edge of traitors, gracious Lord,
That would reduce these bloody days again,
And make poor England weep in streams of blood!
Let them not live to taste this land's increase
That would with treason wound this fair land's peace!
Now civil wounds are stopp'd, peace lives again;
That she may long live here, God say amen!

Richmond's prayer for the future is at once providential, genealogical, and atemporal. It announces the providentially ordained union of York and Lancaster, it describes the genealogical rationale for Tudor legitimacy, and it dissolves the temporal distance that separates the audience from the objects of historical representation.

Although the chapters are organized around a series of binary oppositions, none of the binary oppositions goes unquestioned or uncontested. Divine providence authorizes royal power, and Machiavellian manipulation subverts royal authority; in the case of Richard III, however, divine providence opposes royal power, and in the case of Henry V, Machiavellian manipulation produces royal authority. The disorderly scene of theatrical performance contaminates the desired objects of historical recuperation, but the theater also surpasses historical writing in its ability to revive the dead past and represent the life that eluded historiographic representation. Women represent a constant threat to the legitimacy of patriarchal succession, but they also represent its ultimate warrant. Intersecting but not identical or even homologous, the various oppositions modify and compromise each other to define the conflicted field of Shakespeare's historiographic project. The opposition of masculine and feminine in Chapter 4 is different from the ones between providential and Machiavellian in Chapter 2, between past and present in Chapter 3, and between elite and plebeian in Chapter 5. And all of these are distinct from, although powerfully implicated in, the larger oppositions that inform the various and changing negotiations between written historiographic texts and oral theatrical performance.

Reformulated in subsequent discourse, these structural oppositions recur in the twentieth-century controversies between critics who interpret the plays as expressions of Tudor orthodoxy and those who emphasize their subversiveness, in the construction and contestation of an ahistorical Shakespeare who transcends the limitations of his own historical moment to epitomize the ideal of universal poetic truth, and in contemporary efforts to write the lives of women and ordinary men into the historical record. These concerns, the products of a post-Shakespearean discursive tradition and our own historical moment, determine the disordered and disordering shape of my narrative, which begins by interrogating historical myths of divine providence and royal authority and ends by affirming theatrical representations of nameless plebeian men. With different objects and different objectives, the same historical nostalgia and anachronistic distance that fueled and frustrated the Renaissance project of historical recuperation distort and limit my own.

Writing from our own place in history, we cannot see the plays under the aspect of eternity or even from the perspective of an Elizabethan spectator. The questions with which we approach the past—and, therefore, the answers we seem to hear—are inevitably shaped by our own historically specific concerns. Nonetheless, it seems to me that the attempt at historical reconstruction is worth making even if it inevitably falls far short of its ambition. The emergent culture of Shakespeare's England established the foundations for a world we have not yet entirely lost, Shakespeare's plays provided many of its materials, and the history of post-Shakespearean criticism traces the long process of its construction and deconstruction.[86] Conceived as a continuous process rather than a series of discrete, nostalgic tableaux, history has shaped the very concerns that make us modern, implicating us and inscribing us with the genealogical marks of a past we cannot know.

[86]What Fredric Jameson calls the "organizational fiction" of *The Political Unconscious*—the assumption that "we never really confront a text immediately, in all its freshness as a thing-in-itself"—is particularly relevant to the case of an author like Shakespeare, whose long history of canonicity makes it especially apparent that his "texts come before us as the always-already-read; we apprehend them through sedimented layers of previous interpretations." See *The Political Unconscious: Narrative as a Socially Symbolic Act* (Ithaca: Cornell University Press, 1981), p. 9.

# 2

# Ideological Conflict, Alternative Plots, and the Problem of Historical Causation

Modern criticism of Shakespeare's history plays can be divided conveniently into two main camps, both concerned with the problem of historical causation. First there was the "Tudor myth" school associated with E. M. W. Tillyard, which found in the plays "a universally held," and "fundamentally religious" historical "scheme," governed by divine providence, beginning with the "distortion of nature's course" in the deposition and murder of Richard II and moving purposefully "through a long series of disasters and suffering and struggles" to the restoration of legitimacy and order under the Tudors.[1]

Then—and this side still holds the field—there was the rebellion against the Tudor myth theory, a rebellion that has taken two forms. Sometimes it takes the form of a refusal of ideology. Shakespeare, we are reminded, was always concerned with the

[1] E. M. W. Tillyard, *Shakespeare's History Plays* (New York: Collier Books, 1962), first pub. 1944, p. 362. See also Lily B. Campbell, *Shakespeare's "Histories": Mirrors of Elizabethan Policy* (San Marino, Calif.: Huntington Library, 1947); Irving Ribner, *The English History Play in the Age of Shakespeare* (Princeton: Princeton University Press, 1957); and Andrew S. Cairncross's introductions to the Arden editions of *1, 2,* and *3 Henry VI* (London: Methuen, 1962, 1957, 1964). For more recent examples of providentialist readings, see Robert B. Pierce, *Shakespeare's History Plays: The Family and the State* (Columbus: Ohio State University Press, 1971); and Robert Rentoul Reed, Jr., *Crime and God's Judgment in Shakespeare* (Lexington: University Press of Kentucky, 1984). See also the summaries of twentieth-century criticism of Shakespeare's history plays in *Shakespeare Survey 6* (Cambridge: Cambridge University Press, 1953) and *Shakespeare Survey 38* (Cambridge: Cambridge University Press, 1985).

universal qualities of human nature and experience. Accordingly, an interpretation based on the claim that the plays deal in ideologies belies their rich complexity and literary value by reducing them to political propaganda.[2] Most often, however, the rebellion takes the form of an attack on the Tudor myth itself, either a demonstration that it never existed, except in the minds of Tillyard and his followers, or a demonstration that Shakespeare was actually debunking rather than dramatizing the Tudor myth.

In this view, "Shakespeare was no spokesman for Tudor orthodoxy" but instead "used the stage to undermine" the conventional pieties.[3] In fact, "there is no other Elizabethan writer [who] so acutely and extensively portrays the weakness, folly, incompetence, and wickedness of English kings."[4] Moreover, Tudor opinion was by no means so univocal or conservative as Tillyard and his followers supposed. The myth of the Great Chain of Being was "widely denied," religious skepticism as well as credulity was commonplace, and "insubordination, mutiny and wholesale desertion occurred repeatedly in the princely

[2] Robert Ornstein, in *A Kingdom for a Stage: The Achievement of Shakespeare's History Plays* (Cambridge: Harvard University Press, 1972), is a persuasive advocate for this view. He argues that Shakespeare's "progress in the history plays was a journey of artistic exploration . . . that led almost unerringly beyond politics and history to the universal themes and concerns of his maturest art" (p. 31). "Chaos comes in the History plays as in the tragedies, not when doctrines of obedience are questioned, but when the most intimate human ties disintegrate" (p. 222). More recent critics have argued that the "refusal of ideology" is itself ideologically conditioned. See especially Jonathan Dollimore and Alan Sinfield, "History and Ideology: The Instance of *Henry V*," in *Alternative Shakespeares*, ed. John Drakakis (London: Methuen, 1985), pp. 206–27.

[3] C. G. Thayer, *Shakespearean Politics: Government and Misgovernment in the Great Histories* (Athens: Ohio University Press, 1983), p. viii. Other writers who dispute Tillyard's view include W. Sanders, *The Dramatist and the Received Idea* (Cambridge: Cambridge University Press, 1968); Henry Ansgar Kelly, *Divine Providence in the England of Shakespeare's Histories* (Cambridge: Harvard University Press, 1970); David Riggs, *Shakespeare's Heroical Histories* (Cambridge: Harvard University Press, 1971); John C. Bromley, *The Shakespearean Kings* (Boulder: Colorado Associated Press, 1971); Michael Manheim, *The Weak King Dilemma in the Shakespearean History Play* (Syracuse: Syracuse University Press, 1973); Edna Z. Boris, *Shakespeare's English Kings, the People, and the Law: A Study in the Relationship between the Tudor Constitution and the English History Plays* (Cranbury, N.J.: Associated University Presses, 1974); and Gordon Ross Smith, "Shakespeare's Henry V: Another Part of the Critical Forest," *Journal of the History of Ideas* 37 (1976), 3–26.

[4] Ornstein, p. 29.

armies of this period."[5] There was, moreover, no certain rule or set procedure for determining royal succession, as is attested by "the long list of possible successors to Elizabeth... ample evidence that England lacked a consensus acknowledging order of ascent."[6]

The current division between British cultural materialists and American new historicists opens along the same fault lines. Both new historicism and cultural materialism reject the Tudor myth school's assumption that there was one "Elizabethan mind" whose thinking was everywhere conditioned by a conservative "world picture," and both look beyond canonical literary texts to social, economic, and political history to read those texts in the context of a larger cultural discourse. They have tended, however, to envision that discourse in different terms. For many new historicists, it was finally univocal, a discourse of the elite, shaped by the interests of the dominant classes, whose definitive speaker and auditor and ultimate source of authority was always the sovereign. Cultural materialists, on the other hand, have discovered a polyphonic discourse, where even the voices of the illiterate can never be fully silenced. They have emphasized the role of popular transgression and subversion, while new historicists have tended to construe subversion as always already contained—indeed often produced—by the dominant discourse.[7]

[5]Gordon Ross Smith, "'Princes of Doltish Disposition': Philippe de Comines, *King John*, and *Troilus and Cressida*," *Indian Journal of Linguistics* 8 (July–December 1981), 1–36.

[6]Boris, p. 36.

[7]Of course, as Jean Howard has pointed out, Foucault's theories of deterministic power apparatuses are not quite the same as a providential theory of history, even though both can lead to the erasure of Machiavellian/humanist ideas of agency, etc. For subtle accounts of the similarities and differences magnified and oversimplified here, see the first two essays in *Shakespeare Reproduced: The Text in History and Ideology*, ed. Jean E. Howard and Marion F. O'Connor (New York: Methuen, 1987): Walter Cohen's "Political Criticism of Shakespeare," pp. 18–46; and Don E. Wayne's "Power, Politics and the Shakespearean Text: Recent Criticism in England and the United States," pp. 47–67. Both essays contextualize the differences in the differing cultural situations of British and American academics, and both are accompanied by representative bibliographies. See also the opening chapter in Stephen Greenblatt's *Shakespearean Negotiations: The Circulation of Social Energy in Renaissance England* (Berkeley: University of California Press, 1988), pp. 1–20, where Greenblatt critiques and

Thus, much of the criticism of the history plays during the past forty years[8] has centered on various versions of an issue framed in Shakespeare's time as a conflict between providential and Machiavellian theories of historical causation. Politically conservative, the providential view of history looked backward to an older feudal world and upward to transcendent spiritual authority to oppose change and justify hereditary privilege. The Machiavellian view, by contrast, validates change, mobility, and individual initiative. In the Renaissance, this view was associated with an emergent capitalist individualism; in our time, with a radical opposition to that same capitalism, now transformed by a long process of development and long-entrenched hegemony. In both cases, however, it offers a rationalist demystification of the historical past and ratifies opposition to the status quo. In fact, the modern scholarly controversy even recapitulates the progress of the Renaissance debate: Like the older tradition in Shakespeare's own time, the older tradition in twentieth-century criticism of the history plays emphasized the providential view. The conservative critics of the mid-twentieth century saw the plays as essentially medieval, the expressions of conservative ideology, cautionary tales based upon a political theology that attributed all the sufferings of the Wars of the Roses to the deposition, two generations earlier, of the divinely anointed Richard II. The newer generation, in our time as in the sixteenth century, prefers the Machiavellian version of historical causation, explaining history in terms of force, fortune, and practical politics.

The rejection of Tillyard's providentialism reflects the internal dynamics of any field of literary inquiry: new books have to say something new, and for a time attacking Tillyard was an obvious choice. Like any discursive scheme, the Tudor myth theory called attention to the material for its own refutation, simply by virtue of the emphases and exclusions that characterized its own dealings with Shakespeare's texts. Like the nineteenth-century bowdlerized editions of the plays, which lent themselves readily to prurient reading (that is, reading focused upon the excised

---

modifies his earlier conception of "a single coherent, totalizing system" (p. 19).

[8]I am dating the controversy from 1944, the year when Tillyard first published his *Shakespeare's History Plays*.

passages, which were often preserved in appendices), Tillyard's version inevitably led to a consideration of all the material that had to be left out to make the case. The rejection of the conservative, providentialist view of the history plays also has obvious connections with larger trends in twentieth-century literary study, with the changing populations of university departments of English and history, with the new historical sophistication that refuses, in Stephen Greenblatt's words, to attribute "a single political vision" to an "entire population" or even to an "entire literate class,"[9] and with the movement from the politically conservative New Critical tradition that venerated T. S. Eliot and the American Agrarians to the typically left-wing politics of contemporary European theorists who have influenced Anglo-American literary criticism during the seventies and eighties. In these same years the view of the politics of Shakespeare's history plays has also moved from conservative (or reactionary) to liberal (or radical). From the present vantage point, it is easy to see how Tillyard and his followers projected their own nostalgia for the medieval past and their own distaste for the competitive, individualistic modern age into the plays and only slightly more difficult to see how more recent critics, in constructing a new set of texts for the plays, have been expressing their own rejections of traditionalist mythologies and reifications.[10]

It is not surprising that both sets of critics have found ample ammunition in the plays to defend their claims, for the plays do in fact offer plentiful evidence for both views. Dramatic scripts, open to a variety of directorial emphases and actors' interpretations, the plays lend themselves easily to the kind of interpretive "foregrounding" I have been describing. What the controversy among the critics both fails to acknowledge and demonstrates, however, is that although neither ideological position is clearly or consistently privileged, the conflict between them lies very close to the center of Shakespeare's historical project. Exploring the dramatic implications and exploiting the

[9]Stephen Greenblatt, *The Power of Forms in the English Renaissance* (Norman, Okla.: Pilgrim Books, 1982), p. 5.

[10]Cf. the discussion of twentieth-century literary theory and criticism in Terry Eagleton's *Literary Theory: An Introduction* (Minneapolis: University of Minnesota Press, 1983), especially chap. 1, "The Rise of English."

theatrical potential of rival theories of historical causation, the plays project into dramatic conflict an important ideological conflict that existed in their own time, not only by having dramatic characters speak and act from opposing ideological vantage points but also by inciting these conflicts among their audiences.

The conflict in Renaissance theories of history between providential and Machiavellian views of historical causation involved the most important cultural and social issues of a changing world: the conflicts between feudal values and capitalist practice and the relationship between the two orders of the divine and the human. The demonic Machiavel of the Elizabethan stage expressed a recognition that Machiavelli's theories were irreconcilably opposed to the providential vision of human history that justified the existing social and political order. To a deeply political age, Machiavelli offered the attraction of shrewd political advice, but he also represented what Felix Raab has described as "the horror of atheism, of a political world no longer determined by the Will of a universal Providence manifested in Christian precepts of political morality."[1]

Shakespeare, like his audience, was obviously fascinated with these issues: ten of the thirty-five plays listed at the beginning of the First Folio were English "histories," and in every one of those plays the conflict about historical causation plays a crucial role. The audience at a Shakespearean history play, struggling to make sense out of conflicting evidence and uncomfortably reminded of the difficulty of explaining historical causation, is forced to enact the same conflicts that divided Renaissance historians. The conflicts among the twentieth-century critics illustrate this process: the critics themselves can be seen as a uniquely accessible divided audience, offering conflicting testimony as they describe and rationalize their conflicting responses to the ideological struggles depicted in and incited by the plays. Thus, although the twentieth-century conflict between the Tillyard school of "Tudor myth" advocates on the one hand and their revisionist debunkers on the other can be seen as a response to twentieth-century political and cultural forces, it can also be seen as a response to the rhetoric of the

[1]Felix Raab, *The English Face of Machiavelli: A Changing Interpretation, 1500–1700* (London: Routledge & Kegan Paul, 1964), pp. 69–70.

plays. The ideological conflict between providential and Machiavellian notions of historical causation was built into the plays from the beginning, generating theatrical energy and engaging the audience in the problematic process of historical interpretation.

Herbert Lindenberger, in fact, cites Shakespeare's English histories to illustrate his contention that it is a distinguishing mark of the history play genre to replace "the ordinary suspense of plot" with "a kind of intellectual suspense about the larger causes of action" (that is, about the question of historical causation):

> To what extent are the events of Shakespeare's English historical cycle a working out of providential design (by which the deposition of Richard II must result in the ultimate downfall of the successors of Henry IV until the restoration of order by the first Tudor king) or a result of the weaknesses in character of the various kings (or, for that matter, the stroke of Fortune which cut off Henry V in his prime)? All these questions must, of course, remain unanswered—or, at best, tentatively answered, with new answers following to modify or contradict earlier ones.[12]

— II —

Subjecting conflicting propositions about historical truth and historical causation to the tests of dramatic action, Shakespeare's history plays can be seen as versions of trial by combat. In *Richard II* the ideological conflict between providential legitimacy and Machiavellian power is directly projected into the dramatic conflict between Richard and Bullingbrook. The ideological conflict forms the basis for opposed rhetorical appeals (and opposed modern interpretations)[13] as Richard's theoretical claim to the throne as divinely anointed legitimate heir is supported by providential theory and poetic eloquence but opposed

[12]*Historical Drama: The Relation of Literature and Reality* (Chicago: University of Chicago Press, 1975), p. 133.
[13]Twentieth-century critics reenact this conflict as they argue the relative merits of the two contenders for the throne and the opposed ideologies that support their opposing claims. See especially Ornstein, pp. 13–21.

by Machiavellian logic and the hard evidence of Richard's personal and political failings and Bullingbrook's political and military superiority.[14] It forms the basis for the ironic disparity in the opening scene between Richard's personal weakness (he cannot stop the quarrel between Bullingbrook and Mowbray) and his institutional authority (only he is authorized to adjudicate the quarrel). At the end of the scene, in a speech that expresses his ironic predicament, Richard capitulates in the face of Mowbray and Bullingbrook's stubborn refusal to give up their quarrel:

> We were not born to sue, but to command,
> Which, since we cannot do to make you friends,
> Be ready, as your lives shall answer it,
> At Coventry upon Saint Lambert's day.
> There shall your swords and lances arbitrate
> The swelling difference of your settled hate.
>
> (I.i.196–201)

The first line is a proud assertion of Richard's inherited, institutional authority as king; the second an anticlimactic confession of his inability to exercise it. In the remainder of the speech he calls for a trial by combat, deferring the problem to the only authority superior to his own in the providential scheme that authorizes him, the will of God.

It is significant that Richard calls for a trial by combat, a chivalric ritual that must have had an enormous appeal for Shakespeare's original audience, many of whom would also have flocked to see the extravagant re-creations of medieval tournaments staged by courtiers at Queen Elizabeth's Accession Day tilts and open to the general public.[15] In both cases, the theatrical

---

[14]It is interesting that "Bolingbroke," the usual spelling of Bullingbrook's name in modern editions of *Richard II*, was first adopted by Alexander Pope. Henry St. John, Viscount Bolingbroke (1678–1751), to whom Pope dedicated his *Essay on Man*, was in his own time a leading exponent of the ideology of civic humanism that J. G. A. Pocock has identified as an outgrowth of Machiavelli's theories. See Pocock's *The Machiavellian Moment: Florentine Political Thought and the Atlantic Republican Tradition* (Princeton: Princeton University Press, 1975), pp. 477–86.

[15]On the Accession Day Tilts, see Frances A. Yates, "Elizabethan Chivalry: The Romance of the Accession Day Tilts," in *Astraea: The Imperial Theme in the Sixteenth Century* (London: Routledge and Kegan Paul, 1975), pp. 88–111. On

appeal of extravagant spectacle was reinforced by nostalgia, for both courtly and theatrical enactments of ritual combats evoked an imagined medieval world where divine providence legitimated earthly status.

Shakespeare throws enormous stress on the trial by combat in *Richard II*, deferring it and emphasizing its necessity with an invented scene between John of Gaunt and the Duchess of Gloucester, holdovers (as was the ritual for Shakespeare and his contemporaries) from an earlier world where power and legitimacy were united. The duchess urges Gaunt to avenge Richard's murder of her husband, but Gaunt argues with equal force that there is no way a good subject can avenge that crime without opposing the will of God:

> God's is the quarrel, for God's substitute,
> His deputy anointed in His sight,
> Hath caus'd his death, the which if wrongfully,
> Let heaven revenge, for I may never lift
> An angry arm against His minister.
>
> (I.ii.37–41)

There is nothing Gaunt can do, and nothing the duchess can say to make him change his mind. Faced with a dispute they cannot adjudicate and an ideological dilemma they cannot resolve, both Gaunt and the duchess turn to the trial by combat for providential adjudication. "God's is the quarrel," and only God has the authority to resolve it.

Act I, scene iii, begins with all the formal preliminaries to the trial by combat, the anticipated resolution of the conflict be-

---

Tudor use of the cult of chivalry, see Julia Briggs, *This Stage-Play World: English Literature and Its Background 1580–1625* (Oxford: Oxford University Press, 1983), pp. 132–33; Roy Strong, *The Cult of Elizabeth* (Berkeley: University of California Press, 1977), pp. 161–62; and Arthur B. Ferguson, *The Chivalric Tradition in Renaissance England* (Washington, D.C.: Folger Shakespeare Library, 1986). My account of the conscious anachronism of Shakespeare's use of chivalry is indebted to a fine, unpublished paper by David Scott Kastan, "'I' the Vein of Chivalry': *Troilus and Cressida* and the Politics of Honor." On Shakespeare's use of the cult of chivalry, see also Paul N. Siegel, "Shakespeare and the Neo-chivalric Cult of Honor," in *Shakespeare in His Time and Ours* (Notre Dame: University of Notre Dame Press, 1968), pp. 122–62, especially pp. 133–38, where he discusses Hotspur and Hal; and Ralph Berry, "Shakespeare and Chivalry,"in *Shakespeare and the Awareness of the Audience* (New York: St. Martin's Press, 1985), pp. 109–27.

tween Richard and Bullingbrook (for which the conflict between Mowbray and Bullingbrook has been from the beginning the thinnest of screens) and the anticipated resolution of the ideological dilemma articulated in scene ii. But Richard interrupts the ceremony, refusing, after all the preliminaries have been accomplished, to allow the contest to proceed. When Richard stops the trial by combat he interferes with a symbolic embodiment of his own authority. Trial by combat is a ritual based upon the assumption that right makes might, an assumption that underlies the authority of the whole feudal system, including the authority of God's anointed king. In preventing the symbolic ritual of chivalry, Richard attacks the source of the only authority that makes him king. He also alienates Shakespeare's audience, for they, no less than the characters, have been waiting to see the tournament that Richard now interrupts, depriving them of the anticipated pleasure of seeing on stage a historical spectacle and the anticipated comfort of having their own doubts resolved by a clear, tangible demonstration of God's will.

Late in 2 *Henry IV* (IV.i.123–27), Mowbray's son will recall this scene, attributing enormous historical significance to Richard's reneging:

> O, when the King did throw his warder down,
> His own life hung upon the staff he threw;
> Then threw he down himself and all their lives
> That by indictment and by dint of sword
> Have since miscarried under Bullingbrook.

Regardless of the accuracy of Mowbray's analysis (and it is suspect, since he assumes that his father would have defeated Bullingbrook, had the king allowed the trial to proceed), it serves as a reminder of the importance of Richard's refusal. Trial by combat occupies a central place in the conflict between providential and Machiavellian explanations of history because it forms a nexus of power and authority, a place where those two forces, opposed in the conflict between the two ideologies, are joined together in medieval practice and providential belief. Trial by combat is a crucial ritual in the scheme of divine right because, like the theory of divine right itself, it rests on the assumption that God takes a hand in human events, ensuring that might derives from right, that power derives from authority, and not the other way around.

In the vastly diminished world of *2 Henry VI*, Shakespeare presents a very different trial by combat, parodically reduced to an inept contest between a terrified prentice and his drunken master, but the same issues are involved. This trial ends in a severely qualified version of divine justice when the poor prentice Peter, despite his lack of experience in arms, kills his master, Horner, and Horner confesses with his last breath that Peter spoke the truth when he accused him of the treasonous statement that the Duke of York was rightful heir to the crown (II.iii.94; I.iii.25–27). Shakespeare's modifications of his historical sources for this incident are suggestive. Neither Holinshed nor Hall verifies the servant's story or connects the charge of treason to York's claim to the throne. Both attribute the servant's victory to the master's drunkenness, and both end by reporting the servant's execution. Holinshed, in fact, specifically absolves the master of guilt, both in the marginal description of the episode—"Drunkennese the overthrow of right and manhood"—and in his account of it:

> The said armourer was overcome and slaine; but yet by misgoverning of himselfe. For on the morow, when he should come to the field fresh and fasting, his neighbours came to him, and gave him wine and strong drinke in such excessive sort, that he was therewith distempered, and reeled as he went, and so was slaine without guilt. As for the false servant, he lived not long unpunished; for being convict of felonie in court of assise, he was iudged to be hanged, and so was, at Tiburne.[16]

In Holinshed's account, the servant's story is false, the incident is a warning against drunkenness and a lesson in obedience to earthly masters. Justice comes from the court of assizes rather than the judicial combat. All the implications are secular.

Shakespeare's entire reconstruction of the incident seems designed to raise the issue of providential justice but withhold an

[16]Raphael Holinshed, *Chronicles of England, Scotland and Ireland* (1587; rpt. London: J. Johnson et al., 1808), 3:210. Cf. Edward Hall, *The Union of the Two Noble and Illustre Famelies of Lancastre & Yorke* (1548; rpt. London: J. Johnson et al., 1809), pp. 207–8.

answer. He has Horner confess, departing from his historical sources to validate Peter's story, but he refuses to take the next step and attribute the victory to divine intervention. Henry VI reads the outcome as an unambiguous message from above—"God in justice hath reveal'd to us / The truth and innocence of this poor fellow" (II.iii.102–3)—but York urges Peter to "thank God, and the good wine in thy master's way" (II.iii.95–96). Shakespeare gives Henry the last word in this scene, but Henry's opinion is finally no more reliable than York's, for we have just seen Henry accepting Simpcox's bogus miracle as the work of "God's goodness" (II.i.82). If York has too much interest in discrediting Peter's story to offer reliable testimony, Henry is too credulous. On the one hand, there are Horner's confession and Henry's faith; on the other, York's cynical explanation and the authority of the chronicles. York and Henry offer alternative explanations for Peter's victory, but the world of this play provides no clear standard to adjudicate between them and no clear answer to the riddle of historical causation.[17]

In the providential world of *Richard III*, Richmond's victory will be clearly marked as the will of God, not only by the judgments of the other characters but also by the prophecies, curses, and prophetic dreams that give direct and unambiguous directions for its interpretation. In the world of Henry VI, by contrast, incessant battles between Yorkists and Lancastrians yield no clear pattern of victory, and the rhetoric of those plays yields no clear warrant of legitimacy. In a Machiavellian universe, rival truths have no means of adjudication but the law of force. The verdicts of force, however, are always provisional, always subject to contradiction by the next turn of the fortunes of battle. Trial by combat can only yield an uncontested verdict in a prov-

---

[17]A similar ambiguity about the issue of causation characterizes Shakespeare's representation of Gloucester's death. Initially, it seems to support a Machiavellian reading of history. Shakespeare implies the powerlessness of Gloucester's virtue in the face of his Machiavellian enemies when he has Gloucester deliver the following speech immediately before his summons, arrest, and murder: "I must offend before I be attainted; / And had I twenty times so many foes, / And each of them had twenty times their power, / All these could not procure me any scathe / So long as I am loyal, true, and crimeless" (II.iv.59–63). Nonetheless, before the play is over, Suffolk and Beauford will join their victim in death, Beauford, in fact, by a mysterious, sudden illness that includes among its symptoms the belief that he is haunted by Gloucester's ghost (III.ii.373).

idential universe where victory means vindication because it represents a supernatural justification for the victorious side.

Richard II cannot allow the fight between Mowbray and Bullingbrook to proceed because, unlike the treacherous master in 2 *Henry VI* who expects to win even though he knows he is defending a lie and the cynical Duke of York who attributes Peter's victory to the wine his master drank before the battle, Richard really does believe in trial by combat, and he knows that Bullingbrook's charges are true. But once he throws his warder down, using his ritualistic authority to interrupt the ritual that authorizes him, he abandons the field to another kind of battle—the kind that really is decided by superior military and political power, the kind that Bullingbrook is sure to win.

The interrupted ritual at Coventry may well have been the last formal trial by battle in English history. The chronicles, including Holinshed's, emphasize its importance, and it is pictured in the Harleian MS.[18] It is also the only formal trial by combat in any of Shakespeare's English histories. Richard is the only king in the two tetralogies with an unambiguous hereditary claim to the throne, rooted in an uncontested genealogy and ratified by divine right. The medieval world—and with it the possibility of ritualized judicial combat—disappears with his deposition.

In *King John*, set even farther back in the past but depicting an anachronistically modern world where the relationship between power and legitimacy is endlessly contested, trial by combat ends in frustration and stalemate. The immediate cause of contention is the city of Angiers. The city belongs, as its citizens admit, to the King of England, but neither citizens nor audience can be sure who that king is. John, who sits on the throne, bases his claim on "strong possession much more than . . . right" (I.i.40), but the true heir is a helpless child whose claim on the audience's allegiance is undermined by support from the French king and the Roman pope.

The conflict over Angiers is both the direct result and the direct expression of the larger conflict on which the entire play is based—the conflict between the two claimants to the English

[18]Matthew W. Black, *A New Variorum Edition of The Life and Death of King Richard the Second* (Philadelphia: J. B. Lippincott, 1955), p. 49n.

throne—and its ideological basis, the conflict between power ("strong possession") and authority ("right"). The struggle for legitimacy represented within the play reaches out to engage the audience, who must try to decide where to place their allegiance as they watch the play. Shakespeare makes the analogy explicit in the trial-by-combat scene, where the citizens of Angiers standing on their battlements to watch the two contending armies are compared to an audience "in a theatre" who "gape and point at . . . industrious scenes and acts of death" (II.i.375–76). Both sides have appealed with equal eloquence to the citizens (and the audience) to accept their claims to the city and the English crown, but the citizens (speaking, I believe, for the audience) have refused to admit either claim until one is proved legitimate: "Till you compound whose right is worthiest, / We for the worthiest hold the right from both" (II.i.281–82). Turning to action when words fail, John and Philip try to adjudicate their quarrel in battle, but the audience does not see the battle, which takes place offstage, and at the end of it both sides claim victory. The audience, like the citizens, still has no way to decide, for neither side can present a clear claim to the English throne, and the trial by combat has ended in a draw.

The Bastard's scornful description of the citizens of Angiers exposes the element of voyeurism and theatrical exploitation in all these scenes of trial by combat:

> By heaven, these scroyles of Angiers flout you, kings,
> And stand securely on their battlements
> As in a theatre, whence they gape and point
> At your industrious scenes and acts of death.
>
> (II.i.373–76)

The Bastard's contemptuous metadramatic comparison demystifies the trial by combat, extending the nihilism of his world to encompass the audience in Shakespeare's theater. Debased by theatrical representation, the mortal conflicts of kings and noblemen are reduced to meaningless spectacles designed to amaze and titillate a vulgar public. However, the same theatrical appeal that the Bastard cites to empty the scene of significance and value serves, by merging the audience with the spectators on stage, to engage them in the ideological dilemmas that lie at the center of the plays. The Bastard's demystification exposes the element of vulgar spectacle in all theatrical reenactments of battles, but it elides the ethical and ideological significance of the trial by combat, a significance which is finally theatrical as well. As Herbert Lindenberger points out, "Drama has never thrived well on moral neutrality."[19] The ethical conflicts the trials attempt to resolve constitute an important element of their interest for theater audience as well as characters onstage. Directly or indirectly, the trials represent efforts to clarify the relationship between power and authority and answer the riddle of legitimacy. Appealing to God to adjudicate conflicts that earthly justice cannot resolve and attempting to read God's verdicts in the outcomes of physical conflict, the trials attempt to resolve in dramatic action the crucial and contested issues surrounding the problem of historical causation.

A trial by combat constitutes a miniature plot that stages conflicting propositions about historical truth in the form of physical action, its outcome designed to ratify one proposition and discredit the other. As such, it exhibits in simplified microcosm the dynamics of the larger and more complicated plots of the plays. A plot, as Aristotle explained, is a proposition about causation. If plot is, as he said, the soul of tragedy, it is also the theme of history. A historical plot, whether in a narrative history or in a play about history, constitutes a proposition about historical causation. At the same time, as Michael Quinn points out, "an idea about Providence is an idea about drama."[20] A providential view of history constructs an unbroken chain of historical causation, but a Machiavellian view interrupts that chain, constructing each age as unique, the product of Fortuna, or accident, and individual will.[21] Hence the episodic structure of *King John* and the Henry VI plays and the radical separation of *King John*, the most Machiavellian of all Shakespeare's histories, from the temporal and causal chain that unites the

---

[19]*Historical Drama*, p. 141.

[20]Michael Quinn, "Providence in Shakespeare's Yorkist Plays," *Shakespeare Quarterly* 10 (1959), 45.

[21]It is perhaps for this reason that, as F. J. Levy has observed, Machiavellian historiography tended to deal with "a brief period, such as the reign of one monarch or the story of one event." See *Tudor Historical Thought* (San Marino, Calif.: Huntington Library, 1967), pp. 237–38, where Levy cites Machiavelli's *Prince* and Guicciardini's *History of Italy* as examples.

two tetralogies. The varied structures of Shakespeare's history plays not only produce a variety of dramatic forms and imagined worlds; they also express changing conceptions of historical causation.

— III —

The issue of authority is closely implicated with issues of historical causation and dramatic structure. In a Machiavellian universe, where the hand of God is absent or invisible, so is the hand of the author: the dramatic structure becomes loose and episodic, the principle of causation becomes inscrutable, and the audience has no guidance to help them discover significance or assign value as they watch the action unfold. The issue of authority is also implicit in the long-standing preference of conservative critics for *Richard III* and the plays of the second tetralogy and their superior canonical status to *King John* and the Henry VI plays. Set in a providential universe, graced with aesthetic unity, these plays construct a world where the authority of the playwright as well as that of God is clearly manifest. In *King John* and the Henry VI plays, by contrast, where royal authority is ambiguous and the hand of providence is absent or invisible, the dramatic structure is loose and episodic, as if the hand of the playwright were also effaced. Indeed, many of the earlier critics saw in these plays undigested lumps of chronicle material. To John Middleton Murry, for instance, *3 Henry VI* seemed a "'mere record', with 'no trace of speculation on the causes of things'"; and theories of multiple authorship were often advanced.[22] In these theories, Shakespeare's au-

---

[22]John Middleton Murry, *Shakespeare*, p. 144, quoted by Cairncross in his introduction to the Arden edition of *3 Henry VI*, pp. xlviii–xlix. See Cairncross, p. xli, on the controversy over the question of authorship. On the related questions of royal authority and dramatic unity, the Quarto title pages are revealing. The earliest published version of *3 Henry VI* was entitled "The true Tragedie of Richard *Duke of Yorke, and the death of* good King Henrie the Sixt, *with the whole contention betweene* the two Houses Lancaster and Yorke, as it was sundrie times acted by the Right Honourable the Earle of Pembrooke his servants." In the case of *2 Henry VI* the Quarto title does not even mention the name of the king. Instead, it designates the play as "The first part of the Contention betwixt the two famous Houses of Yorke and Lancaster, with the death of the good Duke Humphrey: and the banishment and death of

thority as playwright was attacked just as the dramatic structure of the plays deposed the king from his expected central role and their represented action attacked the king's authority and that of his office.[23]

At the opposite extreme, in *Richard III*, which delineates a process of providential retribution and restoration, the hand of the playwright is all too apparent; and although the play has a complicated textual history, Shakespeare's authorship has not been seriously questioned. The play has a tight, linear dramatic structure, and the king is a strong, central character, so dominant, in fact, that he has no real antagonist in the play except providence itself. Margaret curses, and she is a powerful dramatic presence, but she has no real part in the plot. Richmond comes in at the end to take Richard's crown, but he is a *deus ex machina* rather than a dramatic presence, and his tiny part in the play could easily be given to a minor actor. The play, in fact, has a large cast of minor characters, but rather than diffusing Richard's dominance, they serve to reinforce it, for most of them could be listed as "assorted victims."

Everyone who dies in *Richard III* is Richard's victim, and, with the exception of the two innocent babes murdered in the Tower, everyone who dies expresses his recognition that he is paying for past crimes. Finally, when all the dying is done, the kingdom is purged of evil and the succession purged of ambiguity. All claimants to the throne except for Richmond and Elizabeth have been killed, and their marriage will unite the warring dynasties. In the Machiavellian universe of *3 Henry VI*, by contrast, death is meaningless or, at best, pathetic, and the play ends with the succession still in question and Richard of Gloucester plotting to take the throne.

Most of the twentieth-century debates about Shakespeare's

---

the Duke of *Suffolke,* and the Tragicall end of the proud Cardinall of *Winchester,* with the notable Rebellion of *Iacke Cade: And the Duke of Yorkes first claime unto the Crowne.*"

[23]As David Kastan has pointed out, Elizabethan objections to "mongrel tragicomedies" expressed similar anxieties, associating the hierarchical logic of the dramatic plot with the hierarchical logic of the unitary state. Kastan made this point in a paper at the 1989 meeting of the Shakespeare Association of America—"'Clownes shoulde speake disorderlye': Mongrel Tragicomedy and the Unitary State"—where he identified the unassimilated intrusions of clowns in the dramatic structure as a register of "what the unitary state would repress."

history plays center on various, related forms of authority: the authority of the king, the authority of God, the authority of the historical source, of the dominant ideology, of the authorial script. In fact, the arguments about Shakespeare's authorship recall (although they do not invoke) the Renaissance analogy between the author of a literary work and the Author of the universe. Julius Caesar Scaliger argued that the poet in the act of literary creation "makes himself another God, as it were."[24] *The Arte of English Poesie* (1589), attributed to George Puttenham, begins:

> A Poet is as much to say as a maker. And our English name well conformes with the Greeke word, for of *poiein*, to make, they call a maker *Poeta*. Such as (by way of resemblance and reverently) we may say of God; who without any travell to his divine imagination made all the world of nought. . . . Even so the very Poet makes and contrives out of his owne braine both the verse and matter of his poeme.[25]

The same analogy (and even more diffidence about making a comparison that might be construed as an irreverent usurpation of divine prerogative) appears in Sir Philip Sidney's *Defense of Poesy* (ca. 1583):

> Neither let it be deemed too saucy a comparison to balance the highest point of man's wit with the efficacy of nature: but rather give right honor to the Heavenly Maker of that maker, who, having made man to His own likeness, set him beyond and over

[24]Julius Caesar Scaliger, *Poetics* (1561) I, i, p. 3DI, in Allen Gilbert, *Literary Criticism: Plato to Dryden* (Detroit: Wayne State University Press, 1962), p. 413. See also Torquato Tasso, *Discourses on the Heroic Poem* (1594): "The operations of art appear to us as though divine and in imitation of God, the first artist" (quoted in Gilbert, p. 492); and Thomas Blundeville, *The true order and Methode of wryting and reading Hystories* (London: Willyam Seres, 1574), E4ʳ-E4ᵛ: "Of those that make anye thyng, some doe make much of nothing, as God dyd in creating the Worlde of naught, and as Poets in some respect also doe, whilest they faine fables and make thereof theyr poesies, and poetical Hystories." Blundeville's treatise is reprinted with an introduction by Hugh G. Dick in *The Huntington Library Quarterly* 3 (1940), 149–70. For a remarkable twentieth-century reinscription of the analogy, see Sigurd Burckhardt's "Notes on the Theory of Intrinsic Interpretation" in *Shakespearean Meanings* (Princeton: Princeton University Press, 1968), pp. 285–313.

[25]G. Gregory Smith, ed., *Elizabethan Critical Essays* (London: Oxford University Press, 1904), 2:3.

all the works of that second nature, which in nothing he shows so much as in poetry, when with the force of a divine breath he brings things forth far surpassing her doings.[26]

Puttenham uses a theological argument to celebrate the work of the poet. Sidney transforms a celebration of literary creativity into an affirmation of religious faith. Both make explicit the deep connections between aesthetic and theological issues implicit in the varied forms of Shakespeare's history plays and the modern scholarly debates about their ideological import. As William Camden wrote in the preface to his *Annals of Queen Elizabeth* (1615), "Although I know that matters military and politic are the proper subjects of an historian, yet I neither could nor ought to omit ecclesiastical affairs (for betwixt religion and policy there can be no divorce)."[27] The growing rift that Camden attempts to bridge lies beneath the dispute about historical causation and the problem of plot as well. As Wlad Godzich points out, "The problem of agency arises in modern times" as a legacy of the secularization that marked the end of the medieval world. For the Scholastics, although "human will could rise in opposition to the divine will . . . it did not have any agential power as such to determine the course of affairs of the world." Secularization, Godzich argues, "let loose all that which had previously been an attribute of God," thus producing the problem of agency and the problem of plot as well.[28] Writing in the time that saw the beginnings of that secularization and reconstructing historical narratives in the shape of dramatic plot, Shakespeare could hardly avoid confronting the problem of historical causation,

[26]*Sir Philip Sidney's Defense of Poesy*, ed. Lewis Soens (Lincoln: University of Nebraska Press, 1970), p. 10.

[27]Trans. Abraham Darcy, reprinted in Peter Burke, *The Renaissance Sense of the Past* (London: Edward Arnold, 1969), pp. 127–28.

[28]"Foreword" to Thomas G. Pavel, *The Poetics of Plot: The Case of English Renaissance Drama*, Theory and History of Literature 18 (Minneapolis: University of Minnesota Press, 1985), p. xx. Cf. Fredric Jameson's observation that "religious and theological debate is the form, in pre-capitalist societies, in which groups become aware of their political differences and fight them out" in "Religion and Ideology: *Paradise Lost*," in *Literature, Politics & Theory: Papers from the Essex Conference 1976–84*, ed. Francis Barker et al. (London: Methuen, 1986), pp. 38–39. For an extensive analysis of the interpenetration between politics and theology in medieval and Renaissance thought, see Ernst Kantorowicz, *The King's Two Bodies: A Study in Medieval Political Theology* (Princeton: Princeton University Press, 1957).

which was also a problem of plot. To say that Shakespeare's English histories cannot be reduced to an extended sermon *pro* or *contra* Machiavel is not to say that the issues raised by the Machiavellian challenge to providential views of history are irrelevant to the plays, only that the ten plays can better be construed as series of dramatic meditations than a sustained univocal sermon.

— IV —

History is always constructed in retrospect. Thus, the criticism of the 1940s and 1950s found in the medieval world, and in Shakespeare's representations of it, a story of national union and English patriotism that answered to their own desires and needs, just as the radical criticism of the present finds a story of conflict and subversion. In both cases, present desire is projected in the form of a historical plot: alternative political agendas construct alternative plots. In Shakespeare's own time, the Tudors, like the conservative critics of the mid-twentieth century, projected the authoritarian world they wished to build into an imagined medieval past.[29] The story that begins with Richard II and ends with Henry VII shows the passage from an idealized medieval England through the crime against God and the state that destroyed it and the long process of suffering and penance that led to its redemption in the divinely ordained accession of the Tudor dynasty. Following the structure of the providential historical plot of the Bible and the medieval cycles that dramatized biblical history, it begins with a myth of the Fall in the deposition and murder of Richard II and ends with a story of redemption in the accession of Henry VII.

The traditional view of Shakespeare's history plays reproduces the teleological providential narrative of Tudor propaganda, focusing on the second tetralogy and *Richard III* to construct a plot that traces the passage from the medieval world

[29]They also recognized that history was a field of ideological contention and that alternative accounts of the past threatened their present political hegemony. See Campbell, *Shakespeare's "Histories,"* pp. 182–92, for an account of the use of Sir John Hayward's history of Henry IV as evidence at the Essex conspiracy trial.

to Shakespeare's own. It starts with *Richard II*, which represents the beginning of the providential narrative Shakespeare found in Hall and depicts a ceremonial, medieval world that looks back to an even more perfect union of authority and power in John of Gaunt's idealized vision of the time of Edward III.[30] It proceeds, in the Henry IV plays, to depict an abrupt plunge into a contemporary, fallen world,[31] where the future Henry V must engage in a long struggle to reconstruct the uncontested union of authority and power that obtained in the older, Edenic world ruled by kings whose power was rooted in unambiguous hereditary authority and validated by divine right. Henry V cannot inherit the Edenic England described by John of Gaunt because it is already lost, but what he can do to reproduce it, he does; when he conquers France, he "achieves" "the world's best garden" (Epilogue.7), as close a postlapsarian approximation to Eden as human endeavor can produce. The final redemption will have to wait for the end of *Richard III* and the advent of Henry Tudor.

An ideological construction, designed in retrospect to ratify the Tudor claim to the throne, this is the story that Shakespeare found in his historiographic sources and twentieth-century conservative critics found in Shakespeare's history plays. It is also implicit in the First Folio arrangement of the plays in a sequence that begins with *King John* and *Richard II* and ends with *Henry VIII*. But it is not the only story Shakespeare could have learned from Tudor historiography, and it is certainly not the only story that modern critics have found in his plays. The plot of Tudor historiography constructs a myth of original order followed by a fall in the deposition of Richard II and leading finally to a glorious redemption in the person of Henry VII, but the order in which Shakespeare composed his English history plays constructs a much more complicated story, whose plot is embedded in the cultural history of his own time. The series of plays that begins with *Henry VI* and ends with *Henry V* replaces the teleological, providential narrative of Tudor propaganda

---

[30]For an especially perceptive version of this reading, see James L. Calderwood, "*Richard II*: The Fall of Speech," in *Shakespearean Metadrama* (Minneapolis: University of Minnesota Press, 1971), pp. 149–86.

[31]Leonard Barkan, "The Theatrical Consistency of *Richard II*," *Shakespeare Quarterly* 29 (1978), 5–19.

with a self-referential cycle that ends by interrogating the entire project of historical mythmaking. The first tetralogy Shakespeare wrote ends in providential redemption; but although the second recapitulates that process, it does so in much more problematic terms. The deposition of Richard II, like the death of Henry V, initiates a period of civil strife, penance, and purgation and ends with the advent of a savior-king, but the redemption depicted in *Henry V* is severely qualified. The order in which Shakespeare produced his two tetralogies follows the progress of Renaissance historiography, towards an increasingly self-conscious and skeptical attitude, not only toward its subjects but also toward the very process of historical production. Increasingly opposing historical fact to literary artifact, Shakespeare exposes the processes of historical mythmaking even as he engages in them.

—— V ——

From the beginning, the plays seem guided by this double agenda: the historical story they tell is also a story of historiographic production. Shakespeare's historical protagonists, in fact, repeatedly conceive their actions as versions of history-writing. In *1 Henry VI*, English heroes identify their struggle to retain Henry V's French conquests as an effort to preserve the historical record of English glory, an identification that recurs in *King John* in the French king's effort to defend Arthur's hereditary right to the English throne, and in *Henry V* with Henry's effort to win his place in history by defeating the French in battle.[32]

In structure as in subject, the plays signal their discursive origins. The retrospective process of historical construction informs the structure of *King John* and *Henry VIII* as well as the entire first tetralogy. The disorderly and disturbing plot of *King John* ends with the assurance that Prince Henry will "set a form upon that indigest / Which [John] hath left so shapeless and so rude" (V.vii.26–27) and the Bastard's ringing declaration that England will never be conquered so long as it "to itself do rest

---

[32]For a fuller discussion of this point, see Chapter 4.

but true" (V.vii.118), denying the subversive implications of its chaotic plot with assurances of future stability and the imposition of a conventional moral lesson.[33] In Henry VIII, the birth of the princess Elizabeth ends a similarly disjointed and painful narrative with similar assurances. The rush of coincidences that resolves the plot in *King John* undermines the concluding rationalizations, making the play increasingly popular with recent critics, who have discovered in it anticipations of their own project of historical demystification.[34] In *Henry VIII* the birth of Elizabeth redeems the preceding action without rationalizing it: like Shakespeare's emphasis on Katherine's virtue even as he depicts her fall, the entire plot seems calculated to demonstrate that the ways of providence are inscrutable. In the first tetralogy, by contrast, the process of retroactive reconstruction is fully realized.

The first three plays are set in a Machiavellian universe. Linked together by open-ended conclusions that conclude nothing but initiate actions to be pursued in the subsequent play, their episodic plots depict an increasingly chaotic and meaningless world and an action that seems devoid of ethical significance or providential purpose until it is explained in retrospect in *Richard III*. At the beginning of *1 Henry VI*, Henry V, the mirror of all Christian kings, has just died; as the *Henry VI* trilogy progresses, the chivalric, civic, patriotic, and ethical virtues associated with Henry V also die, often in the persons of human exemplars like Talbot and the dead king's brothers, Bedford and Gloucester, who retain and exemplify the virtues of an older world. Finally, in *3 Henry VI*, the kingdom is reduced to a Machiavellian jungle where Yorkists and Lancastrians vie with each other in treachery and atrocity, and even the loyalties that bind parent and child are violated in senseless battles in which fathers kill sons and sons kill fathers. Authority is effaced,

---

[33]For especially perceptive discussions of the way this structure interrogates the process of historiographic mythmaking, see John R. Elliott, "Shakespeare and the Double Image of King John," *Shakespeare Studies* 1 (1965), 64–84; and Virginia M. Vaughan, "*King John*: A Study in Subversion and Containment," in *King John: New Perspectives*, ed. Deborah T. Curren-Aquino (Newark: University of Delaware Press, 1989), pp. 62–75.

[34]See the two essays cited in the preceding note and the entire Aquino anthology, especially Larry S. Champion, "The 'Un-end' of *King John*: Shakespeare's Demystification of Closure," pp. 173–85.

power becomes an end in itself, and the crown becomes a commodity, tossed back and forth from one head to another at the
whim of blind fortune and the Earl of Warwick. Even the pre-
tense of hereditary legitimacy and divine right is left behind.[35]

In *3 Henry VI*, a Machiavellian figure erupts from this mael-
strom of history turned savage: Richard of Gloucester, who
promises to "set the murtherous Machevil to school" (III.ii.193),
defining in advance the role he will play in the final play in this
tetralogy. In *Richard III*, however, the ideological tables are
turned. Richard believes (as well he might, given his background in the *Henry VI* plays) that the world runs on Machiavellian principles, but almost from the first the audience is given
reason to believe that he may be mistaken. Prophecies, prophetic dreams, curses that take effect—all suggest that supernatural forces are involved in the events that Richard believes
and claims are completely under his control. For instance, we
have Richard's clever manipulations and self-congratulatory so-
liloquies as he arranges his brother Clarence's death, but we
also have Clarence's prophetic dream and death's-door recognition that his impending doom is, in fact, a recompense for
the crimes he committed in the time of Henry VI.

Richard thinks he is living in a world governed by Machiavellian *Realpolitik*, but Shakespeare places him in a world governed by providence, a dissonance that produces heavy
dramatic irony in the scenes when Richard gloats happily about
the success of his machinations while the audience, informed
not only by their foreknowledge of Richard's historically appointed doom but also by the intimations of a providential
agenda provided by the women's prophecies, know better. At
the end of the play, Richmond, the agent of providence, her-
alded by prophetic dreams and heavenly imagery, kills the tyrant and takes over, but not before Richard has been forced to
suffer the horrified recognition that he does indeed live in a
providential universe, one where he will be punished now and
forever for the crimes he committed in the past.

*Richard III* offers a neat, conventional resolution to the prob-

---

[35]For an excellent account of the shape of the first tetralogy, to which I am
much indebted, see Edward I. Berry, *Patterns of Decay: Shakespeare's Early Histories* (Charlottesville: University Press of Virginia, 1975).

lem of historical causation. All the cards have been stacked in advance, and the entire play reads like a lesson in providential history. In the first English treatise on historiography, *The true order and Methode of wryting and reading Hystories* . . . (1574), Thomas Blundeville advised,

> As touching the providence of God. . . . though things many times doe succeede according to the discourse of man's reason: yet mans wisedome is oftentymes greatlye deceyved. And with those accidents which mans wisedome reiecteth and little regardeth: God by his providence useth, when he thinketh good, to worke marveylous effects. And though he suffreth the wicked for the most part to live in prosperitie, and the good in adversitie: yet we may see by many notable examples, declaring aswell his wrath, and revenge towardes the wicked, as also his pittie and clemencie towardes the good, that nothing is done by chaunce, but all things by his foresight, counsell, and divine providence.[36]

A "notable example" of providential justice, the entire action of *Richard III* is subsumed in the ideological scheme that Blundeville recites. Richard "greatlye deceyves" himself and the other characters, but Shakespeare's audience knows from the beginning that this is a providential universe and that Richard will fall. The audience came into the theater knowing Richard's history and they came to see a play called "The Tragedy of Richard III." That knowledge offers the audience a privileged vantage point, removing them from the flux of human temporality and placing them in the omniscient position of providence itself.

The only threat to that position is Richard himself, who reaches out to seduce the audience by the sheer energy and dramatic force of his characterization. By the end, however, even Richard has been subsumed in the providential scheme, first as the diabolical figure defined, as John Blanpied suggests, "as an antitype of the providentialism it opposes,"[37] and then, like the devil himself, as an unwitting instrument for the fulfillment of a providential plan. Killing off all the characters stained by the lingering guilt of the Wars of the Roses, Richard

[36]F3. Hugh G. Dick points out (p. 149) that Blundeville's was "the first separately printed treatise in English on the art of history."
[37]John W. Blanpied, *Time and the Artist in Shakespeare's English Histories* (Newark: University of Delaware Press, 1983), p. 100.

purges the kingdom to make it ready for Richmond's accession. Counting over Richard's victims and recalling the past crimes which justify their deaths, Margaret concludes,

> Richard yet lives, hell's black intelligencer,
> Only reserv'd their factor to buy souls
> And send them thither. But at hand, at hand
> Ensues his piteous and unpitied end.
> Earth gapes, hell burns, fiends roar, saints pray,
> To have him suddenly convey'd from hence.
> Cancel his bond of life, dear God I pray,
> That I may live and say "The dog is dead."
>                                    (IV.iv.71–78)

Richard is a "factor,"[38] a purchasing agent acting for a superior power, even though he denies the authority of that power and supposes he acts on his own behalf.

In *Richard III* Shakespeare reconstructs the history he has already written, retroactively imposing a providential order that makes sense of the Machiavellian chaos he depicted in the Henry VI plays. The women's litanies of old wrongs and the repeated pattern of Richard's victims recalling just before they die the past crimes for which they are now about to pay subsume the events they recall into a teleological providential plot. Shakespeare brings all the chickens home to roost in *Richard III*, framing and containing the wild melee of human treachery, bloodshed, and injustice he depicted in the Henry VI plays in a totalizing explanatory scheme that purges moral ambiguity and eradicates ideological conflict.

*Richard III* has remained a popular play on the stage, although it is frequently revised for performance, but its neat structure probably did not satisfy Shakespeare;[39] for all the issues so com-

---

[38]On the Machiavellian, commercial implications of the "factor" image, see my discussion in section VI of this chapter of Hal's statement in *1 Henry IV*, III.ii.147–50: "Percy is but my factor, good my lord, / To engross up glorious deeds on my behalf; / And I will call him to so strict account / That he shall render every glory up."

[39]Cf. Blanpied, p. 100, where he too sees *King John* as an expression of Shakespeare's dissatisfaction with *Richard III*, although he defines that dissatisfaction in terms somewhat different from mine: "What he finds he needs, the morning after the *Richard III* blowout, is a strongly centered play that, paradoxically, does not refuse to relinquish control."

fortably resolved in the end of that play are opened up again in *King John*, a "problem history" where the audience has no sure guide through the ideological ambiguities but instead finds itself lost, like the Bastard, "among the thorns and dangers of this world" (IV.iii.141). Historical events take on meaning and coherence only after they have passed into history. Experienced in the present tense, as they happen, "actions outstrip comprehension"; the "truth" a historical narrative constructs is, as Marshall Brown points out, "a reification that only exists outside of time" or after the fact.[40] Of all Shakespeare's English histories, *King John* is set farthest back in the past, and yet of all of them it depicts a world that is least medieval and most insistently present. Caught up in the whirl of events, the audience shares the characters' uncertainties as they find themselves lost together in a "thorny wood" of ideological confusion and confused plot. In *King John* Shakespeare abandons the Tudor historians' anachronistic ascriptions of divine right and providential theory to their medieval ancestors in order to depict a world without faith or ceremony,[41] where failure and success ride on the shifting winds of chance. Late in the play, beset by political and military attack, King John gives "the ordering of this present time" to the Bastard (V.i.77); but it is tempting to speculate that Shakespeare gave it to him from the beginning. The Bastard is a fictitious character; that is, not historically legitimate, and his cynicism and illegitimate birth epitomize the lawless forces that substitute for providential order to motivate the action and move the plot in the confused "present time" of *King John*.

In many ways, *King John* offers a Machiavellian antithesis to the providential thesis so insistently laid down and retroactively imposed upon the entire first tetralogy in *Richard III*. But the second tetralogy would be difficult to read as a synthesis. Moving further into the past and retreating from the providential

[40]Marshall Brown, "'Errours Endlesse Traine': On Turning Points and the Dialectical Imagination," *PMLA* 99 (1984), 11, 21.

[41]Sigurd Burckhardt (in "*King John*: The Ordering of This Present Time," *Shakespearean Meanings*, pp. 116–43) sees *King John* as Shakespeare's critique of the Tudor myth, pointing out that Shakespeare greatly reduces the Protestant propaganda in his source, where John was depicted as a martyr to Roman Catholic wickedness.

resolution he imposed in *Richard III*, Shakespeare reopens the question of historical causation and complicates the conflicts it involves with an increasingly intense interrogation of his own historiographic project. Instead of reconciling the binary oppositions between past and present, providence and Machiavelli, theater and history, the second tetralogy destabilizes them in a whirling dialectic that increasingly calls into question both the adequacy of its own dramatic representations and the possibility of historical knowledge.

At the beginning of the second tetralogy, Shakespeare seems to be replaying the conflicts he staged in the first tetralogy, ringing new changes on the same chimes. *Richard II* begins with a situation exactly opposite to the one in *Richard III*. This time, the king who is the play's protagonist sits on an inherited throne to which he is entitled by divine right. If Richard III thinks he lives in a Machiavellian universe where authority is only another name for power, Richard II thinks he lives in a providential world where authority alone is sufficient to maintain him in office. He imagines that the king's very name can be armed against a would-be usurper—"Is not the king's name twenty thousand names? / Arm, arm, my name! a puny subject strikes / At thy great glory" (III.ii.85–87)—and that angels will fight to defend his title to the crown:

> The breath of worldly men cannot depose
> The deputy elected by the Lord;
> For every man that Bullingbrook hath press'd
> To lift shrewd steel against our golden crown,
> God for his Richard hath in heavenly pay
> A glorious angel: then if angels fight,
> Weak men must fall, for heaven still guards the right.
> (III.ii.56–62)

Shakespeare gives Richard glorious poetry, but he also supplies him with a Machiavellian antagonist, a character who speaks few words but raises large armies and rejects the comforts of imagination and philosophy with the materialistic protest,

> O, who can hold a fire in his hand
> By thinking on the frosty Caucasus?
> Or cloy the hungry edge of appetite

> By bare imagination of a feast?
> Or wallow naked in December snow
> By thinking on fantastic summer's heat?
>                              (I.iii.294–99)

In this play, unlike *Richard III*, it is the Machiavel who wins.

Despite their opposite outcomes, both plays project the ideological conflict into the opposition between a protagonist king and the antagonist who deposes him. In *Richard II*, however, Shakespeare does not simply reverse the terms of the opposition; he also complicates and compromises them. In *Richard III* the principle of historical causation is unambiguous: providentialism and divine right are clearly privileged. The dangerous theatrical power of the Machiavel is contained by his unequivocal definition as a villain. Richmond, the providential figure, is clearly a paragon of royal virtue, his victory the fulfillment of God's plan. No such simple assignment of virtue, vice, or agency can be made in *Richard II*. Richard, the hereditary king who believes heaven will protect his divine right to the throne, is still depicted as being largely at fault in his deposition. Bullingbrook, the usurper, is an enigmatic figure, clearly at fault in taking a throne that he has not inherited, but otherwise not obviously reprehensible, and certainly endorsed with the warrant of success. Moreover, the obscurity of Bullingbrook's motives makes it impossible to determine whether his victory represents the will of God or the triumph of his own Machiavellian strategy.

In the *Henry IV* plays, this duplicity intensifies. All the actions can be explained on two levels, the mystical and the political. As Matthew Wikander points out, "traditional patterns and images refuse to stay put as they do in the earlier history plays. . . . The clear rhetorical lesson that each scene seems to offer is undercut and questioned even as it is taught."[42] The duplicity is probably most obvious in the king's plans to make a pilgrimage to Jerusalem, which are explained both as a political stratagem ("to busy giddy minds with foreign quarrels" "lest rest and lying still might make them look too near unto my state"; *2 Henry IV*: IV.v.211–214) and as a religious obligation ("to wash this blood off from my guilty hand"; *Richard II*: V.vi.50; cf. *1*

---

[42]*The Play of Truth and State*, p. 27.

*Henry IV*: I.i.19–27), but it characterizes every component of the king's action. Hal's wildness is both a political problem (How will civic order be maintained in the future if the king is a riotous wastrel?) and a supernatural affliction.[43] The rebellions that beset the king throughout his reign have a similar duplicity, sometimes rationalized as retributions for Bullingbrook's crime against Richard, sometimes explained as the ambitious strivings of power-hungry nobles. Thus, *Henry IV* is a play that can be understood on either or both of two levels, like the Tudor histories that, acknowledging that all things have their first causes in the will of God, still found it profitable and useful to explore their second causes in the deeds of men.

In *Henry V*, the last play in the second tetralogy, the two views are deliberately clashed against each other. We get not only two interpretations of the action but two accounts of the action, one in the discourse of the chorus and one in the dramatic representation staged before us; and the two accounts not only differ from each other but also insist upon each other's inadequacies. Moreover, instead of reconciling the two views at the end of the play or discarding one for the other, Shakespeare lets both of them stand, directing our attention to the abyss at the center of the historiographic project: the impossibility of recovering the past or of getting behind the historiographic text (whether that text be a written record or a dramatic representation) to discover the always postulated and never graspable fiction called historical truth.

The two emblems of royal perfection, English triumph, peace, and prosperity that frame the first tetralogy—Henry V at the beginning, Henry VII at the end—are never problematized. Indeed, Henry V never even appears on stage, and Henry VII appears only at the very end of *Richard III* and only as Richmond, not as the ideal king he will become. Both, therefore, exemplify an authority that is never really seen or subjected to the tests and strains of theatrical representation. In the second tetralogy,

[43]Henry IV is characteristically skeptical: "I know not whether God will have it so / For some displeasing service I have done / That in his secret doom, out of my blood / He'll breed revengement and a scourge for me; / But thou dost in thy passages of life / Make me believe that thou art only mark'd / For the hot vengeance, and the rod of heaven, / To punish my mistreadings" (1 *Henry IV*: III.ii.4–11).

by contrast, Shakespeare subjects his icon of royal authority to those tests and strains, exploring the theatricality of royal authority and the fictiveness of historical truth even as he creates their dramatic embodiments. Henry VII, briefly introduced at the end of *Richard III* as England's savior, is never anything but God's soldier, the destined king who will unite the red rose and the white to found the Tudor dynasty. Henry V and his England, recalled with nostalgic longing as the world of his son sinks into chaos, is projected in the *Henry VI* plays in unproblematic terms as an image of lost perfection. In the second tetralogy, however, Shakespeare complicates that image by showing the process of its creation.

The second tetralogy depicts a world where "miracles are ceas'd; / And therefore we must needs admit the means / How things are perfected" (*Henry V*: I.i.67–69). The Henry we see on stage in the second tetralogy anticipates the Tudors in using the resources of theatrical role-playing to produce the perfect image of royal authority that he could not inherit from the ambiguous genealogy that left him the throne. Producing himself as "the mirror of all Christian kings," Henry appropriates the legitimating emblems of an older world to authorize himself.[44] Just as Henry VII looked to the dim mists of legendary Welsh history to ratify his claim to the English throne, Henry V invokes a tortuous, distant genealogy to ratify his claim to France. Just as Elizabeth's aspiring courtiers engaged in mock tournaments and her newly rich merchants purchased genealogical titles to authorize their newly acquired gentility, Henry appropriates Hotspur's chivalric honor to reproduce the anachronistic ideals of the world his father destroyed when he usurped the English throne.[45]

[44]Like a playwright or actor, Henry is characterized from the very beginning as an "imitator." Note, for instance, his first soliloquy in *1 Henry IV* (I.ii.197), where he announces that he will "imitate the sun." As Alexander Leggatt points out, the "promise to imitate the sun takes us back to *Richard II*; but while Richard, as rightful king, was naturally identified with the sun, Hal can only promise to *imitate* it—to produce, as his father did, a good performance in the role of king." *Shakespeare's Political Drama: The History Plays and the Roman Plays* (London: Routledge, 1988), p. 89.

[45]David Norbrook, *Poetry and Politics in the English Renaissance* (London: Routledge & Kegan Paul, 1984), p. 99, points out that "despite the archaising feudal costumes they wore at court entertainments," many of the "members of Leicester's circle were essentially nouveaux riches" and that no less a person than

—— VI ——

There is a sense in which Shakespeare's progress as a writer of English history seems to run against the current of Renaissance historiography, which moved from providential to Machiavellian explanations of historical causation. In the Machiavellian world of the Henry VI plays, Shakespeare celebrates the pagan virtues of heroic warriors like Talbot and good citizens like Alexander Iden. Moreover, these plays, like *King John*, highlight the forces that subvert the project of patriarchal history. The characters who dominate the worlds of these plays act on the Machiavellian principle of self-interest, and they prevail because they live in a Machiavellian universe governed by force and fortune rather than the providential hand of God. Moving in *Richard III* and the second tetralogy to a providential universe, Shakespeare depicts history in mythic, Christian terms, thus, it would seem, inverting the progress of Renaissance historiography, which developed in the direction of rational analysis and demystification. But there is another way to see this progress; for at the same time that Shakespeare's historical representations became more providential, they also became more self-consciously theatrical, increasingly complicated by metadramatic allusions that emphasize their status as theatrical representations. Even as he celebrates the glamor of Richard II and the perfect royalty of Henry V and depicts the working out of God's holy purpose in English history, Shakespeare emphasizes the theatricality of his own representations. The metadramatic self-consciousness of the plays of the second tetralogy invokes the growing rift between historical fact and fictional artifact to emphasize the constructed character of all historical representation.

Moving backward to the mystified medieval past of Richard II, Shakespeare's second tetralogy self-consciously reconstructs the providential order that was deconstructed in the Henry VI plays, but it also moves forward into Shakespeare's own theatrical future. Reconstituting a providential universe in explicitly theatrical terms, the plays of the second tetralogy expose their

---

the Queen's Champion at the Accession Day tilts, Sir Henry Lee, "owed much of his wealth to enclosures."

own compromised status as theatrical performances to inter-
rogate the process of historical representation that produces
images of authority and the myths that authorize them. Henry
V, the great image of royal authority in the second tetralogy, is
depicted from the first as a player of roles. Conquering France,
unifying the English nation, submitting himself first to the legal
counsel of churchmen and finally to the verdict of God in
heaven, Henry V frames his story in providential terms; but his
continual recourse to theatrical strategies to achieve those ends
also identifies Henry as a Machiavel. As Kenneth Burke points
out, Machiavelli's *Prince* "can be treated as a rhetoric insofar as
it deals with the *producing of effects upon an audience.*"[46] Separating
moral virtue from political efficacy and private character from
public mask, Machiavelli conceived politics in theatrical terms,
as, in Wylie Sypher's words, "a form of role-playing."[47]

In Shakespeare's history plays there is a persistent association
between Machiavellianism and theatricality. Richard III, the
only one of Shakespeare's English kings explicitly associated
with Machiavelli, is also the most theatrical. Images of the theater hover around Richard from the beginning. Contemplating
his impending death at Richard's hands, Henry VI asks, "What
scene of death hath Roscius now to act?" (*3 Henry VI*: V.vi.10).
Plotting with Buckingham to seize the English throne, Richard
prepares him for a theatrical performance where he will "counterfeit the deep tragedian" (*Richard III*: III.v.1–9). It is significant,
moreover, that Richard announces himself as a Machiavel in
the same speech wherein he announces himself as an actor:

---

[46] *A Grammar of Motives and a Rhetoric of Motives* (Cleveland: Meridian Books,
1962), p. 682.

[47] Wylie Sypher, *The Ethic of Time: Structures of Experience in Shakespeare* (New
York: Seabury Press, 1976), p. 28. Cf. Jonas Barish, *The Antitheatrical Prejudice*
(Berkeley: University of California Press, 1981), p. 97: "Machiavelli rarely asks
whether the prince should practice such and such a vice . . . or should possess
such and such a virtue . . . but rather whether he should be *thought* to practice
it. . . . The image is all, the reality nothing." Recent critics, especially American
new historicists and especially during the Reagan presidency, have been fascinated with the Renaissance theatricalization of power. For an influential early
exploration, see Stephen Orgel, *The Illusion of Power: Political Theater in the
English Renaissance* (Berkeley: University of California Press, 1975); for an especially committed later one, see Leonard Tennenhouse, *Power on Display: The
Politics of Shakespeare's Genres* (New York: Methuen, 1986).

Why, I can smile, and murther whiles I smile,
And cry "Content" to that which grieves my heart,
And wet my cheeks with artificial tears,
And frame my face to all occasions.
I'll drown more sailors than the mermaid shall,
I'll slay more gazers than the basilisk,
I'll play the orator as well as Nestor,
Deceive more slily than Ulysses could,
And like a Sinon, take another Troy.
I can add colors to the chameleon,
Change shapes with Proteus for advantages,
And set the murtherous Machevil to school.
                                   (III.ii.182–93)

Richard describes his diabolical theatrical power in the same terms that Renaissance writers typically used to describe actors. Both Edward Alleyn and Richard Burbage, the actor who first played Richard's role, were compared by admiring contemporaries to Proteus the shape-shifter;[48] but in Richard's self-description, the reference to Proteus slides inexorably into the reference to Machiavelli, a far more sinister symbol of perfect hypocrisy, who was also associated with Proteus in contemporary thought.

Although Richard represents the apotheosis of the Machiavellian forces in the first tetralogy, he has numerous and varied antecedents. Subverters of history, opponents of true royalty and the English state, characters like Joan, Margaret, and Jack Cade deceive their fellow characters and seduce the audience with a dangerous theatrical energy. They pursue a power to which they have no legitimate claim with the ruthless, amoral ambition that associated the image of Machiavelli in Elizabethan thought with the new commercial forces that threatened the status quo. Deceitful, ambitious, scornful of traditional restraints and traditional notions of honor, the Machiavel represented the threats to traditional order posed by emergent capitalism.

The associations between actor, merchant, and Machiavel are

[48]For a good summary of Elizabethan descriptions of actors, including those of Alleyn and Burbage, see Louis Adrian Montrose, "The Purpose of Playing: Reflections on a Shakespearean Anthropology," *Helios* n.s. 7.2 (1980), 56–57. On the image of Proteus, see Barish, pp. 99–107.

explicit in Thomas Heywood's satiric pamphlet, *Machiavel as He lately appeared to his deare Sons, the Moderne Projectors* (1641). Of one group of projectors, Heywood writes, "Their scene was the whole Kingdome. In every part of which, they stoutly acted their well seasoned interlude, which now at last is proved the Tragedie of the Actors themselves."[49] In fact, Heywood's description of the Machiavellian deceptions of "A Projector in generall" employs the same images that Richard uses in his self-characterization as a Machiavel. Just as Richard can "frame [his] face to all occasions" and "add colors to the chameleon," Heywood's projector can "change himself into as many shapes as Painters can doe colours." Like Richard, the projector has "more wit than honestie," and like him, he uses his Machiavellian devices to rise in the world and acquire titles that bespeak a nobility he does not possess.[50] The Protean, shape-shifting actor, the ruthless image of the Florentine and the new commercial adventurer merge in a single figure that combines subversive threat with theatrical power. Cut loose from the traditional bonds that unite feudal society and define the place of individuals in terms of hereditary rights and obligations, no longer subsumed under the old generic categories that reduced individuals to representations of their classes, these strikingly individualized characters represent the emergence of individual subjectivity in a changing world.[51]

Like the "new men" of emergent capitalism that Heywood satirizes, the Machiavellian subverters of established order provide the subjects for sharply individualized characterizations.

[49](London, 1641), D2ʳ.

[50]Sigs. B3–B4. For a perceptive discussion of Renaissance associations between theatrical deception and commercial trickery, see Jean-Christophe Agnew, *Worlds Apart: The Market and the Theater in Anglo-American Thought, 1550–1750* (Cambridge: Cambridge University Press, 1986), pp. 1–148. On pp. 76–77 Agnew cites Heywood's pamphlet to illustrate the way "English dramatists forced on Machiavelli's principles an association with commercial trickery that would have horrified the Florentine."

[51]On the intellectual roots of the conjunction between Machiavellianism and this new sense of personality, see Hugh M. Richmond, "Personal Identity and Literary Personae: A Study in Historical Psychology," *PMLA* 90 (1975), 209–21, especially pp. 215–18. On the roles of social change and theatrical representation in the Renaissance production of a new concept of subjectivity, see Catherine Belsey, *The Subject of Tragedy: Identity and Difference in Renaissance Drama* (London: Methuen, 1985).

Intensely theatrical, they represent not only a new kind of dramatic characterization that substitutes individual for generic attributes but a new conception of personal identity. No longer imposed by an inherited social position, the new man's identity is constructed in action: the theatrical principle of present performance replaces the historical principle of hereditary status as its defining ground.

The most compelling dramatic presences in the first tetralogy, these characters speak with distinctive dramatic voices that emerge from the undifferentiated blank verse that constitutes most of the dialogue. Nonetheless, despite the lively dramatic particularity of their voices and personalities, they are all contained ideologically within the binary opposition that defines them as enemies to royal authority and established order. The French peasant Joan and the English queen Margaret, the great Cardinal Beauford and the knavish priest John Hume, the noble lady Eleanor Cobham and the poverty-stricken Simpcox, the bricklayer's son Jack Cade and the Plantagenet pretender to the throne range in characterization from the heights of aristocratic pride to the depths of poverty and humiliation. Their languages range from learned eloquence to inarticulate illiteracy, but they all share the Machiavellian attributes of treachery and selfish, amoral ambition that define them as demonic Others. Peasant rebels, aristocratic traitors, and noble usurpers are all contained within the binary opposition between legitimate authority and Machiavellian subversion.

In *King John* and the second tetralogy, these characters become increasingly prominent, and their theatrical power becomes increasingly dangerous, reaching out to the audience with a seductive, amoral appeal and influencing the course of the action by the sheer force of their personalities. Character, in fact, emerges along with Machiavellianism as a motive force in Shakespeare's historical universe. In the providential universe of the morality play, as in the paradigmatic expressions of universal rules of causality that Aristotle found in tragedy,[52] character is subordinated to plot. As Catherine Belsey points out, the protagonist of a morality play is "a fragmented and frag-

---

[52]*Poetics*, VI. 9–11, in *Aristotle's Theory of Poetry and Fine Art*, ed. S. H. Butcher, 4th ed. (New York: Dover, 1951), pp. 24–27.

mentary figure," the battlefield for a struggle between Christ and Satan "which exists before he is born and continues after his death."[53] Character, however, becomes increasingly important in the increasingly secularized worlds of Elizabethan drama (and in the increasingly secularized world of Elizabethan England), as human agency rather than transcendental teleology comes.to motivate the action. This opposition between providential plot and Machiavellian character can be seen in the first tetralogy, where the emblematic flatness of the characters who act in the name of God and country and the uniformity of their language contrast with the vivid particularity of the characters who oppose providential order to pursue their own agendas. In the later plays, however, although characters like the Bastard in *King John* and Falstaff in the Henry IV plays exhibit many of the traits that marked their dramatic antecedents as Machiavels, they are no longer contained within the simple binary scheme that opposes character to plot and Machiavellian subversion to legitimate authority.

With the deposition of Richard II, royal authority is dispersed, and so is the subversive force that opposes it. In the second tetralogy, Machiavellianism is no longer contained by association with characters who threaten to destroy or usurp royal authority. In *1 Henry IV* the rebels Worcester and Northumberland are marked as Machiavels by their calculation and duplicity, but so is the king, the man Hotspur calls "this vile politician, Bullingbrook" (I.iii.241). The most ruthless act of Machiavellian cunning in the Henry IV plays is used, significantly, to *subdue* rebel forces. Prince John deceives the rebels at Gaultree Forest when he swears "by the honor of my blood" and gives his "princely word" (IV.ii.55–66), corrupting and compromising the very authority he invokes to win an ignoble victory. The characterization of the royal prince as a cold-blooded Machiavellian deceiver shows how far royal authority has been compromised in the second tetralogy, for the same historical personage, grown old, was depicted in *1 Henry VI* as a paragon of the old chivalric virtues, the "valiant Duke of Bedford" (III.ii.87), the subject of Talbot's eulogy, "A braver soldier never

[53]Belsey, *The Subject of Tragedy*, p. 15.

couched lance, / A gentler heart did never sway in court"
(III.ii.134–35). It is Bedford who leads the chorus of praise and
mourning for Henry V in the opening scene and Bedford whose
gallant courage inspires the English victory at Rouen. Old and
sick, Bedford refuses to leave the battlefield,

> for once I read
> That stout Pendragon in his litter sick
> Came to the field and vanquished his foes.
> Methinks I should revive the soldiers' hearts,
> Because I ever found them as myself.
>                               (III.ii.94–98)

Bedford's emblematic characterization is completely subsumed
within the binary scheme that associates noble English valor
with a heroic, historic past.

In the world of Henry IV, by contrast, the only character who
is thoroughly animated by the old feudal values is Hotspur, and
it is in the name of those values, of personal honor and Mortimer's hereditary right to the throne, that Hotspur rebels
against the king. Hotspur's honor is never questioned in the
play, but the very absoluteness of his commitment to honor
serves to compromise honor itself. To Douglas, Hotspur is the
very "king of honor" (IV.i.10); and even the king he opposes
calls him "the theme of honor's tongue" (I.i.81). Personified in
Hotspur, the old knightly honor is doubly compromised, not
only by the slightly comical enthusiasm with which he embraces
it but also by the fact that it inspires him to rebel against the
king.

Royal authority is compromised too. Not only opposed by
Hotspur in the plot, but also characterized as the calculating,
political antithesis to the impetuous, idealistic young rebel, the
king has none of the honor that should belong to royalty. Prince
Henry is perfectly aware that he must appropriate the honor he
needs from Hotspur. He tells Hotspur before their battle, "all
the budding honors on thy crest / I'll crop to make a garland
for my head" (V.iv.72–73). Earlier, he used the same chivalric
language, even the same metaphor, when he promised his father that he would "redeem" his shame "on Percy's head":

> And stain my favors in a bloody mask,
> Which wash'd away shall scour my shame with it.
> And that shall be the day, when e'er it lights,
> That this same child of honor and renown,
> This gallant Hotspur, this all-praised knight,
> And your unthought-of Harry chance to meet,
> For every honor sitting on his helm,
> Would they were multitudes, and on my head
> My shames redoubled!
>
> (III.ii.132–44)

Hal's promise is a heroic vaunt in the old chivalric tradition. He promises to "die a hundred thousand deaths / Ere break the smallest parcel of this vow" (III.ii.158–59). But even in the course of making that promise, he slips into another idiom, contaminating the language of chivalry with gross terms taken from the new commercial economy. When he swears to "make this northren youth exchange / His glorious deeds for my indignities" (III.ii.145–46), the prince transforms glorious deeds and indignities into objects of commercial exchange:

> Percy is but my factor, good my lord,
> To engross up glorious deeds on my behalf;
> And I will call him to so strict account
> That he shall render every glory up,
> Yea, even the slightest worship of his time,
> Or I will tear the reckoning from his heart.
>
> (III.ii.147–52)

The "factor" image defines in advance Hal's victory over Hotspur in knightly combat as a repossession of the honor that rightly belongs to royalty, but it also compromises that honor by terms—"factor," "render up," "engross," "strict account" and "reckoning"—that reduce the chivalric battle to a closely calculated financial transaction.[54]

Like the aspiring commercial men of Shakespeare's time, the future Henry V must struggle to achieve a status he did not inherit. Unlike Richard II, who had a clear, hereditary claim to the throne, Henry V must *earn* his legitimacy. The honor he could not inherit from the "vile politician Bullingbrook," he

---

[54]Cf. Leggatt, *Shakespeare's Political Drama*, p. 94: "The thinking is that of a chivalric hero, but the words belong to the counting-house."

must acquire from Hotspur in battle. The "cold blood he did naturally inherit of his father" he warms by drinking "good and good store of fertile sherris," in Falstaff's company (2 *Henry IV*: IV.iii.118–21).[55] Like the son of a rich tradesman sent to university to acquire the education that will make him a gentleman, Hal revels and carouses, but he also "studies his companions" (2 *Henry IV*: IV.iv.68) and acquires new languages. Learning the names of his humble subjects and mastering the terms in which they speak, he wins their recognition as the "king of courtesy" (1 *Henry IV*: II.iv.5–11). The two parts of *Henry IV*, in fact, depict a long educational process in which Prince Hal learns the skills and assumes the attributes that constitute the "mirror of all Christian kings" he will become in *Henry V* (II.Chorus,6). Like the new gentility that successful commoners were acquiring by their own efforts, the royal authority that Henry V finally represents is an achievement, not an inheritance.

What Henry V does inherit is a taint—his father's guilt for usurping Richard II's crown. The hereditary taint of his father's low origins and dishonorable ascent threatens Henry's own aspirations for worldly power and success: "Not to-day, O Lord!," he prays before his climactic battle of Agincourt, "O not to-day, think not upon the fault my father made in compassing the crown" (IV.i.292–94). Henry's struggle for France represents an effort to wipe out that taint and legitimate his status as King of England. "No king of England, if not king of France" (II.ii.193), Henry uses Agincourt as an enormous trial by combat to establish the legitimacy of his rule and earn his place in providential history. The providential legitimation, in fact, is the sole purpose of the battle. Refusing to accept any credit for the victory, he insists, "Take it, God, / For it is none but thine!" and he threatens his soldiers, "be it death proclaimed through our host / To boast of this, or take that praise from God / Which is his only" (IV.viii.111–16). The stridency of the threat exposes the anxiety that produced it, the keen sense of the absence of divine

---

[55]This speech is placed, significantly, at the end of the Gaultree Forest episode. Celebrating the virtues of sherris-sack to explain the difference between the heat and valor of Prince Henry and the cold-blooded calculation of Prince John, Falstaff emphasizes that Henry's virtues are achievements and not inheritances.

right that Henry attempts to fill by the exercise and mystification of earthly power.

It takes three plays for Henry to reconstruct the royal authority that was lost when Bullingbrook usurped the English throne, and although he finally succeeds in producing the perfect icon of royal authority in Henry V, the authority he reconstructs is deeply compromised by his recourse to Machiavellian strategies of political manipulation and theatrical display.[56] His constant role-playing celebrates the power of theater to produce the perfect image of royalty, but it also compromises the authority it produces by associating it with the ambiguous figures of actor, Machiavel, and merchant.

The authority of the playwright is also compromised. The playwright of *Richard III* conceived his authorial role in the same exalted terms that Sidney used to describe the poet. Contriving his plot to show "virtue exalted and vice punished,"[57] he distributed rewards and punishments with a poetic justice that bespoke the providential order it imitated. Like God, he created and ruled a providential universe, and he ended his play with a prayer, designed to inspire his audience to piety and patriotism. In the second tetralogy, the authorial role is divided against itself by the social and ethical differences that separated Sidney's gentleman poet writing to inspire his readers from a commercial playwright manufacturing public entertainments for financial gain.[58] As a poet, the dramatist works in imitation of divine providence to teach the ways of righteousness and draw

[56]For an extended discussion of Hal's Machiavellianism, see Blanpied, chap. 9, especially pp. 160–66. On the ways the mere fact of theatrical representation threatened to compromise royal authority, see Franco Moretti, "'A Huge Eclipse': Tragic Form and the Deconsecration of Sovereignty," *Genre* 15 (1982), 7–40, reprinted in *The Power of Forms in the English Renaissance*; and David Scott Kastan, "Proud Majesty Made a Subject: Shakespeare and the Spectacle of Rule," *Shakespeare Quarterly* 37 (Winter 1986), 459–75.

[57]*Defense*, p. 21.

[58]On Sidney's association of social rank with poetic quality, see Norbrook, *Poetry and Politics in the English Renaissance*, p. 92. See also Stephen Greenblatt, "Murdering Peasants: Status, Genre, and the Representation of Rebellion," in *Representing the English Renaissance* (Berkeley: University of California Press, 1988; originally published in *Representations* 1 [1983]), pp. 17–18 for a perceptive discussion of Sidney's anxious efforts to mark the status boundaries between himself as a gentleman amateur and the commoner who practices art as a profession.

his audience "to as high a perfection as our degenerate souls, made worse by their clay lodgings, can be capable of."[59] As a commercial playwright, he deceives and manipulates for his own profit like a Machiavel.

A deep contradiction, therefore, divides the subject of Shakespeare's English history plays from their medium, opposing the patriotic piety of historical mythmaking to the Machiavellian subversion of theatrical performance. The theater, in fact, was associated with every sort of transgression of the social and religious order that the historical myths were designed to support.[60] Common players acting the parts and wearing the clothes of kings and noblemen transgressed the hierarchical status system; providential order and genealogical history supported it. The rhetoric of antitheatrical polemic, denouncing the theater as a seat of dangerous allure "whereunto more people resort than to sermons or prayers," set the playhouse in diametrical opposition to the house of God: "More have recourse to Playing houses, then to Praying houses."[61] Sidney's poet inspired his readers to virtuous action, but the playwright of the antitheatrical tracts provided the "springs of many vices, and the stumbling blocks of godliness and virtue," seducing his audience to "adulterie and uncleannesse," and every sort of "ungodly desires," crimes, and treason:[62]

if you will learne to . . . blaspheme both Heaven and Earth: . . . If you will learn to rebel against Princes, to commit treasons . . . if you will learne to contemne GOD and all his lawes, to care nither for heaven nor hel, and to commit al kinde of sinne and mischeef,

---

[59]Sidney, *Defense*, p. 13 et passim.

[60]Many writers have explored the ways the Elizabethan theater constituted a site of transgression, but see especially Montrose, "The Purpose of Playing"; Peter Stallybrass and Allon White, *The Politics and Poetics of Transgression* (Ithaca: Cornell University Press, 1986), chap. 1; and Steven Mullaney, *The Place of the Stage: License, Play, and Power in Renaissance England* (Chicago: University of Chicago Press, 1988).

[61]Samuel Cox, letter of January 15, 1591, and I. H., *This World's Folly. Or a Warning-Peece discharged upon the Wickednesse thereof* (1615), both reprinted in E. K. Chambers, *The Elizabethan Stage* (Oxford: Clarendon Press, 1923), 4: 237, 254.

[62]George Whetstone, *A Touchstone for the Time*, printed as an "Addition" to *A Mirour for Magestrates of Cyties* (1584), and Gervase Babington, *A very Fruitful Exposition of the Commandements* (1583), reprinted in Chambers, 4:227, 225.

you need to goe to no other schoole, for all these good Examples
may you see painted before your eyes in enterludes and playes.[63]

This final statement, taken from Phillip Stubbes' *Anatomie of
Abuses*, represents an extreme example of antitheatrical invective, and the theater had its defenders as well.[64] The statement
is significant, however, because it reveals the extent to which
the subversive power of the theater was associated with rebellion against the authority of God and the king, the same authority that providential history was designed to justify.

— VII —

*Henry V* ends the two tetralogies in a play of unresolved
contradictions. The action Shakespeare dramatizes contradicts
the story the chorus tells. The king's recourse to Machiavellian
plotting contradicts his representations of his achievements as
manifestations of providential purpose, and his role-playing
contradicts his characterization as a true embodiment of royal
authority. The chorus constantly urges the audience to suppose
that the historical persons and events the play depicts are actually present, and just as constantly reminds them that they
are only watching a theatrical representation that falls far short
of the historical reality it attempts to imitate.

The final chorus echoes these contradictions even as it attempts to deny them. Cast in the form of a sonnet, the chorus
employs the familiar sonnet strategy of translating existential
contradiction into verbal antithesis and paradox[65] and resorting
to rhetorical appeal to escape from logical impasse:

> Thus far, with rough and all-unable pen,
> Our bending author hath pursu'd the story,

[63]Phillip Stubbes, *The Anatomie of Abuses: Contayning a Discoverie, or briefe
Summarie of such Notable Vices and Imperfections, as now raigne in many Christian
Countreyes of the Worlde: but (especiallie) in a verie famous Ilande called Ailgna*
(London, 1583), in Chambers, 4:224.

[64]For an account of these defenses, and of the deep instability of contemporary conceptions of the theater, see Chapter 3, section III.

[65]I am indebted to an unpublished paper of Myra Jehlen's for the distinction
between paradox and unresolved contradiction.

In little room confining mighty men,
Mangling by starts the full course of their glory.
Small time; but in that small most greatly lived
This star of England. Fortune made his sword;
By which the world's best garden he achieved,
And of it left his son imperial lord.
Henry the Sixt, in infant bands crown'd King
Of France and England, did this king succeed;
Whose state so many had the managing,
That they lost France, and made his England bleed;
Which oft our stage hath shown; and for their sake,
In your fair minds let this acceptance take.

The chorus's description of Henry's French conquest ("Fortune made his sword: / By which the world's best garden he
achieved") redeems that Machiavellian and commercial implications of "fortune" and "achieved" with the providential warrant implied by the allusion to Eden. And the sestet erases the
distinction the chorus has emphasized throughout the play—
the intractable difference between the historic past and Shakespeare's dramatic representations. The sestet moves impercep-
tibly from England's historical future in the troubled reign of
Henry VI to Shakespeare's theatrical past in the successful plays
he had written about that reign, from the painful history of
bleeding and loss to the pleasing theatrical spectacles that represented that history.

Refusing to distinguish between historical event and theatrical
performance, the sestet of the final sonnet also denies the ir-
reconcilable opposition between past pain and present pleasure.
Conflating bloody battles with theatrical pleasure, the chorus
now elides the social and ethical differences that separate participation in heroic history from attendance in a commercial
theater. At the end of the first tetralogy, Richmond invited
Shakespeare's audience to join him in a patriotic prayer for a
common future of "smooth-fac'd peace," "smiling plenty" and
"fair properous days." At the end of *Henry V* the chorus asks
the audience to approve a theatrical performance. The playwright of the second tetralogy takes on a divided role, compromising the notable image of virtue he produces in Henry V and
the providential plot that depicts Henry's triumph with the Machiavellian taint of his own theatrical, commercial contrivance.

When the Bastard in *King John* compared the citizens of Angiers to the members of a theater audience who "gape . . . at . . .
industrious scenes and acts of death" (II.i.375–76), he exposed
the debasement and commodification of the heroic past in the
hands of professional actors working for the pleasure of a low-
born audience and their own profit. At the beginning of *Henry
V*, the Prologue addressed the same problem when he com-
plained about the inadequacy of "this wooden O" to contain
the heroic past and wished for "princes to act, and monarchs
to behold the swelling scene"; only then, he said, would "warlike Harry" be "like himself." He wished, as David Kastan
points out, "that the contradictions of playing would disappear." Purified of the social contamination of bourgeois actors
and a socially heterogeneous audience, the representation of
the heroic past "would be simply presentation and history plays
would be history itself."[66] In the final sonnet, he papers over
all these deficiencies and contradictions—the social deficiencies
of actors and audience and the inadequacy of the theatrical
representation—when he submits himself and the play to the
public theater audience he actually has. The sonnet ends with
a rhetorical appeal to the audience that is also a commercial
appeal—if the audience does not accept the play, the play will
not make money. The appeal rests on an ambiguous pronoun—
the "their" in "for their sake"—that conflates the authority of
history with the popularity of the Henry VI plays.

The final chorus's reference to the Henry VI plays defines the
place of *Henry V* in Shakespeare's historical plot. Not only the
last play in the two tetralogies, it is also their center; for the plot
of Shakespeare's historical reconstruction bends the teleological,
chronological line of his historiographic sources into a circle,
beginning and ending with the death of Henry V. The circle is
joined at the point that represents the moment of loss, and, like
the "wooden O" of Shakespeare's theater, it circumscribes an
absence—the heroic past and royal authority that the name of
Henry V denotes. It replaces the purposeful, linear progress of
history with the endless work of historiography and the endless
repetition of theatrical performance, obsessively moving about
a lost center they can never recover. Enacting the obsessive

---

[66]Kastan, "Proud Majesty Made a Subject," pp. 473–74.

movement it describes, the image of the circle itself circles back
to the first act of 1 *Henry VI* to recall Joan's resonant lines:

> Glory is like a circle in the water,
> Which never ceaseth to enlarge itself,
> Till by broad spreading it disperse to nought.
> With Henry's death the English circle ends,
> Dispersed are the glories it included.
>
> (I.ii.133–37)

Here too the circle encloses an absence, and here too it is associated with Henry's death and the erasure of English heroic
history.

The desired object of theatrical recuperation, the king who
presided over the transcendent moment when the English star
"most greatly lived" is finally revealed as the product of his
own theatrical recuperation, his providential authority the
product of Machiavellian manipulation. The unresolved contradictions of *Henry V* are those of Shakespeare's entire historiographic project. Infused by nostalgic yearning, the plays
begin in a heroic effort to recuperate a lost, heroic past, but they
end by calling attention to the ineluctable absence of that past
and their own compromised status as commercial, theatrical
representations.

# 3

## Anachronism and Nostalgia

The Douglas, says Prince Hal, is reputed to be such a good shot that he can kill a flying sparrow with his pistol (II.iv.345–46). The Variorum edition of *1 Henry IV* reminds us that pistols were not yet invented in the days of Henry IV; but without such a footnote, modern readers are likely to miss the anachronism. Even if we do notice it, we have been thoroughly instructed that neither Shakespeare nor his original audience was troubled by such inconsistencies.

Critical thinking about Shakespeare's use of temporality has changed very little in the two hundred years since Dr. Johnson wrote his own footnote on Douglas's pistol—"Shakespeare never has any care to preserve the manners of the time,"[1]—and his own famous rebuttal of the neoclassical critics who thought Shakespeare's Romans not sufficiently Roman and his kings not sufficiently royal:

[1]Reprinted in *A New Variorum Edition of Henry the Fourth Part I*, ed. Samuel Burdett Hemingway (Philadelphia: J. B. Lippincott, 1936), p. 157n. For other examples of Shakespeare's use of anachronisms, see the indexes and notes to the Variorum editions; Paul Stapfer, *Shakespeare and Classical Antiquity: Greek and Latin Antiquity as Presented in Shakespeare's Plays*, trans. Emily J. Carey (London: C. Kegan Paul, 1880), pp. 107–10; Wilhelm Creizenach, *Geschichte des neuren Dramas* (1909, rev. ed. 1911), translated as *English Drama in the Age of Shakespeare* (Philadelphia: Lippincott, 1916), pp. 156–57; and chapter 4: "Sequel, Anachronism, and Multiple Time," in Clifford J. Ronan's book in progress, "Antique Romans: Semiotics of Power in Roman Plays of Shakespeare's England, 1585–1635."

His characters are not modified by the customs of particular places, unpractised by the rest of the world; by the peculiarities of studies or professions, which can operate but upon small numbers; or by the accidents of transient fashions or temporary opinions: they are the genuine progeny of common humanity, such as the world will always supply, and observation will always find.[2]

Celebrating Shakespeare as the universal poet, Johnson ascribed to Shakespeare's representations of the historical past the same ahistorical validity that he found represented in Shakespeare. Denying Shakespeare's historical specificity and distance, he anticipates the nineteenth- and twentieth-century Shakespeare criticism that refused either to confine the "Shakespeare" it constructed within the limitations of his own temporality or to acknowledge that Shakespeare's representations of the historical past were conditioned and compromised by a deep sense of anachronism.[3] Johnson remains enough a man of his own rationalist age to arm himself against "superstitious veneration" by constructing a list of Shakespeare's faults. In comparison to the eloquent paean to Shakespeare's universal genius, however, the list of faults seems flat and perfunctory, as if Johnson felt constrained by the neoclassical requirement for judicious appraisal that forced him to look for deficiencies in the author in whom he had invested his own ideal of poetic truth. Apparently groping for examples, he reintroduces the issue of Shakespeare's anachronisms, this time acknowledging that they are "faults."

[2]From the Preface to Johnson's edition of Shakespeare's plays, reprinted in Hazard Adams, ed., *Critical Theory since Plato* (New York: Harcourt Brace Jovanovich, 1971), pp. 331, 330.

[3]I do not, of course, mean to imply that these critics were simply echoing Johnson. In fact, although Johnson's defense of Shakespeare's anachronisms opposed the prevailing critical opinion of his time, the antihistorical bias of his argument identifies it with a dominant tradition in western thought. The binary opposition that privileges universal truth over particular fact can be seen, e.g., in Aristotle's argument that poetry "is a more philosophical and a higher thing than history" (*Poetics*: IX.3), in the medieval thought that ignored the accidents of time and place to subsume all human history under the unchanging, atemporal light of eternity, and in Sidney's conflation of the two in the claim that poetic invention reveals ideal truths inaccessible to historical report. See *Sir Philip Sidney's Defense of Poesy*, ed. Lewis Soens (Lincoln: University of Nebraska Press, 1970), pp. 8–10, 19–23.

> He had no regard to distinction of time or place, but gives to one age or nation, without scruple, the customs, institutions, and opinions of another, at the expense not only of likelihood, but of possibility. . . . Shakespeare, indeed, was not the only violator of chronology, for in the same age Sidney, who wanted not the advantages of learning, has, in his *Arcadia*, confounded the pastoral with the feudal times, the days of innocence, quiet and security, with those of turbulence, violence, and adventure.[4]

The reference to Sidney has the immediate effect of exonerating Shakespeare from the "fault" of anachronism; it also situates Shakespeare's practice in the context of contemporary discourse. Nonetheless, Johnson never attributes either to Shakespeare or to Shakespeare's contemporaries the consciousness of anachronistic distance from a lost historical past that would refute Johnson's own notion of universal, atemporal truth, not only as an attribute of Shakespeare's historical representations but also as the ideal that animated his own.

For Johnson, the anachronisms can only be faults, either faults to be blamed as the embarrassing evidence of Shakespeare's lack of education or faults to be excused as the products of an unenlightened age or the by-products of a genius too preoccupied with the essence of universal truth to trouble itself with the accidents of transient fashions or temporary opinions. These positions, in fact, pretty much exhaust the range of commentary on Shakespearean anachronism from Johnson's time to our own. In the eighteenth century, editors noted the places where Shakespeare was "guilty of an anachronism," attributing the errors either to Shakespeare's ignorance or to the benighted age in which he lived.[5] They historicized Shakespeare's practice, but only at the cost of denying that Shakespeare and his contemporaries were capable of historicizing their own past.

Swimming in the high tide of bardolatry, nineteenth-century critics dismissed their predecessors' objections as irrelevant quibbles. They expressed their disdain for the mundane details

---

[4]Adams, p. 333.

[5]Edmond Malone (ed. 1790), cited in the note to III.ii.32–33 in the Variorum edition of *1 Henry IV*. Although recent criticism has been remarkably silent on the question of Shakespearean anachronism, the Variorum editions of the plays provide the materials for a capsule history. See, for instance, the notes on *1 Henry IV*, II.i.25 and III.ii.103; on *Coriolanus*, I.iv.82 and II.ii.108 and on *Antony and Cleopatra*, II.v.6.

of historical chronology, the pedantry of the eighteenth-century editors, and the inadequacies of Shakespeare's theater in order to celebrate the transcendent poetic genius they found exemplified in Shakespeare. Writing at the beginning of the twentieth century, the German critic Wilhelm Creizenach manages to include what seems to have been the full range of available positions:

> Anachronisms play a great part in the dispute over the extent of Shakespeare's education, which aroused so much eager controversy among the English critics during the eighteenth century. ... But in most cases these anachronisms appear to have been due to the indifference of genius rather than to intention. ... In addition ... it would have been impossible, even with the best intentions, for a poet to maintain any accuracy of historical setting at a period when the arts of scenic mounting and costume were completely inadequate for the purpose.[6]

Creizenach celebrates the transcendent genius of his author by insisting on Shakespeare's indifference to historical fact, but he also invokes the specificity of time and place—history, in other words—in order to sneer at the misguided fastidiousness of eighteenth-century English critics and the technological inadequacy of the sixteenth-century English theater. As a "poet," Shakespeare stands above history: the nature of his education is irrelevant, the material practice of his theater "inadequate" to realize his sublime intentions.

During the last fifty years, criticism has had almost nothing to say about Shakespeare's use of anachronisms, perhaps the legacy of the bardolatry that attributed the anachronisms to the negligence of a mind preoccupied with higher things, perhaps on the assumption that neither Shakespeare nor his audience would have noticed them.[7] With his eye on the eternal verities, Shakespeare could hardly be expected to anticipate the cavils

[6]*English Drama in the Age of Shakespeare,* pp. 156–57.

[7]A notable exception is Sigurd Burckhardt's brilliant argument in *Shakespearean Meanings* (Princeton: Princeton University Press, 1968), pp. 4–11, that the clock in *Julius Caesar* is a deliberate anachronism, designed to signify to the audience that "time is now reckoned in a new, Caesarean style" (p. 9). Although I am not entirely convinced by Burckhardt's interpretation of the clock's significance, his argument that the anachronism is deliberate has been an important influence in this chapter.

of pedants that the conspirators in *Julius Caesar* wear anachronistic hats and Antony's Cleopatra lived too soon to play at billiards and the Douglas kills sparrows with a not-yet-invented firearm. With *their* eyes dimmed by the ignorance of a benighted age, the members of Shakespeare's original audience were not likely to be disturbed when they saw Posthumus wave a glove in the first-century England of Cymbeline any more than they worried about the location of the seacoast in Bohemia.

We know, however, that at least one of Shakespeare's contemporaries *did* worry. William Drummond's record of his conversations with Ben Jonson in 1619 reports Jonson's observation that "Sheakspear in a play brought in a number of men saying they had suffered Shipwrack in Bohemia, wher there is no Sea neer by some 100 Miles."[8] More learned than most of his contemporaries and also more committed to the new ideals of accurate historical scholarship and realistic dramatic representation, Jonson anticipates the eighteenth-century editors' objections to Shakespeare's anachronisms.[9] Shakespeare, along with the majority of his contemporary playwrights, was no more meticulous about the dates of historical events than he was about the literal details of geography, but the requirement for factual accuracy that was transforming the practice of historiography would soon transform the practice of dramatic imitation as well. Moreover, the issue of anachronism was not only a subject of consciousness in Shakespeare's world; it was also hotly contested, for it marked both the emergent boundary between history and fiction and the cultural transformation that produced it.

Medieval and early Renaissance poets, like their contemporary historians, displayed no sense of anachronism, and many writers besides Shakespeare continued to use anachronisms right through the sixteenth century. Apropos of the Douglas's pistol, for instance, George Steevens noted that "Beaumont and Fletcher, in *The Humorous Lieutenant* [a play written around 1620]

---

[8]See "Conversations with Drummond" in *Ben Jonson*, ed. C. H. Herford and Percy Simpson (Oxford: Clarendon Press, 1925), 1:138.

[9]Stapfer, however, notes that on at least one occasion Jonson "forgot himself so far as to observe, in describing the character of obsequious clients, in 'Sejanus' (I.i.), that they observe their patron 'as his watch observes his clock'" (p. 112). For other examples of Jonsonian anachronism, see Creizenach, p. 158.

have equipped one of the immediate successors of Alexander the Great with a pistol."[10] The issue, then, is not whether or not Shakespeare and his contemporaries *used* anachronisms; everyone knows that they did. The issue is whether or not they knew what they were doing when they used them.

Both medieval and Renaissance representations of the past use anachronisms. What distinguishes the Renaissance is the *sense* of anachronism, the recognition of temporal distance that alienated a nostalgic present from a lost historical past. Typically, medieval writers of history display no sense of anachronism, although they use it constantly. When a thirteenth-century Florentine chronicler reports that once when the wife of Catiline was at mass in the church of Fiesole on Easter morning, a centurion went up and spoke to her, he uses an anachronism.[11] When the Fool in *King Lear* says, "This prophecy Merlin shall make, for I live before his time" (III.ii.95), he expresses a sense of anachronism.

Herman L. Ebeling has traced the modern usage of the term "anachronism" to mean "an error in respect to dates" or "an error which implies the misplacing of persons or events in time" to a text written during this period.[12] It expressed a new awareness of the difference and distance that separate a historiographic text from the history it purports to represent. Designating the place where the newly distinct categories of past and present came together, anachronisms were purged from historiographic narratives because they marked a site of repression, the growing recognition that history is always and inevitably constructed in retrospect. Still permitted in poetic fictions, they also marked the different purposes and methods that now distinguished poet from historiographer and, as a result, the radical instability of Shakespeare's hybrid genre.[13] This insta-

---

[10]Cited in the Variorum edition of *1 Henry IV*, p. 157n. For other examples of anachronisms in the work of Shakespeare's contemporaries, see Ronan, chapter 4; Creizenach, pp. 155–58, and Stapfer, pp. 111–13.

[11]Quoted by Peter Burke, in *The Renaissance Sense of the Past* (London: Edward Arnold, 1969), p. 1.

[12]"The Word 'Anachronism,'" *MLN* 52 (1937), 120–21. He cites the 1629 edition of Joseph Justus Scaliger's *De Emendatione Temporum* (1583).

[13]The use of anachronisms in poetry was much debated. Castelvetro criticized Sophocles for having a chariot race at the Pythian games reported in his *Electra* because "history makes evident" that the race was not part of the games at

bility was political as well as epistemological: the multiply conflicted site designated by anachronism was also the point where
historiographic representation, whether in the form of written
narrative or dramatic reenactment, could take on a dangerous
present relevance.

Dignified and distanced by antiquity or elevated into the transcendent reaches of atemporal universal truth, historical
representation could be defended against present political
censure.[14] This is the strategy Ralegh employs in the Preface to
his *History of the World*. Mindful that "whosoever, in writing a
modern history, shall follow truth too near the heels, it may
happily strike out his teeth," he declares his intention "to write
of the eldest times," but he also feels the necessity to disclaim
any intention to "point at the present" or "tax the vices of those
that are yet living, in their persons that are long since dead."[15]
Anachronisms were likely to be taken as clear evidence of an
intention to "point at the present." On the day before their
unsuccessful uprising against Queen Elizabeth, followers of the

---

the time represented in the play ("Commentary on the Poetics of Aristotle"
[1571], trans. Allen H. Gilbert, in *Literary Criticism: Plato to Dryden*, ed. Allen
H. Gilbert [Detroit: Wayne State University Press, 1962], pp. 356–57). Torquato
Tasso compared a poet who uses anachronisms to "a painter of little judgment
who presents a figure of Cato or Cincinnatus clothed according to the fashions
of the young men of Milan or Naples" or gives Hercules "a doublet and Helmet
as Giraldi [Cinthio] did in his poem" (*Discourses on the Heroic Poem* [1594],
Gilbert, pp. 482–83). Cinthio, by contrast, argued that although historians are
obliged to report the past accurately, poets who write of ancient affairs "seek
to harmonize them with their own customs and their own age, introducing
things unlike those of ancient times and suitable to their own. . . . in order to
give at once profit and delight by satisfying the men of that age in which they
write, a thing that is not permitted to those who write histories" ("On the
Composition of Romances" [1549], Gilbert, pp. 270–71). Note that Cinthio de-
fends the poets' use of anachronisms as deliberate choices, dictated by the
differences between poetry and history, not as insignificant lapses unlikely to
be noticed by an audience, and that he associates them with a poet's obligation
to make the history he represents relevant to the concerns of his present
audience.

[14]Marcus, *Puzzling Shakespeare: Local Reading and its Discontents* (Berkeley:
University of California Press, 1988), pp. 26–30.

[15]*The Works of Sir Walter Ralegh, Kt., now first collected* (1829; rpt. New York:
Burt Franklin, 1966), 2:lxiii. Cf. the example cited by Janet Clare, in "'Greater
Themes for Insurrection's Arguing': Political Censorship of the Elizabethan
and Jacobean Stage," *Review of English Studies* n.s. 38 (1987), 170, of the censorship of certain passages from the second edition of Holinshed's *Chronicles*
because they recounted "matters of later yeeres that concern the State."

Earl of Essex sponsored a performance of Shakespeare's *Richard II*, apparently hoping that the play would incite its audience to join their rebellion. A tiny anachronism, not likely to attract attention in a modern theater, occurs in act II, scene i, when one of the fourteenth-century conspirators against King Richard charges that the king has used benevolences to extort money from his subjects. Shakespeare may have known that Richard II never used the forced loans called benevolences; Holinshed, his source for most of the history plays, states that benevolences were introduced by Edward IV, who reigned late in the following century. And the authorities in Elizabeth's England certainly knew that Richard II never used benevolences because this very anachronism, present not only in Shakespeare's play but also in a seditious *Life of Henry IIII* by Sir John Hayward, was cited at the trial of Essex as evidence that "the times of Elizabeth rather than those of Richard II were in question."[16]

Not every anachronism had such profound or dangerous implications; many of them must have passed without comment. Often, Shakespeare simply takes advantage of a customary poetic license to rearrange events within the historical time frame of his play, telescoping two or three battles into one decisive encounter, altering the order in which events occurred, or manipulating the ages of historical characters to make a dramatic point. Thus, in *1 Henry IV* Hotspur, historically three years older than the king, is made the contemporary of Prince Hal so that he can serve as a foil to the heir apparent, and thus Henry VI's Queen Margaret (dead in France in 1482) is kept alive in the England of Richard III to rail at the Yorkists and remind the audience of the past crimes that make their present sufferings justified.[17]

[16]Lily B. Campbell, *Shakespeare's "Histories": Mirrors of Elizabethan Policy* (San Marino, Calif.: Huntington Library, 1947), p. 201. Modern scholars disagree on the extent—in fact, on the presence—of political allegory in the play, but even the Arden editor, Peter Ure, who minimizes the political allegory, comments on the significance of this anachronism (see the Arden edition, London: Methuen, 1961, p. 65n). For a brief (although not unbiased) summary of the controversy, see the Arden edition, pp. lvii–lxii.

[17]However, even these anachronisms are suggestive. Appearing only twice on stage (I.iii and IV.4), both times as an eavesdropper who enters the ongoing dialogue to demand and foretell the divine vengeance that will descend upon the Yorkists, Margaret speaks, like a voice from the dead, from a vantage point beyond that of the represented historical action. For a discussion of the sig-

Anachronisms like these, involving alterations of the order of events within a historical context, may or may not be noticed by an audience, for all the events remain situated within history: they are still told, as it were, in the past tense. On the other hand, anachronisms that disrupt the historical context to create direct confrontations between past and present are more radical in their effect. The very essence of history is that it deals with the past, with events that have already taken place. Therefore, any invocation of the present in a history play tends to create radical dislocations: it invades the time-frame of the audience, and its effect is no less striking than that of a character stepping off the stage to invade the audience's physical space or addressing them directly to invade their psychological space.

Those dislocations are remarkably double-edged. On the one hand, they can produce an illusion of presence. Breaking the frame of historical representation, anachronisms can dissolve the distance between past events and present audience in the eternal present of dramatic performance. On the other hand, and especially in conjunction with metadramatic allusion, anachronisms can also produce a kind of alienation effect. Thus, when the conspirators in *Julius Caesar* say, "How many ages hence / Shall this our lofty scene be acted over / In states unborn and accents yet unknown! / How many times shall Caesar bleed in sport" (III.i.111–14), Shakespeare's English audience was reminded of their situation in the playhouse and the actors' status as actors representing an event that had taken place so long ago that even the English language the actors were in fact speaking was yet unknown. The anachronistic reference to the present theatrical occasion reminds the audience of the vast gulf of time and awareness that separates them from the historical events represented on stage and the barrier of mediation implicit in the bodies of the actors and the translated words they speak.

In a very important sense, anachronism is built into the entire project of history-making, since the historian always constructs the past in retrospect, imposing the shapes of contemporary

---

nificance of Shakespeare's alteration of Hotspur's age, see section V of this chapter.

interests and desires on the relics of a former age. Historiographic texts, however, tend to restrain this anachronism, for
they are written in the past tense, that is, in a form that enforces
the temporal separation between past historical events and present historiographic representation. The texts of history plays,
by contrast, are much less stable. Generic hybrids, they conflate
the absent past of historical representation with the embodied
presence of dramatic performance. Written in the present tense,
presenting the past, they constitute a medium for the mingling
of past and present that Renaissance theorists taught us to call
anachronism. Staging the English past in the volatile and ideologically conflicted arena of present theatrical performance,
Shakespeare's English history plays threatened, by the conditions of their production, to expose the present ideological motives that implicitly determined the shape that history took and
subject them to public contest. Perhaps that is the reason that
so many of Shakespeare's most striking anachronisms take the
form of metadramatic references to the present theatrical occasion.

—— II ——

When Richard III compares himself to the murderous Machevil, he speaks anachronistically. Richard died in 1485, when
Machiavelli was only sixteen years old. *The Prince* was not written until 1513, not printed until 1532.[18] Like the Bastard's metadramatic comparison between the citizens of Angiers and the
theater audience that watches industrious scenes and acts of
death, Richard's anachronistic references to the Machevil and
the chameleon player break the frame of historical representation by reminding the audience of the present theatrical occasion. In the century between Richard's death and Shakespeare's
play, "the Machevil" had been transformed from a historical
Florentine writer to a stock character on the English stage.[19]

[18]Felix Raab, *The English Face of Machiavelli: A Changing Interpretation, 1500–
1700* (London: Routledge and Kegan Paul, 1964), p. 30.
[19]For an account of sixteenth-century English responses to Machiavelli, see
Raab, chap. 2, "Machiavelli's Reception in Tudor England," pp. 30–76.

Along with the reference to Proteus, which recalls the `chame-
leon player of the antitheatrical tracts, it alludes to a theater
that was a recent innovation, inconceivable in the world
of Richard III.

As these examples suggest, anachronistic juxtapositions of
past and present involve many of the same conflicts that are
implicated in the opposition between providential and Machiavellian conceptions of historical causation. The past is the locus
of transcendent value, the present the site of theatrical mediation and social debasement. Defending the theater against
charges of subversiveness, Thomas Heywood invoked classical
precedent to describe the physical playhouse as a model and
microcosm of the traditional order of society. In Heywood's
account of the theater built by Julius Caesar, ornaments, structure, and seating arrangements all serve to enforce a hierarchical
social order:

> So had the starres their true and coelestiall course; so had the
> spheares, which in their continuall motion made a most sweet
> and ravishing harmony: Here were the Elements and planets in
> their degrees. . . . In briefe, in that little compasse were compre-
> hended the perfect modell of the firmament. . . . In the principall
> galleries were special remote, selected & chosen seats for the
> Emperour, *patres conscripti*, Dictators, Consuls, Pretors, Tribunes,
> Triumviri, Decemviri, Ediles, Curules, and other Noble Officers
> among the Senators: all other roomes were free for the plebe, or
> multitude.[20]

The Roman theater Heywood describes serves as a perfect
instrument of ideological control, but things were radically dif-

[20]*An Apology for Actors* (London: Nicholas Okes, 1612), D2$^v$-D3$^r$. As Leo
Braudy points out, "The seating arrangement [Heywood describes] was a per-
fect mirror of the hierarchy of society." See Braudy's *The Frenzy of Renown:
Fame and Its History* (New York: Oxford University Press, 1986), pp. 317–18.
Cf. the description of classical drama as an instrument of ideological control
in *The Arte of English Poesie. Contrived into three Bookes: The first of Poets and Poesie,
the second of Proportion, the third of Ornament* (London: Richard Field, 1589), in
*Elizabethan Critical Essays*, ed. G. Gregory Smith (Oxford: Oxford University
Press, 1904), 2:32–39. Although the text was published anonymously, it is
usually attributed to George Puttenham. See also Jonathan V. Crewe, "The
Hegemonic Theater of George Puttenham," *English Literary Renaissance* 16
(1986), 71–85.

ferent in the actual theaters of Heywood's own time, where each viewer's place was determined, not by the protocols of a traditional status system but by the amount of money he or she had paid for that day's admission. As Jean Howard has pointed out, the public theater of Shakespeare's time was first and foremost "a commercial venture," a place where "one's money, not one's blood or title, decide[d] how high and how well one sat, or whether, indeed, one stood."[21] The subversive effects of this practice were recognized as early as 1574, when the Merchant Taylors decided to discontinue the performance of plays in their common hall:

> Whereas at our comon playes and such lyke exercises whiche be comonly exposed to be seene for money, everye lewd persone thinketyh himself (for his penny) worthye of the chief and most comodious place withoute respecte of any other either for age or estimacion in the comon weale, whiche bringeth the youthe to such an impudente famyliaritie with theire betters that often tymes greite contempte of maisters, parents, and magistrats foloweth thereof, as experience of late in this our comon hall hath sufficyently declared, where by reason of the tumultuous disordered persones repayringe hither to see suche playes as by our schollers were here lately played, the Maisters of this Worshipful Companie and their deare ffrends could not have entertaynmente and convenyente place as they ought to have had.[22]

The Merchant Taylors had better uses for their hall. The new public theaters, by contrast, were sites where place and privilege continued to be bought and sold, and newly determined at every performance. As a result, they provided graphic demonstrations of the power of money to disrupt the traditional order of society.

Within those theaters, the use of metadramatic anachronisms focused the radical contradictions implicit in the entire project

---

[21]"Crossdressing, the Theatre, and Gender Struggle in Early Modern England," *Shakespeare Quarterly* 39 (1988), 440. Howard also develops this point, to which I am much indebted, in a brilliant paper entitled "Scripts versus/and Playhouses: Ideological Production and the Renaissance Public Theater," presented at the 1988 annual convention of the Modern Language Association.

[22]Chambers, *Elizabethan Stage*, 2:75.

of historical recuperation on stage. As anachronisms, they break the frame of historical representation to mark the difference between historical past and present reconstruction of that past. As metadramatic allusions, they call attention to the present reality of theatrical performance—the scene, not only of the desired recuperation of an idealized past but also of the present degeneration that made the recuperation desired. The objects of Shakespeare's representation, the medieval aristocrats and kings who perform the roles assigned by God in a providential script, participate in the historiographic project of ideological mystification, a project always vulnerable to subversion by references to the present scene of theatrical performance.[23]

Although all Shakespeare's metadramatic allusions are, ipso facto, anachronistic, not all of his anachronisms are metadramatic. Nonetheless, even those anachronisms that do not invoke the fact of theatrical performance often debase the objects of historical representation by associating them with the forces of present social change and disruption. When the French soldiers in *1 Henry VI* use anachronistically modern weapons against their English enemies, they use a new technology that was perceived as degrading the older practice of war as a noble vocation governed by the aristocratic code of chivalry. The anachronistic rapier with which Fitzwater threatens Aumerle in *Richard II* carries similar connotations. Aumerle remains loyal to the old king, Richard. Declaring his allegiance to the soon-to-be-crowned usurper, Henry IV, Fitzwater threatens Aumerle with the new weapon of a Renaissance courtier (IV.i.40). By contrast, the good Duke Humphrey in *2 Henry VI*, the last survivor of an older, better world, has an old-fashioned "two-hand sword" (II.i.45). In each case, anachronistically modern weapons serve as images of debasement, associating the users with the disturbing forces of change that motivated the countervailing construction of an idealized medieval past.

[23]As Walter Cohen points out, "However aristocratic the explicit message of a play, the conditions of its production introduced alternative effects." *Drama of a Nation: Public Theater in Renaissance England and Spain* (Ithaca: Cornell University Press, 1985), p. 183.

A similar use of new military technology to express the new world's debasement of the old appears in *King John*. Set farthest back in the past of all Shakespeare's English history plays, *King John*, as I argued earlier, is also the most anachronistically contemporary in Shakespeare's representation. Defending by force a throne to which he has no legitimate hereditary right, John immediately threatens to assault his enemies with anachronistic cannon (I.i.26).[24] Cannon play a major role in the inconclusive battle for Angiers, where they are employed by both armies. Coupled with the Bastard's comparison between the citizens watching the battle and the audience in an Elizabethan theater, the repeated references to cannon (II.i.37, 210, 251, 382, 461, 462) displace the war from its medieval setting, transforming it from a chivalric contest to settle the issue of divine right to a modern battle where both the point of contention and the means of determining the verdict are reduced to physical power and material wealth.

Insofar as the entire project of Renaissance historiography— its construction in the Tudor chronicles and its representation on Shakespeare's stage—was driven by nostalgia, anachronistic intrusions of present reality tend to contaminate the idealized object of desired recuperation. The anachronistic "benevolences" (II.i.250) that Richard II uses to extort money from his subjects help to express Richard's profanation of the royal legacy he inherited from his glorious Plantagenet ancestors.[25] Although the historical Richard was known for lavish personal expenditure,[26] Shakespeare represents his extravagance in terms that associate it with the luxurious modern self-indulgence of sixteenth-century courtiers:

[24]See my discussions of *King John* in Chapters 2 and 4. For a full account of the ways anachronistic invocations of Elizabethan reality serve as images of debasement in *King John*, see Virginia M. Vaughan, "*King John*: A Study in Subversion and Containment," in Deborah T. Curren-Aquino, ed., *King John: New Perspectives* (Newark: University of Delaware Press, 1989), pp. 62–75.

[25]Benevolences were not introduced until the time of Edward IV. See note 16, this chapter.

[26]See, e.g., Raphael Holinshed, *Chronicles of England, Scotland and Ireland* (1587; rpt. London: J. Johnson et al., 1808), 2:868, for a description of the ways in which Richard "kept the greatest port, and mainteined the most plentifull house that ever any king in England did either before his time or since."

Report of fashions in proud Italy,
Whose manners still our tardy, apish nation
Limps after in base imitation.
Where doth the world thrust forth a vanity—
So it be new, there's no respect how vile—
That is not quickly buzz'd into his ears?
(II.i.21–26)

Depicted in terms of novelty and anachronism, Richard's ex-travagance is associated with that of the "Italianated English-man" who was a familiar object of satire in the sixteenth, but not the fourteenth, century.[27] Like the absentee landlords of the sixteenth century who betrayed the old feudal traditions of no-blesse oblige to enclose their property and exploit it for money to spend on lavish displays at court, Richard has reduced the sacred land of his fathers to a source of ready cash, degraded his office from king to "landlord" (II.i.113).

Money, like modern artillery, functions as an image of de-basement whenever it intrudes into the idealized feudal world of the histories. The two were connected in material practice as well as symbolism. Because, as Maurice Keen points out, the new military technology involved unprecedented expense, it "put the maintenance of any effective army beyond the reach of all purses save the public, princely one," thus contributing to the disempowerment of the feudal aristocracy, as it lost its traditional military function, and also to the ever-present fiscal problems of the Tudors.[28] In Shakespeare's account, although not in Holinshed's, Richard's outrageous fiscal exactions as well as his confiscation of Gaunt's estate are motivated by his need for money for Irish wars, the same need that constituted Queen Elizabeth's major financial burden in the late 1590s.[29] In *King John* the anachronistically modern army not only fights with cannon; it also fights for personal financial gain. As Virginia Vaughan points out, the troops are described in terms "that can

---

[27]See Ure, ed., The Arden Edition of *King Richard II*, pp. 48–49n.

[28]Maurice Keen, *Chivalry* (New Haven: Yale University Press, 1984), pp. 241–42.

[29]See act I, scene iv, and Peter Ure's note in the Arden Edition, pp. 39–40. See also Alan G. R. Smith, *The Emergence of a Nation State: The Commonwealth of England 1529–1660* (London: Longman, 1984), p. 248.

only apply to Elizabeth's own soldiers of fortune."[30] "All th' unsettled humors of the land," they are "fiery voluntaries" who "have sold their fortunes" and bear "their birthrights . . . on their backs, / To make a hazard of new fortunes" in France. (II.i.66–71). As such, they anticipate Pistol's anachronistic contamination of Henry V's war in France. Henry conceives his invasion as a divinely sanctioned effort to reclaim his hereditary right to the French throne. Pistol plans to follow in the manner of "horse-leeches": "to suck, to suck, the very blood to suck" (II.iii.55–56).

Perhaps the best example of the way money and commerce function as images of anachronistic degradation is John of Gaunt's description of the ways Richard has debased the ideal England of his forefathers:

> This land of such dear souls, this dear dear land,
> Dear for her reputation through the world,
> Is now leas'd out—I die pronouncing it—
> Like to a tenement or pelting farm.
> England, bound in with the triumphant sea,
> Whose rocky shore beats back the envious siege
> Of wat'ry Neptune, is now bound in with shame,
> With inky blots and rotten parchment bonds.
>
> (II.i.57–64)

The pun on "dear" reduces the incommensurable value of what is loved to the commercial value of an expensive commodity; the pun on "bound" expresses a similar degradation, from the triumphant sea and the rocky shore that beat back the medieval siege of the classical god of the sea to the instruments of a sordid new commercial economy.[31] The enduring, immanent value of land and sea (*real* estate) has been replaced by the fluctuating, mediated value of the market, represented by legal documents.

The debasement of feudal honor into monetary wealth is conceived as an ethical betrayal, but it is represented in terms that

[30]"*King John*: A Study in Subversion and Containment," p. 68.
[31]See Murray Krieger, *A Window to Criticism: Shakespeare's Sonnets and Modern Poetics* (Princeton: Princeton University Press, 1964), pp. 133–36, for a discussion of Shakespeare's Sonnet 87, which uses a similar pun on "dear" to express the reduction from the dream of a world of faith to the "late, post-chivalric, pragmatic world that we recognize as the world of that mixed hero, Bolingbroke."

carry strong connotations of social disarray and degradation. When Gaunt charges that Richard has degenerated from England's king to its "landlord," he associates him with the beneficiaries of a new commercial economy that was transforming land from a mark of hereditary status to a source of new wealth. The same degrading transformation of aristocratic honor into money recurs in the debate between Henry IV and the Duke of York in act V, scene iii. Offering a royal gift to a loyal subject, the king proposes to pardon York's son for his intended treason:

> O loyal father of a treacherous son!
> Thou sheer, immaculate, and silver fountain,
> From whence this stream through muddy passages
> Hath held his current and defil'd himself!
> Thy overflow of good converts to bad,
> And thy abundant goodness shall excuse
> This deadly blot in thy digressing son.
> (V.iii.60–66)

This speech is couched in the same vocabulary of precious jewels, earth and water, and good and evil that Gaunt used to celebrate the ideal glory of England and ground it in nature and religion. Gaunt's England was a "precious stone set in the silver sea" (II.i.46). York's virtue, diminished in scale but not yet transvalued, is a "sheer, immaculate, and silver fountain." The contaminating effects of the new commercial economy, dimly adumbrated in the "deadly blot" that echoes Richard's "inky blots and rotten parchment bonds" (II.i.64), will give way, in Bullingbrook's account, to the superior force of York's virtue.

Rejecting the king's proposal, York refigures the offer of royal largesse as a degrading commercial transaction. The king proposes to reward York's virtue by giving him the gift of pardon for his son. York redefines the gift as a commodity, his honor as the coin that will purchase it. If the king pardons Aumerle, he says, "he shall spend mine honor with his shame, / As thriftless sons their scraping fathers' gold" (V.iii.68–69). In York's construction of the pardon, his aristocratic honor will be transformed into money to be "spent" and he himself degraded from a great medieval nobleman into the money-grubbing, miserly father of a spendthrift son, a stock character with a disquieting resemblance to Shakespeare's Shylock or to an ambitious Elizabethan merchant.

The same association of anachronistic modernity with social lowering can be seen in Shakespeare's representations of plebeian characters. If his feudal aristocrats and kings are degraded by allusions that associate them with the emergent bourgeoisie of late sixteenth-century England, his plebeian characters have no place at all in the past, living instead in an eternal Elizabethan present.[32] Shakespeare locates his highborn men in a variety of historical worlds, but his commoners belong to the emphemeral present moment of theatrical performance, the modern, and socially degraded, world of the Renaissance public theater.[33]

It is not Prince Hal but Poins who wears the peach-colored silk stockings that were a new fashion in sixteenth-century England, and not Henry IV's court but Mistress Quickly's tavern where Hal indulges in the sack that no one in England drank before the time of Henry VIII.[34] The Boar's Head, in fact, was the name of at least six real taverns in Shakespeare's London, one of them used for a theater.[35] Shakespeare represents his Boar's Head as a kind of theater, as well. Frequented by a disorderly, heterogeneous crowd, it is also the scene of playacting: Falstaff pretends to be Hal, Hal pretends to be Falstaff, and both degrade the dignity of royalty by playing the part of the reigning king. It is also the scene of Hal's degradation. In the court and on the battlefield, Hal plays out his historical role as future king.

[32]Cf. the illustration of the scene from *Titus Andronicus* and the discussion of it in Chapter 1. With its anachronistic mixture of Roman aristocrat and Elizabethan commoners, the drawing probably follows the practice of the actors. Titus wears a costume that situates him in ancient Rome, but the common soldiers are dressed in contemporary Elizabethan garments, as is the Gothic queen. As I argue in Chapters 4 and 5, women and commoners have no history because both are excluded from the aristocratic masculine world of written historical representation. Represented as a malignant foreigner, set apart from the historical world inhabited by noble Roman men, Tamora anticipates the characterization of the French women in *1 Henry VI* (see the discussion in Chapter 4).

[33]For a fuller discussion of this point, see Chapter 5, section II.

[34]On the stockings, see Muriel St. Clare Byrne, "The Social Background," in *A Companion to Shakespeare Studies*, ed Harley Granville-Barker and G. B. Harrison (New York: Doubleday, 1960), pp. 191–92. On the sack, see Hemingway, p. 174n.

[35]See Chambers, *The Elizabethan Stage*, 2: 443–45; and Andrew Gurr, *The Shakespearean Stage, 1574–1642*, 2d ed. (Cambridge: Cambridge University Press, 1980), p. 117.

In the Boar's Head Tavern, he plays practical jokes and rubs elbows with a dissolute crew whose social rank is far beneath his own. He behaves, in short, like an aristocrat at an Elizabethan public theater.

— III —

Invoking a degenerate present and a disreputable scene of theatrical performance to degrade the idealized past, Shakespeare's anachronisms usually function as tokens of debasement. If history could be contaminated by theatrical performance, however, it could also be redeemed. The English history play was, in fact, a deeply ambivalent medium, the place where two discursive fields, each unsettled in itself, came together in a new hybrid genre, with no established tradition and no uncontested protocols to govern the complicated negotiations between its unstable components. In most ways, the status of *historia* in Shakespeare's England was far above that of the public theater. Celebrating a heroic national past and constructing an ideological justification in heredity for the present status system, history was an honorable and much-honored institution. Identified with every sort of threat to the personal virtue of subjects and the good order of society, the new commercial theater often seemed to exemplify the disruptive forces that threatened the status quo. Nonetheless, neither history nor theater was as stable or unambiguous as this account implies. History was undergoing profound changes, and the public commercial theater was an innovation too recent to have acquired a clear institutional status or cultural significance.

Driven by nostalgia, humanist historians struggled to recuperate a lost feudal past to validate a bewildering, unstable present. But the new secular ideals of scientific empiricism that were transforming the practice of historiography made that project increasingly difficult, riven by contradictions and divided against itself, painfully aware of the anachronism implicit in the entire project of historical recuperation. As Renaissance historiography became increasingly secular in its orientation and scientific in its methodology, historians became increasingly aware of the limitations of their own enterprise—the mutability and unreliability of historical records, the inscrutability of human motives, and the enormous gulf of time and awareness that separated the history-writing present from the historical past. During this period of transition, historiography was an unstable discourse, a new discipline in the process of defining its purpose, its subject matter, and its methodology. The new definition restricted historiography to the analysis of second causes and reduced its didactic function to lessons in practical politics and military strategy, but historians still mystified the outcomes of political and military conflicts in divine providence and rationalized misfortunes as punishment for evildoing. The new methodology confined historiography to the discovery of verifiable facts, but historians continued to invent eloquent speeches and personal motivations for the heroes they represented, even though such invention was now, strictly speaking, the work of the poet.

The new conception of historiographic discourse also entailed a redefinition of poetry. The construction of history as a scientific discipline designed to discover the objective truth about the past also constructed a binary opposition between historiographic fact and fictional artifact. Increasingly defined in opposition to historical fact, poetic fiction assumed the lofty ambitions that historians were forced to relinquish in order to pursue the new ideal of scientific objectivity. Defenders of poetry celebrated its power to repair the deficiencies of historical knowledge and to perform the earlier functions of history: to inspire virtuous acts and reveal the will of God, to transcend the limitations of temporality and resuscitate the dead past in full presence. Sidney's *Defense of Poesy* makes this process explicit.[36] Arrogating to poetry the traditional praise of history as a teacher of virtuous action, Sidney argues,

---

[36]See, e.g., *Defense*, p. 6. Appropriating for poetry traditional prerogatives of historians, Sidney legitimates his procedure by charging the historians with a prior act of appropriation: "And even historiographers (although their lips sound of things done and verity be written in their foreheads) have been glad to borrow both fashion and perchance weight of the Poets. So Herodotus entitled his history by the name of the nine Muses, and both he and all the rest that followed him either stole or usurped of poetry their passionate describing of passions, the many particularities of battles (which no man could affirm) or, if that be denied me, long orations put in the mouths of great kings and captains (which it is certain they never pronounced)."

that which commonly is attributed to the praise of history in respect of the notable learning is got by marking the success, as though therein a man should see virtue exalted and vice punished, truly that commendation is peculiar to poetry and far off from history.[37]

"Captived to the truth of a foolish world," the historian cannot show the perfect pattern of virtue or vice. "Freely ranging within the zodiac of his own wit," the poet can depict the higher truths obscured by the accidents of a fallen world:

If the poet do his part aright, he will show you in Tantalus, Atreus, and such like, nothing that is not to be shunned, in Cyrus, Aeneas, Ulysses, each thing to be followed, where the historian, bound to tell things as things were, cannot be liberal (without he will be poetical) of a perfect pattern but, as in Alexander or Scipio himself, show doings, some to be liked, some to be misliked, and then how will you discern what to follow but by your own discretion, which you had without reading Quintus Curtius.[38]

The new demand that historians confine themselves to fact not only interfered with history's traditional ability to provide notable examples of virtue and vice, it also deprived the historian of a function very close to the heart of the entire historiographic enterprise, the discovery of historical causation.[39] Aspiring to write a universal *History of the World*, Ralegh is, nonetheless, keenly aware that no human historian can speak infallibly of history's first cause in God's will: "For all histories do give us information of human counsels and events, as far forth as the knowledge and faith of the writers can afford; but of God's will, by which all things are ordered, they speak only

[37]*Defense*, p. 21.

[38]*Defense*, pp. 22, 9, 20.

[39]On the importance of historical causation and its relation to history's didactic function, see *The Mirror for Magistrates*, ed. Lily B. Campbell (New York: Barnes & Noble, 1938), p. 198: "But seeing causes are the chiefest thinges / That should be noted of the story wryters, / That men may learne what endes al causes bringes / They be unwurthy the name of Croniclers, / That leave them cleane out of their registers. / Or doubtfully report them: for the fruite / Of reading stories, standeth in the suite."

at random, and many times falsely."[40] Locked in the infinite reaches of divine providence, the first cause of history was inaccessible to human knowledge, but so too were its second causes in human desire and action:

> The heart of man is unsearchable; and princes, howsoever their intents be seldom hidden from some of those many eyes which pry both into them and into such as live about them, yet sometimes, either by their own close temper, or by some subtle mist, they conceal the truth from all reports. . . . [Moreover] matters of much consequence, founded in all seeming upon substantial reasons, have issued indeed from such petty trifles, as no historian would either think upon, or could well search out.[41]

Here too, poetic fiction was summoned to perform a task that history could no longer accomplish. Humanist historians had claimed that reading the past could provide practical lessons for the present by revealing the universal principles of causation, but the new scientific history was forced to concede this function to poetic fiction. "Historians," Ralegh admits, "do borrow of poets, not only much of their ornament, but somewhat of their substance. Informations are often false, records not always true, and notorious actions commonly insufficient to discover the passions, which did set them first on foot."[42] Moreover, even if a scientific historian could come in possession of all the facts, he would still be unable to speak with certainty about their causes. As Sidney argues, an account of facts, in and of itself, cannot yield universal principles; the historian, resting his case upon the "bare *was*" of recorded facts, is like someone who

[40]Book II, chap. xxi, sec. vi (4:612): "A digression, wherein is maintained the liberty of using conjecture in histories." Cf. Matthieu Coignet, *Politique Discourses upon trueth and Lying*, trans. Sir Edward Hoby (London: Ralfe Newberie, 1586), p. 72: "Albeit that *Sainct Augustine*, attributed much to histories, yet doth he adde, that hee can not see how all that which is written by the witte of man can bee in everie point true, consideringe that all men are lyers, and that it commeth to passe often tymes, that they which follow the reason of man in anye historie, builde upon the brutes of the vulgar sorte, and are abused by the passions of sundrie men, which report nothinge of certayne. . . . But in the holye historie, they oughte to feare no suche thinge since that it proceedeth of the holye ghoste, and thence a man maye take out certayne witnesses."
[41]Ralegh, *History*, II, xxi, sec. vi (4:614–15).
[42]*History*, II, xxi, sec. vi (4:613).

argues "because it rained yesterday, therefore it should rain today." "Many times," Sidney concludes, the historian "must tell events whereof he can yield no cause, or if he do, it must be poetically."[43]

Although Sidney bases most of his *Defense* on nondramatic poetry, arranged in a strict generic hierarchy with the epic firmly placed on top, he also includes the drama. Poetic justice, he argues, makes the stage a better teacher than history of virtuous action and political loyalty:                                              ·

> If evil men come to the stage, they ever go out (as the tragedy writer answered to one that misliked the show of such persons) so manacled as they little animate folks to follow them. But the historian, being captived to the truth of a foolish world, is many times a terror from well-doing and an encouragement to unbridled wickedness. . . . See we not the virtuous Cato driven to kill himself and rebel Caesar so advanced that his name yet after sixteen hundred years lasts in the highest honor. . . . History . . . indeed can afford you . . . I know not how many more of the same kennel that speed well enough in their abominable injustice of usurpation.[44]

Sidney's extravagant claims for the edifying effects of dramatic fiction rest on classical tradition and elite texts. The "tragedy writer" he cites in defense of plays is Euripides;[45] when he turns to the popular drama of his own time, his tone becomes contemptuous. But the same arguments could also be raised in defense of the public theater and extended to the lowliest and most ignorant members of their audiences. The antitheatrical pamphlets represented only half the story, one side of an impassioned debate in which the new public theater had its defenders as well as its detractors. If the opponents of the stage argued that it incited its audiences to personal vice and political subversion, its defenders could argue just the opposite. Portrayals of moral virtue and heroic patriotism could provide uplifting models for their audiences, and dramatizations of sub-

---

[43]*Defense*, p. 20.

[44]*Defense*, pp. 22–23.

[45]Identified by Soens on p. 22, n.63. Note, however, that Francis Meres's "Comparative Discourse of Our English Poets with the Greeke, Latine, and Italian Poets" associates Shakespeare with Plautus and Seneca. See his *Palladis Tamia, Wits Treasury* (1598), in *Elizabethan Critical Essays*, 2:317–18.

versive actions need not themselves inspire subversion. By playing out the evil consequences of feigned rebellions on stage,
they could, in fact, help to prevent actual ones in the world.

Recent critical debates about the place of the stage in Renaissance culture reenact in many ways the Renaissance controversy
between opponents of the English commercial theater and its
defenders. Both debates center on the political implications of
theatrical performance, and both illustrate that the place of the
stage in Shakespeare's world was deeply ambivalent. The Renaissance public theater drew on a complex heritage, at once
learned and popular, literary and theatrical, sacred and profane,
authoritarian and subversive. Its sources range from medieval
liturgical drama to irreverent popular festivals, from elite literary
tradition to vulgar public entertainment.[46] Its medieval religious
heritage associated it with the transcendent power of sacred
ritual. Its contemporary use as a commercial enterprise associated it with the degrading power of money and the social
disruptions created by new economic practices. The status of
players and playwrights was equally ambivalent. The players
were authorized by royal and aristocratic patrons, but they depended for their living on appealing to the heterogeneous
crowds who paid to see them perform. Insofar as the playwright
was a poet, he was authorized by an elite tradition dating back
to the classics. Insofar as he was a player or sold his wares to
the players, he was subjected to the social degradation and
ethical contamination of the new commercial economy.

The product of a rapidly changing world, the new commercial
theater was associated with the forces that threatened the established order. But it was also associated with the institutions
of power—the aristocratic and royal patrons who authorized
the players, the public processions and court masques that authorized *them*. This ambivalence is reproduced in the work of
current critics. Some see the theater as an instrument of ideological control, a site for what Leonard Tennenhouse has called
"power on display," "disseminating an iconography of state"
that helped to authorize the power of the ruling elite. Others
see it as a site of subversion, undermining the dominant ideology not only by the nature of the material it represented but

---

[46]Many writers make this point, but see especially Cohen, *Drama of a Nation*.

also by the very fact of theatrical representation and the disorderly conditions of theatrical performance.[47]

As Paul Yachnin has remarked, the "subversion/containment debate" in current scholarship "parallels the original controversy as exemplified by Stubbes' vilification of the stage as 'sathans synagogue' (that is, as a focus and disseminating agent of radically subversive ideas) and by Nashe's encomium of stage-plays as 'a rare exercise of vertue' (as an entertainment devoted to the promulgation of civic virtue amongst the audience)."[48] The one indisputable conclusion to be drawn from both debates is that the theater for which Shakespeare wrote had not yet acquired a clearly defined discursive position. A radically innovative practice, the public commercial theater of early modern England had no cultural precedent and no established institutional position within a culture that was itself undergoing a process of radical transformation. The theater served as a focus for the anxieties, contradictions, and deep cultural conflicts that

[47] *Power on Display: The Politics of Shakespeare's Genres* (London: Methuen, 1986), p. 186. The leading exponent of the view that the theater is to be understood as an instrument of the dominant class and that representations of subversion are ultimately contained by and subsumed within its hegemonic agenda has been Stephen Greenblatt. See especially his influential early work, *Renaissance Self-Fashioning: From More to Shakespeare* (Chicago: University of Chicago Press, 1980) and his subtle reconsideration of the issue in "Invisible Bullets: Renaissance Authority and Its Subversion, *Henry IV* and *Henry V*," in *Political Shakespeare: New Essays in Cultural Materialism*, ed. Jonathan Dollimore and Alan Sinfield (Ithaca: Cornell University Press, 1985). Among the critics who emphasize theatrical subversion are Jonathan Dollimore and Michael Bristol. See especially Dollimore's *Radical Tragedy: Religion, Ideology, and Power in the Drama of Shakespeare and His Contemporaries* (Chicago: University of Chicago Press, 1984) and Bristol's *Carnival and Theater: Plebeian Culture and the Structure of Authority in Renaissance England* (New York: Methuen, 1985). For a thoughtful analysis of the differences between the two groups, see Walter Cohen, "Political Criticism of Shakespeare," in *Shakespeare Reproduced: The Text in History and Ideology*, ed. Jean E. Howard and Marion F. O'Connor (New York: Methuen, 1987), pp. 18–46.

[48] Professor Yachnin makes this point in "The Powerless Theater," forthcoming in *English Literary Renaissance*. Although I do not agree with all of his conclusions regarding the depoliticizing and the powerlessness of the theater during this period, I am grateful to him for permission to read and cite this important essay. The quotation from Stubbes comes from *The Anatomie of Abuses* (1583), in Chambers, 4:223, the quotation from Nashe from *Pierce Penilesse his Supplication to the Divell* (1592) in Chambers, 4:238.

attended the passage from feudal to capitalist social organization in early modern England.[49]

More than any other dramatic genre, the history play was conditioned by the discursive instabilities that produced the ambivalent position of the theater and the ambivalent roles of playwright and player. The same capacity to transform its audiences that gave the theater its dangerous potential to incite subversive behavior could become in the history play an unequaled instrument of social control. Moving uneasily between the debased world of the theater and the elite province of poetry, the playwright was located both below and above the historian. Conceived as a mercenary theatrical entertainer, the playwright degraded the history he represented to provide gross spectacles for vulgar eyes. Conceived as a poet, he drew his authority from an idealized and idealizing tradition that elevated history from a bare record of facts to a coherent and inspirational myth of national destiny and personal heroism.

Both opponents and defenders of the theater played on fears of class conflict and popular subversion. Antitheatrical polemics condemned the theater as the source of every kind of personal and political corruption, but they emphasized its dangerous effects on the poor and the ignorant. A 1574 act of the Common Council of London claimed that the theater allured "poore and fond persons" to the "unthriftye waste of [their] monye," corrupting them with the "utteringe of popular busye and sedycious matters."[50] Phillip Stubbes' *Anatomie of Abuses* (1583) warned that the theater taught its audiences to "rebel against Princes."[51] Appealing to the same anxieties, defenders of the theater described it as the perfect instrument for the ideological indoctrination of those same potentially disorderly masses, especially when it took its subjects from the inspiring records of English history. Thomas Heywood's *Apology for Actors*

[49]Many recent critics make this point, but see especially Steven Mullaney, *The Place of the Stage: License, Play, and Power in Renaissance England* (Chicago: University of Chicago Press 1988); Cohen, *Drama of a Nation*, especially chap. 2, "Renaissance Theater and the Transition from Feudalism to Capitalism"; and Howard, "Crossdressing, the Theatre, and Gender Struggle."

[50]In Chambers, *Elizabethan Stage*, 4:274.

[51]In Chambers, 4:224.

(1612), for instance, emphasized the beneficial effects of English history plays as lessons in obedience to the "ignorant" and "the unlearned":

> Playes have made the ignorant more apprehensive, taught the unlearned the knowledge of many famous histories, instructed such as cannot reade in the discovery of all our *English* Chronicles. . . . Playes are writ with this ayme, and carryed with this methode, to teach the subjects obedience to their King, to shew the people the untimely ends of such as have moved tumults, commotions, and insurrections, to present them with the flourishing estate of such as live in obedience, exhorting them to allegeance, dehorting them from all traytorous and fellonious stratagems.[52]

As this quotation indicates, defenders of the theater found some of their most powerful ammunition in historical drama. Sidney invoked the conventional hierarchy of poetic genres to make the epic the capstone of his *Defense*. In the same way, although antitheatrical polemics focused obsessively on the corrupting effects of bawdy comedies and the licentious behavior they incited among their audiences, defenders of the stage emphasized the inspirational power of the English history play. The same hierarchy of poetic genres can be seen in both defenses, and in both cases it cuts across and compromises the social and discursive hierarchy that separated the elite written discourse of "poesy" from the vulgar spoken medium of public performance in a commercial theater. In the case of the epic, Sidney could write, "There rests the heroical, whose very name, I think, should daunt all backbiters." In the case of comic poetry, he feels compelled to answer "arguments of abuse" and to grant that "naughty play-makers and stage-keepers have justly made [it] odious."[53] Opponents of the theater could point to the ill effects of comedy, but advocates could invoke the authority of epic tradition and English history to defend theatrical performance as an inspiration to civic virtue and heroic patriotism. In Sidney's defense of poetry, comedy is tainted by association with the disreputable vulgar stage. In defenses of the theater,

---

[52]Book III, F3$^r$–F3$^v$.
[53]For Sidney's celebration of the epic, see the *Defense*, pp. 30–31; for the statement about comedy, see p. 28.

the history play is elevated by association with elite written genres.

The same power of impersonation that made the "chameleon player" a threat to the hierarchical order of society when he stepped out of his own social location to enact a part he was never born to could also make him, when he portrayed a historical English hero, an inspiration to reverence for the authority he impersonated. Heywood, for instance, uses "our domesticke hystories" to illustrate the beneficial effects of theatrical impersonation:

> what English blood seeing the person of any bold English man presented and doth not hugge his fame, and hunnye at his valor, pursuing him in his enterprise with his best wishes, and as being wrapt in contemplation, offers to him in his hart all prosperous performance, as if the Personator were the man Personated, so bewitching a thing is lively and well spirited action, that it hath power to new mold the harts of the spectators and fashion them to the shape of any noble and notable attempt. What coward to see his countryman valiant would not bee ashamed of his own cowardise. What English Prince should hee behold the true portrature of that amous King *Edward* the third, foraging France, taking so great a King captive in his owne country, quartering the English Lyons with the French Flower-delyce, and would not bee suddenly Inflam'd with so royall a spectacle, being made apt and fit for the like atchievement. So of *Henry* the fift.[54]

Written historiographic texts could record the glorious past, but only the theater could make that past present. This contrast between historical representation and theatrical presence is, in fact, the first argument that Thomas Nashe adduces when he sets out to demonstrate the many values of theatrical performance:

> Nay, what if I proove Playes to be no extreame; but a rare exercise of vertue? First, for the subiect of them (for the most part) it is borrowed out of our English Chronicles, wherein our forefathers valiant acts (that have line long buried in rustie brasse and worme-

---

[54]*An Apology for Actors* (1612), Book I, B4ʳ. Compare Sidney's praise of the epic: "As the image of each action stirs and instructs the mind, so the lofty image of such worthies most inflames the mind with desire to be worthy" (pp. 30–31).

eaten bookes) are revived, and they themselves raised from the Grave of Oblivion, and brought to pleade their aged Honours in open presence. . . . How would it have joyed brave *Talbot* (the terror of the French) to thinke that after he had lyne two hundred yeares in his Tombe, hee should triumphe againe on the Stage, and have his bones newe embalmed with the teares of ten thousand spectators at least (at severall times) who, in the Tragedian that represents his person, imagine they behold him fresh bleeding? I will defend it against any Collian, or clubfisted Usurer of them all, there is no immortalitie can be given a man on earth like unto Playes.[55]

Safer than plays for public consumption, the ideologically motivated and carefully censored texts of printed historiography nonetheless lacked the almost supernatural power of living theatrical performance. Like the antitheatrical polemics, the defenses associate theatrical performance with sorcery.[56] Heywood rests his argument on the "bewitching" power of plays to "new mold the harts of the spectators and fashion them to the shape" of the actions it represents. Nashe claims that the players confer new life on the heroes they impersonate. Like necromancy, the theater could raise the dead; like witchcraft, it could transform the living. Moreover, the association of dramatic performance with witchcraft was not confined to the debates about the stage. Stephen Greenblatt demonstrates in "Shakespeare and the Exorcists" how pervasive the connection between the supernatural and the theatrical was in contemporary religious controversy.[57] If Heywood and Nashe found a kind of bewitching in theatrical performance, Samuel Harsnett, Richard Baddeley, and Erasmus all found a kind of theatricality in exorcism. These comparisons were used, as Greenblatt explains, to demystify the supernatural pretensions of exorcists, but they were also used to express the mysterious power of theatrical impersonation. The opening chorus of *Henry V* suggests the necromantic power of theatrical

[55]*Pierce Penilesse his Supplication to the Divell* (1592), in Chambers, IV:238–39.

[56]On the importance of magic in the antitheatrical pamphlets and its associations with the power of the theater to transform its spectators, see Laura Levine, "Men in Women's Clothing: Anti-Theatricality and Effeminization from 1579 to 1642," *Criticism* 28 (1986), 123–28.

[57]In *Shakespearean Negotiations: The Circulation of Social Energy in Renaissance England* (Berkeley: University of California Press, 1988), pp. 94–128.

performance even in the act of denying it: the actors are "flat unraised spirits" and the theater is a "wooden O."

Both exorcism and theatricality were sites of intense contestation, alternately mystified and demystified, honored and denounced as the contradictions between an emergent scientific rationalism and a residual religious mysticism were marshaled in support of equally contradictory political agendas. If the theater could be invoked in religious controversy as an image of deception or condemned in antitheatrical polemic as a site of diabolical transformation, it could also be defended as a powerful ritual of personal and political redemption.[58] In Shakespeare's theater as in the medieval mystery plays, theatrical performance could create a kind of atemporal ceremonial space to repair the ravages of mortality and eradicate the temporal distance that separated the audience from the objects of nostalgic desire.[59]

What is most striking about Nashe's defense is that he places theatrical performance *above* historiographic writing. The ideological premises and political agenda of Nashe's defense are impeccable, but he argues that the disreputable practice of commercial theatrical display could better serve that agenda than the officially sanctioned texts of Tudor historiography. Nashe invokes the old dream of the humanist historians, to recover the glorious past and confer earthly immortality upon its heroes, to argue that by the end of the sixteenth century, this dream

[58]The old, medieval association of theatrical performance with sacred ritual seems to lie behind the account Greenblatt cites of a 1610 performance by a group of travelling players for a recusant Catholic family of *King Lear, Pericles,* and "a 'St. Christopher Play'" (pp. 121–22). On the diabolical power of the theater, see not only the antitheatrical arguments cited and excerpted in Chambers, vol. 4, appendix C, but also Greenblatt's example from the Catholic *Book of Miracles* of an account of a devil "grievously tormented" when an exorcist "caused to be drawn upon a piece of paper, the picture of a vice in a play, and the same to be burned with hallowed brimstone" (p. 110).

[59]For the relations between Shakespeare's dramaturgy and medieval theatrical tradition, see Robert Weimann, *Shakespeare and the Popular Tradition in the Theater: Studies in the Social Dimension of Dramatic Form and Function,* ed. Robert Schwartz (Baltimore: Johns Hopkins University Press, 1978). Walter Cohen points out (in *Drama of a Nation,* p. 126) that most of the Chester cycle was actually composed in the sixteenth century; and Samuel Schoenbaum points out in *William Shakespeare: A Compact Documentary Life* (New York: Oxford University Press, 1977), pp. 111, 161, that Shakespeare could easily have seen the mystery plays performed.

could only be realized on the stage. Just as Sidney appropriated history's mission for poetry, Nashe appropriates it for the theater; but while Sidney degraded *historia* to assert the superiority of an elite poetic tradition, Nashe degrades it to assert the superiority of the public, commercial theater.

Sidney depicted a silly, pompous historian, "a wonder to young folks and a tyrant in table-talk" "loaded with old mouse-eaten records" in order to deflate the traditional humanist celebration of *historia* as "the witness of time, the light of truth, the life of memory, the governess of life, the herald of antiquity";[60] but the imagery Nashe uses in his defense of the stage performs an even more radical transformation. Sidney's homely, comical image of the domestic bore with his mouse-eaten records invokes the materiality and mutability of historical writing to deride the proud Ciceronian claim, but Nashe's worm-eaten books recall the resonant traditional iconography and the horrifying physical reality of the worms who eat the corpses of the dead. Nashe's metaphors depict historical writing as a "Grave of Oblivion" where the historical past lies forever "buried." They invoke the imagery of human mortality to express the disillusioned recognition that historiography itself is subject to the same destructive power that the nostalgic project of Tudor historiography was designed to overcome.

In place of historiography, Nashe puts the stage. Only in dramatic performance, he argues, can the past be preserved, the dead come to life, the absent past of historical representation return in full, living presence. Sidney's poet could reveal the perfect patterns of virtue and vice because he was not bound by the requirement that he report the facts of this world or limited by the inadequacies of historical records. In Nashe's defense, the theater takes on that same transcendent power. The wooden O of Shakespeare's theater circumscribed a temporal absence, but it could also serve as a conjuror's circle to raise the spirits of the dead, or even as a symbol of eternity, the clear, unchanging light that revealed abiding truths obscured by the ravages of time and the deficiencies of historiographic discourse.

[60]*Defense*, p. 15.

—— IV ——

Shakespeare's audience, as Nashe reminds us, was attracted to English history plays by the same nostalgic sense of anachronism, the same perception of temporal distance that fueled (and finally frustrated) the Tudor project of historiographic recuperation. Only the theater, Nashe argued, could provide direct contact with the heroic past that was celebrated but also obscured by the "worm-eaten" books of history. Only the living presence of dramatic performance could bring the dead historical records back to life.

Writing in or before 1592, Nashe uses Talbot to exemplify that past, probably in a reference to Shakespeare's *1 Henry VI.*[61] But the play where Shakespeare most fully exploits, and also interrogates, the nostalgic appetite for representations of an idealized feudal past is *Richard II,* written about three years later. Insofar as Tudor historical mythology identified a moment of loss, it was the deposition of Richard II, the last of the medieval kings who ruled England, as Tillyard emphasizes, "by hereditary right, direct and undisputed, from the Conqueror," uniting present power and historical authority in "the full sanctity of medieval kingship."[62] A secularized but not entirely secular analogue to the Fall, Richard's deposition marks the loss of the idealized feudal world that formed the object of sixteenth-century longing, but the very centrality of Richard's story to the project of ideological mystification also made it a privileged site for interrogating that project and the nostalgia that motivated it.[63]

[61]For the date of *Pierce Penilesse his Supplication to the Divell,* see *The Works of Thomas Nashe,* ed. Ronald B. McKerrow, reprinted from the original edition with corrections and supplementary notes by F. P. Wilson, vol. 1 (Oxford: Basil Blackwell, 1966), pp. 137–41; on the reference to Talbot, see 4:134.

[62]E. M. W. Tillyard, *Shakespeare's History Plays* (New York: Barnes and Noble, 1944), p. 289. Tillyard's entire discussion emphasizes the medievalism of the play.

[63]Although nostalgia was not named or defined until the seventeenth century, it forms a constant feature of Renaissance thought. Combining the Greek words *nostos* ("homecoming") and *algos* ("pain, sorrow"), it was first used in the *Dissertatio medica de nostalgia* (Basel, 1688) by the Swiss physician Johannes Hofer to describe the homesickness suffered by Swiss mercenary soldiers. Both these associations—with the Swiss and with a longing for a distant place (home)

Tudor historical accounts of Richard, in fact, exemplify the difficulty of historical reconstruction at a time when history was being reconceived as a form of secular, scientific inquiry that displaced historical causation from the will of God to the deeds of men. Richard's deposition was interpreted in terms of first causes as a transgression against God for which the entire country would have to suffer until the crime was finally expiated in blood and the land redeemed by Henry Tudor. Nonetheless, Richard's deposition was also explained in terms of second causes—Richard's faults and errors as a ruler, his bad luck, and the enmity of powerful nobles. Moreover, Richard's reign was interesting to the Elizabethans not only because it marked the point of separation from a lost, feudal past but also because of its immediate, present relevance. The teleological reading of history that located the restoration of the royal legitimacy lost in Richard in the union of Henry VII and Elizabeth of York, Queen Elizabeth's grandparents, established a direct line of providential purpose between the long-ago-deposed Plantagenet king and the reigning Tudor queen. Even more to the point, Elizabethan analogies between Richard II and Elizabeth I served as disquieting reminders that the tragic process might yet be reenacted on the stage of history as well as Shakespeare's theater. Queen Elizabeth's often-quoted comment, "I am Richard II, know ye not that?"; the sponsorship by Essex's followers of a performance of an old play about Richard II (probably Shakespeare's) on the afternoon before their rebellion; and the suppression of the deposition scene in Shakespeare's play during the queen's lifetime all indicate that for Shakespeare's audience the play was not simply an exercise in historical recreation or an occasion for nostalgia. Janus-faced, the history of

---

that was also a longing for a lost time (childhood)—persisted through the eighteenth century, and it is interesting that both seem to be anticipated in *Richard II*. They appear, for instance, in Mowbray's promise to go anywhere in pursuit of his quarrel with Bullingbrook, "even to the frozen ridges of the Alps" (I.i.64) and its ironic fulfillment when he laments his banishment in act I, scene iii. Conflating the experience of banishment with the experience of old age, Mowbray complains (I.iii.170–71) that he is now "too old . . . too far in years" to learn a new language. For the early history of nostalgia, see Jean Starobinski, "The Idea of Nostalgia," *Diogenes* 54 (1966), 84–103, and Fred Davis, *Yearning for Yesterday: A Sociology of Nostalgia* (New York: Macmillan, Free Press, 1979), pp. 1–4.

Richard II looks backward to a lost medieval past, but also looks forward to a disquieting Elizabethan present.

A similar duplicity characterized the conventions of representation in Shakespeare's theater, which occupied a liminal position between the atemporal ritual drama of the Middle Ages and the spatial and temporal specificity of classic realism. In dramatizing the story of Richard II, Shakespeare moves between these two modes of representation, which also constitute two temporal perspectives for the audience, representing the action sometimes as a distant historical pageant, told in the past tense, of actions already completed and reduced to the stasis of formal tableaux and sometimes as a disturbing present process that reaches out to involve and implicate the audience in the theater. It is a commonplace in criticism of *Richard II* that the play presents a conflict between two contrasting worlds—the static, picturesque, ceremonial world of Richard's medieval court and the active, modern, practical world of Bullingbrook and his successors.[64] The corollary of this proposition—that the audience must shift its perspective during the course of the play, sometimes taking a long, historical view of the action and sometimes seeing it as insistent, present reality—has not been so well developed, yet those manipulations of temporality provide the means by which Shakespeare interrogates his own difficult project of historiographic recuperation.

Actually, there are three temporal perspectives developed in *Richard II*. In the first, Richard's world is displayed as a remote historical pageant, colored by nostalgia. The members of the audience are cast as spectators, contemplating the scene of dramatic action from a distance, but not involved in it. This perspective might be called chronological: separating the audience from the action, it marks the temporal distance between past (the historical objects of representation) and present (the audience in the theater). The second perspective might be called achronic, since it erases the fact of temporality. Here, as in the medieval mystery cycles, there are no temporal boundaries to separate present audience from past events, and the members

---

[64]For an especially perceptive reading of this aspect of the play, see Leonard Barkan, "The Theatrical Consistency of *Richard II*," *Shakespeare Quarterly* 29 (1978), 5–19.

of the audience are implicated as participants in the actions performed on stage. If the first perspective displays a historical pageant for the audience's detached contemplation, the second dissolves temporal distance to engage them in the performance of the action. Moving between them, Shakespeare exploits the temporal fluidity of his bare stage to manipulate the distance between the audience and the objects of historical representation. Finally, there is a third perspective, one that might be called anachronistic. Unlike the other two, it calls attention to its own theatricality and to the anachronism that is finally inseparable from the project of historical recuperation. It separates the audience from the historical action represented on stage by reminding them that they are, after all, simply an audience in a theater. Exploiting the instability of dramatic illusion, which can at any moment be taken for truth or falsehood, this final perspective directs an audience's attention to the differences between past and present, stage and audience, that are obscured by the other two. In so doing it exposes the contradiction that lies at the heart of the project of historical recuperation.

Shakespeare's representation of the story of Richard II begins as a period piece, designed to thrill its sixteenth-century audience with a glimpse of an exotic medieval world. The elaborate pageantry of the opening scene, with its royal ceremony and formal verse, evokes the remote world of Richard's fourteenth-century court. The first line, "Old John of Gaunt, time-honored Lancaster," in addition to its obvious literal meaning as the king's address to his venerable uncle, also sets the medieval scene for Shakespeare's audience by its reference to the legendary John of Gaunt, Chaucer's patron, who was indeed "time-honored" by the sixteenth century.[65] The conclusion of the scene, Richard's order for the judicial combat between Bullingbrook and Mowbray, promises more feudal pageantry, in the spectacle of what Tudor historians had reported as the last of the great medieval trials by battle.

The beginning of *Richard II* anticipates Richard's final conception of his history as a tale "of woeful ages long ago betid"

[65]On the appeal to an audience of local color and the appearance of well-known historical figures in historical drama, see Herbert Lindenberger, *Historical Drama: The Relation of Literature and Reality* (Chicago: University of Chicago Press, 1975), pp. 105–6.

(V.i.41–42). The medieval trappings of the opening scene, like Spenser's archaic, "medieval" language, use a temporal equivalent of local color to represent the past in terms of distance and difference. But that distance is quickly erased. Richard, initially identified with an idealized feudal past, is quickly debased by associations with the forces of modernity and change that separate the audience from the object of their nostalgic desire. In the second scene, Gaunt and the Duchess of Gloucester identify Richard's murder of Gloucester as a crime against the old order and its emblems: the "sacred blood" of Edward III and the genealogical tree that springs from "his most royal root" (I.ii.17–18). At the end of scene iii, it is Richard who deprives the audience of the historical spectacle of a medieval trial by combat; in the following scenes (I.iv. and II.i.) he is debased by association with a new commercial economy and the elaborate self-indulgence of an aristocracy reduced from feudal warriors to effeminate courtiers.

The redefinition that associates Richard with the objects of present anxiety also serves to engage the audience in the historical action represented on stage. The anguished debate between Gaunt and the Duchess of Gloucester about the proper response to Richard's murder of Gloucester articulates an impossible dilemma that also confronts the audience: what is a good subject to do (or desire) when the king has committed a crime against the same authority that the king himself embodies and in whose name he claims their allegiance? In the first half of act I, scene iii, the audience shares the characters' frustration when Richard prevents the combat that they, along with the characters, have been anticipating since the end of the opening scene. And the second half of that scene (154–309) is devoted to Mowbray and Bullingbrook's laments at the prospect of their banishment—anticipatory expressions of the bitter longing for a lost homeland that provide a powerful emotional bond with the nostalgic audience.

The imagined medieval past is now relocated into a time before Richard's. Gaunt, the dying representative of a previous generation, becomes its spokesman. Richard's contemptuous treatment of Gaunt and his cynical plan to appropriate Bullingbrook's inheritance complete his redefinition as an enemy of the old feudal order, and also complete the engagement of

Shakespeare's audience in the action represented on stage. By the end of act II, scene i, Shakespeare has reconstructed the last of the indisputably legitimate medieval kings as a bad ruler in almost every way that Elizabethan theory recognized. He is luxurious and effeminate; he is a bad warrior and administrator; he imposes high and unfair taxes; he listens to flatterers, and he scorns Gaunt's good counsel. Most important, Richard has been thoroughly identified with the forces that oppose the objects of nostalgic historical longing.

The idealized vision of feudal England is reconstituted in Gaunt's famous set speech, "This royal throne of kings," which locates it in a time before the dramatic action began. Gaunt belongs to an older generation, dead and dying. Speaking from his deathbed, he is effectively identified with the ideal values he ascribes to England, and his death is associated with the death of those values. Gaunt's speech, probably the fullest and most explicit description of the idealized vision of an Edenic feudal England in any of the history plays, locates the object of his celebration in an irretrievable past. The speech begins with an extraordinary nineteen-line series of appositive phrases ("This royal throne of kings, this sceptred isle, / This earth of majesty, this seat of Mars," etc.), grammatical constructions of his subject as an ideal substance beyond the reach of historical process. The exemplary object of nostalgic desire, Gaunt's England is both transcendent and prior, both timeless and past. The paradox can be described in psychological terms as a yearning for one's own beginnings or in logical terms as the conflating of the temporal priority of origins with the logical priority of essence.[66] Longing for a lost past, Gaunt imagines it as an un-

---

[66]See Kenneth Burke's discussion of "The Temporizing of Essence" in *A Grammar of Motives* (Cleveland: Meridian, 1962), pp. 430–40. As Burke explains, "Because of the pun whereby the logically prior can be expressed in terms of the temporally prior, and *v.v.*, the ways of transcendence, in aiming at the discovery of *essential* motives, may often take the historicist form of symbolic regression. That is, if one is searching for the 'essence' of motives, one can only express such a search in the temporal terms of imaginative literature as a process of 'going back.' And conversely, one given to retrospect, as Proust in his 'remembrance of things past,' may conceptualize his concern as a search for 'essence.'" Among other examples, Burke also cites Freud's use in *Totem and Taboo* and in *Group Psychology and the Analysis of the Ego* of Darwin's theory of the "primal horde": Because Freud's "analysis of the patriarchal family convinced him that certain kinds of rivalry and allegiance are essential to it,"

changing ideal. Imagining an ideal England, Shakespeare's contemporaries located it in a lost past.

Situated both before time and beyond it, Gaunt's "demi-
paradise" is projected to a point outside of history. His construction of England as an "other Eden" associates it with that
exemplary object of nostalgic yearning, an ideal world that existed in the beginning before the advent of time, change, or
death. Imagined in defiance of mortality, it reconstitutes the lost
past as an unchanging ideal beyond the reach of historical
change. Like the historiographic project it motivated, the nostalgic ideal was fraught with the contradictions that produced
it. Living in a time of radical social and economic transformation,
Shakespeare's contemporaries idealized the world they were
losing. Attempting to retrieve and preserve a lost past, the nostalgic ideal describes a world that is always already lost. The
ultimate object of the historical search for origins, it is never
retrievable in history because it is necessarily *pre*historic.
Changeless, it cannot even be represented in the form of narrative. Gaunt can only describe it in a long series of nominal
phrases.

In the twentieth line, Gaunt supplies the predicate for all those
celebratory appositive phrases, "is now leas'd out." With the
verb, he moves into history and into the present tense, invoking
the degrading commercial forces of present change to describe
the profane use to which Richard has put the sacred land.
Gaunt's mercantile image puts the final touch on the case against
Richard, as it completely transvalues his significance for Shakespeare's audience. Initially identified with a lost medieval world,
Richard is now associated with the emergent capitalism that
was transforming English society in Shakespeare's own time,
with the same threatening mercantile forces that produced the
longing for an idealized feudal past which must have drawn
many of Shakespeare's original audience to see the play in the
first place.

---

he invoked Darwin's theory of the primal horde to hypothesize "(a) that such
a condition had existed in its purity in some past era, and (b) that the lineaments
of this original extreme form were still observable as more or less attenuated
survivals." Burke's use of Freud as an example is especially apt, because Freud-
ian theory provides an exemplary instance of the conceptual strategy of ground-
ing claims for essence and universality in hypotheses of genesis and priority.

By the time the audience learns that the rebels have set sail from France to take Richard's throne, Richard's personal faults and his inadequacies as a king have been so vividly portrayed and Richard has been so thoroughly identified with the forces that oppose the objects of nostalgic desire that the audience is enlisted on the side of the rebels. Holinshed finds "a verie notable example" in the fact that Bullingbrook had "the helpe and assistance (almost) of all the whole realme" in rebelling against Richard.[67] He draws two familiar lessons from the example, that "the providence of God is to be respected" and that "deceivable" human judgement, "not regarding things present with due consideration, thinketh ever that things to come shall have good successe, with a pleasant and deliteful end." Following Holinshed's account, Shakespeare twice alludes to the universal dissatisfaction with Richard's government and support for Bullingbrook's rebellion (II.i.246–88; III.ii.112–19). He also contrives the rhetoric of his play to evoke in his audience the same almost universal complicity in the rebellion that Holinshed attributes to Richard's subjects. Shakespeare's descriptions of the subjects Richard has offended ("the commons," "the nobles") and the crowds that have taken up arms on Bullingbrook's side ("white-beards," "boys with women's voices," "distaff-women," "both young and old") emphasize their heterogeneity. They could stand equally well for descriptions of the heterogeneous crowds that attended his own theater.[68] Dissolving historical distance, the rhetoric of the play merges Shakespeare's sixteenth-century audience with Richard's rebellious fourteenth-century subjects. No longer spectators watching a medieval pageant, the audience has been drawn back by the rhetoric of the play into the fourteenth century and confronted with the same situation that confronted their fourteenth-century ancestors. With the historical scene recast as present action, the audience is encouraged to reenact the mistaken choice described by Holinshed: "not regarding things present with due consid-

[67]*Chronicles*, 2:855.

[68]Cf. the descriptions quoted in Alfred Harbage, *Shakespeare's Audience* (New York: Columbia University Press, 1961), pp. 83–86, and appendix I in Andrew Gurr's *Playgoing in Shakespeare's London* (Cambridge: Cambridge University Press, 1987), pp. 191–204, which lists and describes the 162 known playgoers between 1567 and 1642.

eration," they are likely to side with the usurper against the true king.[69]

Because that choice is both guilty and mistaken, it serves to discredit the promise of historical recuperation even at the moment of its fulfillment. Instead of the desired return to prelapsarian innocence, the dissolution of temporal distance has produced a twofold contamination: Richard defiled by anachronistic association with the objects of present anxiety, the audience corrupted into vicarious participation in the rebellion. Instead of the desired perfection of historical knowledge, the return to the past actually produces a kind of blindness. Erasing the temporal distance between past events and present spectators, these scenes also erase the knowledge that would not become available until the events had received their historiographic construction. They require a willing suspension, not only of the audience's disbelief, but also of their historical knowledge. In fact, the price of the audience's engagement in the historical action is, precisely, history—the history of subsequent events, and their historiographic construction as a teleological causal chain of national disaster and providential retribution.

The same antithesis between historical recuperation and historical knowledge is implicit in the garden scene, which restores historical knowledge but only at the cost of theatrical presence and audience engagement. Here, the audience is released from the characters' temporality by a curiously remote, self-

[69]I realize that my attempts to postulate a kind of "role" for the audience in the dramatic action are highly arguable. The responses of Shakespeare's original audience are inaccessible to any closer knowledge than learned conjecture. Any hypotheses I make will be conditioned by my own historical distance and difference, and they will also be singular and partial, while Shakespeare's original audience was plural and heterogeneous. Nonetheless, it seems to me that the risk is worth taking. Shakespeare's strategy, in play after play, works to implicate the audience in the action and to transgress the comfortable demarcation between stage and audience that a safer, more objective criticism seeks to preserve. Such a criticism preserves the illusion of its own integrity but only at the cost of reducing Shakespearean theater to a spectator sport in which only the actors move and only the characters suffer and change. For a fuller account of the ways the responses of the audience are orchestrated in *Richard II*, see my article, "The Role of the Audience in Shakespeare's *Richard II*," *Shakespeare Quarterly* 36 (1985), 262–81.

consciously medieval tableau in which a gardener and his helper, speaking as no real gardeners can be imagined to speak, develop an elaborate allegorical argument condemning both Richard's dereliction of royal duties and Bullingbrook's usurpation of Richard's divinely appointed throne.[70] In the preceding scenes, the audience was induced to share the characters' temporality and their action. Here action is reduced to stillness, and the characters' temporality recedes into a distant perspective where the audience no longer participates but simply observes. The characters are utterly stereotypical and inhuman, the faceless speakers of conventional judgments couched in conventional terms.

The stylized unreality of the garden scene distances the audience from the characters' medieval time-situation and reminds them that what they are watching is a representation of an exemplary tale, an action completed long ago whose interpretation is not disputable but an established convention. This convention, which the audience has violated in giving their allegiance to Bullingbrook, will be carefully elaborated at the beginning of the deposition scene when Carlisle delivers an eloquent speech that foretells the divine vengeance the deposition will incur when "future ages groan for this foul act" (IV.i.138). Echoing the language of Tudor homilies and sermons as well as Holinshed's history, Carlisle's prophecy recalls the historical past of Shakespeare's sixteenth-century audience at the same time that it predicts the historical future of his own time.[71]

The temporal perspective of Carlisle's prophecy might be de-

---

[70]The allegory comparing the kingdom to a garden together with the queen's reference to the gardener as "old Adam's likeness" (III.iv.73–76) brings up the traditional *topos* of the garden of Eden. Note that this scene, then, like the deposition scene, alludes to medieval mystery cycles and also to providential history, the kind of history not bound by the ordinary limits of time. The interesting difference is that the deposition scene implicates the audience while this scene distances them. I believe this might have something to do with the subject. Eden is "Other" not only because of its remoteness in time but also because it deals with an unfallen state from which fallen humanity is necessarily excluded and because it deals with a world that is still, in a very important sense, timeless, since it is a world in which there is no such thing as death.

[71]On the resemblances between Carlisle's speech and various Tudor pamphlets and homilies, see the notes in the Arden edition of *Richard II*, ed. Peter Ure, pp. 132–33.

scribed as future perfect, that of the garden scene as past. Taken together, they reconstitute the represented action as history. The garden scene represents it as a historical tableau, remote and distant, Carlisle's prophecy as a historically significant event, its meaning informed by the knowledge of later events and their construction in subsequent historical narratives. Reconstituting the audience's temporal separation from the action, they also begin the process of reconstituting Richard and his England as the lost object of nostalgic desire. As long as the audience shared the characters' temporal situation, the action was cast in the present tense and its outcome was indeterminate; the audience could then join in the characters' fatally mistaken choice to depose Richard. With the action restored to the past tense, no choices are possible because no choices remain to be made.

In a literal sense as well, no choices remain to be made. Richard, we learn in the garden scene, is about to be deposed; in the next scene, we will see that deposition, the central historical event in the play. Everything in the play hinges on this scene: the entire action—what is to come as well as what is past—is encapsulated. It depicts an event so momentous and with such far-reaching consequences and paradigmatic significance that the Tudor historians of subsequent reigns repeatedly advert to it and Queen Elizabeth's censors, two centuries later, will feel the need to excise it from Shakespeare's play.

Shakespeare makes the deposition scene paradigmatic in his play as well, for in it he erases temporality altogether. More than any other scene in Shakespeare's histories, it answers the nostalgic desire to make the past present. It situates the action in an atemporal ritual space that dissolves the divisions separating the present audience from the historical objects of representation. But here, just as in Gaunt's speech, the nostalgic moment is fraught with paradox: the point at which the audience can finally achieve the desired recovery of the lost world of Richard II is also the point that dramatizes its loss. *Richard II* recalls Nashe's celebration of the power of dramatic performance to resuscitate the past in full presence, but it does so ironically. Even in the act of satisfying the desire for historical recuperation, Shakespeare disappoints the longing for a lost time of innocence and purity that animates that desire. The past he depicts is finally as conflicted and contaminated as the present. The nostalgic effort to erase the effects of time and change is also an attempt to deny guilt. The longing for Eden is not only a longing for a lost place that existed before the advent of time and change, but also a longing for a lost state of innocence. As Renato Rosaldo has recently argued, nostalgia is a form of mystification that attempts "to establish one's innocence and at the same time talk about what one has destroyed." Locating its origins in the late seventeenth century, Rosaldo identifies various forms of imperialist nostalgia, including the nineteenth-century North American deification of "nature and its Native American inhabitants" that "developed at the same time that North Americans intensified the destruction of the human and natural environment."[72] But a similar process was already apparent in Tudor England, where the same dynasty that attempted to create an absolutist state on the European model also mystified its newly acquired power in the emblems of native tradition and feudal authority and the same upstart gentlemen who profited from a new commercial economy draped themselves in the trappings of the very traditions they were helping to destroy. Nostalgia for an idealized medieval past, then, was not simply an expression of mourning for the passing of an older, better world. It was also a denial of guilt for complicity in the destruction of that world.

These contradictions come into sharp focus in the history play, where the objects of representation celebrate a lost feudal past while the conditions of performance reflect and serve the opposing forces of commercial capitalism and social change. In the commercial theater, history became a commodity and the scene of historical representation was open to anyone who was willing to pay the price of admission. As early as 1559 a royal proclamation prohibited the performance of plays "wherin either matters of religion or of the governance of the estate of the common weale shalbe handled or treated, beyng no meete matters to be wrytten or treated upon, but by menne of aucthoritie, learning and wisedome, nor to be handled before any audience, but of grave and discreete persons."[73] As Walter

---

[72]"Imperialist Nostalgia," *Representations* 26 (Spring 1989), 108–9.
[73]Chambers, 4:263.

Cohen points out, "any drama of state performed in the public theater automatically converted a heterogeneous and, it seems, largely popular audience into judges of national issues, a position from which most of its members were excluded in the world of political affairs."[74] By the very acts involved in attending the play—of buying into the disordered and disorderly crowd of spectators, of voyeuristic intrusion in the world of their betters, of presuming to judge in matters of state—the members of the audience became complicit in the destruction of the historical world they came to see celebrated on stage.

Guilt, the repressed component of the audience's nostalgia, is projected in *Richard II* as a motive force for the represented action. The play begins with Bullingbrook's attempt to place the guilt for Gloucester's murder; it ends with his resolution to wash away his own guilt for Richard's. Richard's association of his betrayers with Pilate, the biblical archetype for a futile attempt to deny guilt (IV.i.239–42), is prefigured at the beginning of act III, scene i. when Bullingbrook declares his intention "to wash your blood [Bushy and Green's] from off my hands" (5-6) and echoed at the end of the play in his resolution "To wash this blood [Richard's] off from my guilty hand." The issue of the guilt for Gloucester's murder recurs at the beginning of act IV, scene i.; and the issue of Aumerle's pardon, a parodic version of the audience's own need for absolution at this point in the play, takes up most of Act V.

The conflicted union of guilt and nostalgia comes to the foreground and implicates the audience in the deposition scene, where the issue of the audience's guilt becomes the immediate subject of dramatic conflict. No sooner has the deposition been accomplished than Northumberland demands that Richard read a confession of his crimes so that "the souls of men may deem that [he is] worthily depos'd" (IV.i.226–27).[75] Neither Richard

---

[74]*Drama of a Nation*, p. 183.

[75]The articles drawn up against Richard are recorded both in Edward Hall, *The Union of the Two Noble and Illustre Famelies of Lancastre & Yorke* (1548; rpt. London: J. Johnson et al., 1809), pp. 9–11, and in Holinshed 2:859–61, but neither reports that Richard was required to read them; the conflict between Richard and Northumberland over the reading of the document seems to be Shakespeare's invention. Richard's rejection of the document (insistently present on stage but never read aloud) can stand for a rejection at this point in the play of the mediation of historical writing; his substitution of direct address

nor Shakespeare is willing to comply, however, for the souls
the rebels would satisfy include all those who have given
their "soul's consent" to the deposition—Shakespeare's
sixteenth-century audience along with Richard's fourteenth-
century subjects—and the dialogue that follows is designed
to make them *dis*satisfied. Refusing to read the confession,
Richard turns on Northumberland and reminds him of his
own guilt, "mark'd with a blot, damn'd in the book of
heaven," for deposing a rightful king. Then he broadens the
indictment:

> Nay, all of you that stand and look upon me
> Whilst that my wretchedness doth bait myself,
> Though some of you, with Pilate, wash your hands,
> Showing an outward pity, yet you Pilates
> Have here deliver'd me to my sour cross,
> And water cannot wash away your sin.
>
> (IV.i.237–42)

In these lines, Richard implicates all of those who "stand and
look upon" him, audience in the theater as well as characters
on the stage, in the crime against the king that replicates the
paradigmatic crime of the crucifixion.

The implication becomes stronger in the lines that follow. At
first, Richard claims that he cannot read the account of his crimes
because he is weeping: "Mine eyes are full of tears, I cannot
see" (IV.i.244). The water image associates Richard with the rest
of the traitors, all Pilates, all trying to wash away an ineffaceable
guilt. Moreover, when Richard finally acknowledges his guilt
in the next lines, his self-indictment again implicates the audience as well. Richard says,

> I find myself a traitor with the rest
> For I have given here my soul's consent
> T' undeck the pompous body of a king

---

to the audience moves the action into the immediacy of ritual drama (or dramatic ritual).

Made glory base, [and] sovereignty a slave;
Proud majesty a subject, state a peasant.
(IV.i.248–52)

Like Richard and like the usurpers, members of the audience
have given their souls' consent to the deposition they stood and
looked upon. Like Richard and the usurpers, they have made
glory base and proud majesty a subject to their rebellious desires.[76] The words Richard uses to describe the guilt he shares
with his spectators—"For I have given here my soul's consent"—insist upon the presence of the action. Time and space
have collapsed, uniting the "here" of Richard's fourteenth-century court with the "here" of Shakespeare's sixteenth-century
theater. Like the crucifixion scenes in medieval drama evoked
by Richard's references to his "sour cross" and "you Pilates,"
Richard's deposition transforms the scene of theatrical performance into a ritual space where all time is eternally present. It
erases the temporal distance between the outrageous historical
event it depicts and the guilty contemporary audience that has
come to see it enacted. Like Christ speaking from the cross to
a medieval audience, the deposition scene engages the audience
directly in an event that is not seen as reenacted or represented
but as present action.[77]

Unlike those medieval crucifixions, however, Richard's deposition, which takes place in act IV, does not end the play. At
this point, Shakespeare seems to anticipate Marx's famous observation that "all great incidents and individuals of world history occur, as it were, twice . . . the first time as tragedy, the
second as farce."[78] The movement forward in history is also a

[76]Cf. David Scott Kastan, "Proud Majesty Made a Subject: Shakespeare and
the Spectacle of Rule," *Shakespeare Quarterly* 37 (1986), 459–75.

[77]Anne Barton's eloquent description in *Shakespeare and the Idea of the Play*
(London: Chatto and Windus, 1962), pp. 22–23, is worth quoting: "The Crucifixion . . . becomes almost frighteningly real in those plays in which Christ
appeals directly from The Cross to the people standing about the pageant. . . .
He speaks to those spectators gathered together at Golgotha who were actually
responsible for His death, but also to fourteenth-century Christians. Moments
like this illuminate and make manifest that marriage of time present with time
past upon which the mysteries are based."

[78]"The Eighteenth Brumaire of Louis Bonaparte" (1852), reprinted in *The
Portable Karl Marx*, ed. Eugene Kamenka (New York: Penguin 1983), p. 287.

generic lowering, from the tragic romance of feudalism to the grim farce of a suddenly modern world.[79] The grand poetry of the earlier parts of the play gives way to doggerel, and the sublime metaphors of royal state and cosmic significance are replaced by homely images of riding boots and beggars and the weary knees of an old man. The conflict that initiates the tragic action, the mutual challenges of Bullingbrook and Mowbray, is recapitulated at the beginning of act IV, but now there are six disputants instead of two, and the gages drop on stage with such profusion that one of the characters is finally obliged to borrow a gage before he can answer a challenge (IV.i.83). Instead of two parties ranged symmetrically on either side of the king, the audience sees an unruly crowd of contending nobles; and, until they speak, neither the audience nor the other participants know which side each of them will take (see, for example, lines 56–64). This wildly indecorous scene, usually cut from stage productions because of the nervous laughter it elicits, distances the audience from the action, which is now reduced to farce.[80]

The comic wrangling in act V between the Duke of York and his duchess about whether or not their son should be executed for treason constitutes a similar degeneration, recapitulating in the form of farce the tragic dilemma that confronted John of Gaunt when he was forced to participate in sentencing his own son to exile (I.iii). York, earlier represented with the formal dignity that befits his exalted rank and historical importance, is now degraded to a caricature who conceives his aristocratic

[79]The phrase "tragic romance of feudalism" comes from Graham Holderness, Nick Potter, and John Turner, *Shakespeare: The Play of History* (Iowa City: University of Iowa Press, 1987), but the point about generic lowering and modernity comes from Leonard Barkan's excellent article, "The Theatrical Consistency of *Richard II*," *Shakespeare Quarterly* 29 (1978), 5–19, which anticipates my analysis at many points. The same homology between progression forward in time and downward in genre seems to inform Northrop Frye's *Anatomy of Criticism* (Princeton: Princeton University Press, 1957). Although Frye arranges his taxonomies in cycles, the sequence of the phases within each cycle constitutes a narrative of degradation, or, as Frye puts it in his account of the modes of fiction, a lowering, over time, of the "center of gravity" (pp. 34–35).

[80]See Arthur Colby Sprague and J. C. Trewin, *Shakespeare's Plays Today* (Columbia: University of South Carolina Press, 1970), pp. 42–43. See also Barkan, 5–19.

honor as a miser's treasure and wrangles with his wife in ridiculously rhymed couplets and ludicrously mixed metaphors in a frantic effort to ensure that his own son will be executed for treason (V. iii).[81]

Originally a venerable spokesman for the idealized England of the previous generation, "the last of noble Edward's sons" (II.i.171) has become simply old. His transformation is marked, significantly, by references to his aging body: the "signs of war about his aged neck" that mark the beginning of his degeneration in act II, scene ii; the arm "now prisoner to the palsy" that prevents him from chastising the rebellious Bullingbrook in act II, scene iii; and the "weary joints" of his legs that make even the act of kneeling a painful business for him in act V, scene iii. No longer dignified by association with the Edenic world of John of Gaunt, that imagined oldest time of all which is also the time of youth, York is now old in the real time of a fallen world.

The speech that depicts York's transformation also marks the audience's final separation from the action, and it constitutes a direct antithesis to the deposition scene. York compares the crowds who watched Bullingbrook's triumphant return to London to the audience in a sixteenth-century theater, but unlike the onstage spectators who merged with the theater audience that watched Richard's deposition, the London crowd York describes never appears on stage. Instead of incorporating the present theater audience into the action, York's simile serves to mark their antithetical difference from the entire world from which he speaks. It replaces the deposition scene's erasure of temporality with the anachronism that insists upon temporal distance, and the immediacy of Richard's direct address to "all

---

[81]These scenes have not received much critical attention, and they are often cut in stage productions, largely because of the oddly comic tone that seems to undercut the seriousness of their subject matter. The comic debasement serves a crucial function, however, for it provides the mechanism by which the audience can escape its complicity in the impending crime of Richard's murder. Two notable exceptions are Barkan's "The Theatrical Consistency of *Richard II*," which argues that the scenes "help establish Shakespeare's vision of kingship in the modern world" (p. 18); and Sheldon P. Zitner's "Aumerle's Conspiracy," *Studies in English Literature* 14 (1974), 239–57, which sees them as mockeries "of the vision of life as historical pageant." For a fuller account of the ways these scenes work, see my "Role of the Audience," pp. 273–75.

of you that stand and look upon me" with the metadrama that calls attention to the mask of theatrical mediation:

> As in a theatre the eyes of men,
> After a well-graced actor leaves the stage,
> Are idly bent on him that enters next,
> Thinking his prattle to be tedious,
> Even so, or with much more contempt, men's eyes
> Did scowl on gentle Richard. No man cried "God save him!"
> No joyful tongue gave him his welcome home,
> But dust was thrown upon his sacred head,
> Which with such gentle sorrow he shook off,
> His face still combating with tears and smiles,
> The badges of his grief and patience,
> That had not God, for some strong purpose, steel'd
> The hearts of men, they must perforce have melted,
> And barbarism itself have pitied him.
> But heaven hath a hand in these events,
> To whose high will we bound our calm contents.
> To Bullingbrook are we sworn subjects now,
> Whose state and honor I for aye allow.
>                                    (V. ii. 23–40)

The procession York describes is a mirror image, and therefore a reversal, of the theatrical action the audience has been watching and the historical narrative they know. Henry IV is following Richard II, not preceding him, as king of England, and the king preferred by the verdict of the Tudor historians was Richard and not Henry. Moreover, Richard is also the "well-graced actor" in Shakespeare's theater. Richard's is the leading role in the play: no acting company would give the smaller and less demanding role of Bullingbrook to its best actor and deny him the chance to play Richard. York's anachronistic comparison provides the final adjustment of the audience's perspective on the action. Alienated from the action on stage, first by York's reminder that they are in fact "in a theatre" and that their judgments, informed by historical hindsight, are more reliable than his, and then by the extravagantly farcical scenes that follow this speech, the audience can withdraw from complicity in Bullingbrook's rebellion and applaud the reassuring pieties with which the play ends. Bullingbrook's own final judgment on Richard's murderer—"the guilt of conscience take thee for thy labor"—rendered in the course of a series of comfortably conventional couplets (V.vi.38–52) does not implicate the audience. It simply reiterates the familiar judgment of Tudor historians and allows the audience to leave the theater, a bit drained, perhaps, but restored to its own time and place.

The play ends by reaffirming the received, historical interpretation of Richard's story, but only in retrospect and only at a distance. The last act interposes an impassable barrier between the audience and the objects of historical representation. York's anachronistic, metadramatic speech invokes the barriers of temporal distance and dramatic mediation; the farcical scenes that follow dissipate emotional involvement in scornful laughter, and the formulaic final speech completes the process of disengagement. Delivered over the coffin that contains Richard's corpse, the speech brings history back to death. Like Nashe's image of the worm-eaten history books that entomb the dead remains of a historic past, it constitutes the antithesis of the theatrical necromancy that brings that past to life.[82] Richard's coffin marks the loss of the nostalgically imagined medieval world and with it the possibility of re-creating the timeless, ritual space of medieval drama where past and present could come together under the aspect of eternity.

— V —

In *Richard II* Shakespeare's mode of representation is as medieval as its objects. The dialogue abounds in biblical allu-

---

[82]See Susan Stewart's antithesis between the relic and the souvenir in *On Longing: Narratives of the Miniature, the Gigantic, the Souvenir, the Collection* (Baltimore: Johns Hopkins University Press, 1984), p. 140: "The antique as souvenir always bears the burden of nostalgia for experience impossibly distant in time. . . . Because they are souvenirs of death, the relic, the hunting trophy, and the scalp are at the same time the most intensely *potential* souvenirs and the most potent antisouvenirs. They mark the horrible transformation of meaning into materiality more than they mark, as other souvenirs do, the transformation of materiality into meaning. If the function of the souvenir proper is to create a continuous and personal narrative of the past, the function of such souvenirs of death is to disrupt and disclaim that continuity. Souvenirs of the mortal body are not so much a nostalgic celebration of the past as they are an erasure of the significance of history. . . . these souvenirs mark the end of sacred narrative and the interjection of the curse." Cf. my discussion in Chapter 4 of Joan's speech over Talbot's corpse: the moment of demystification that displays the material physical remains of the dead hero in a movement against history.

sions that associate its secular historical subject with the
timeless subjects of medieval mystery plays. Like the ritual
quality of many of its scenes and Richard's direct address to
the spectators in the deposition scene, they recall the conventions of a dramatic genre that was historically associated with
feudalism.[83] With the accession of Henry IV, medieval England recedes into the past. Medievalism, in fact, becomes
anachronistic. Hotspur, who attempts to live by the code of
feudal chivalry, seems misplaced in the world of Henry IV.[84]
Shakespeare lowers the age of the historical Hotspur by a
generation to make him contemporary with Prince Hal; but
the terms of his characterization seem to recall his original
historical location as well as his anachronistic relocation in
Shakespeare's play.[85] Motivated by an extravagant and single-
minded pursuit of chivalric honor, Shakespeare's Hotspur is
represented as a belonging to an earlier (and therefore, like
the character himself, an anachronistically youthful) time.
The failure of Hotspur's efforts and the tinge of the ridiculous as well as the pathetic that attends his enthusiastic pursuit of honor expose the impossibility of the old feudal ideals
in the pragmatic new world of Henry IV.

In *Henry V*, the chorus constantly yearns for a theater that
will revive the heroic king and reenact his glorious deeds in a
timeless transcendent present and just as constantly reminds
the audience that no such thing can be achieved. After the
deposition of Richard II, Shakespeare's historiographic representation, like the history it represents, seems to fall into
time. The atemporal ritual space of medieval drama can
never be re-created in the divided, modern world of the Lancastrian kings. A postlapsarian world, it juxtaposes but does

[83]On the ritual quality, see Tillyard, pp. 280–287. On the association of medieval drama with feudalism, see Cohen, *Drama of a Nation*, chap. 1: "Medieval
Theater and the Structure of Feudalism," pp. 33–81. Cf. *Henry VIII*, where the
episodic series of falls from high estate, each ending in a speech of moral (and
moralized) enlightenment, recalls the conventions of representation in an earlier Tudor genre, exemplified in *A Mirror for Magistrates*.

[84]As Alexander Leggatt points out, "Hal's tribute to [Hotspur] as the bravest
gentleman 'To grace this latter age with noble deeds' (*1 Henry IV*: V.i.92)
suggests a picturesque throwback." *Shakespeare's Political Drama: The History
Plays and the Roman Plays* (London: Routledge, 1988), p. 85.

[85]The historical prototype of Shakespeare's character was three years older
than Henry IV and Richard II.

not unite the *platea* of plebeian theatrical presence in the Boar's Head Tavern with the *locus* of elite historical representation.[86] The linear, causal structure of *Richard II* is replaced in the Henry IV plays by a proliferation of subplots that cannot be subsumed under the temporal principle of teleology; instead, they are tenuously connected by the spatial principles of analogy, parody, contrast, and juxtaposition. The homogeneous, empty time of modern narrative and modern consciousness which relates disparate events only by calendrical coincidence has replaced the medieval sense of historical connection under the aspect of eternity. The spatial boundaries that define modern nations replace the chronological links that define feudal dynasties.[87]

The movement from *Richard II* to *Henry IV* resembles the movement in Renaissance historiography from chronicle to chorography, from the history of royal dynasty to the maps and geographical descriptions that assembled a picture of national identity from the component parts of the land. In *Richard II* York describes the medieval conception of time as genealogical connection even as he foretells its loss once the chain of patrilineal inheritance is broken:

> Take Herford's rights away, and take from Time
> His charters and his customary rights;
> Let not to-morrow then ensue to-day;

[86]*Locus* and *platea* are taken from Robert Weimann's theory of *Figurenposition*, derived from the conditions of medieval staging, where the playing area included public streets and marketplaces as well as elevated pageant wagons or scaffolds. Weimann distinguishes the *locus*, the upstage site of mimetic illusion, from the *platea*, the forestage site of clowning and of direct address to the audience. See Weimann's *Shakespeare and the Popular Tradition in the Theater: Studies in the Social Dimension of Dramatic Form and Function*, ed. Robert Schwartz (Baltimore: Johns Hopkins University Press, 1987), pp. 73–85, 224–26. For Weimann's most recent formulation of this distinction, see his "Bifold Authority in Shakespeare's Theatre," *Shakespeare Quarterly* 39 (1988), 401–17.

[87]For this formulation, I am indebted to Benedict Anderson's *Imagined Communities: Reflections on the Origin and Spread of Nationalism* (London: Verso, 1983), pp. 28–40, and also to Homi K. Bhabha's unpublished paper, "Dissemination." The structure of the Henry IV plays resembles that of the modern newspaper, which Anderson uses to exemplify the secular modern sense of temporality, the "meanwhile" that provides an arbitrary link between disparate events. Each day's newspaper, he points out, reports a collection of unrelated events, united only by the date on which they occurred.

Be not thyself; for how art thou a king
But by fair sequence and succession?

(II.i.195–99)

Substituting land for king as the embodiment of national identity and space for time as its medium, the new genre of chorography constructed the nation as a material place rather than a royal domain.[88] In the England of Henry IV, the nostalgic binary opposition between a degraded present and an idealized medieval past is replaced by multiple divisions that mark off distinct spheres of action separated by physical and social location, by different antecedents and different languages, and by the diversity of the representational modes that construct them on Shakespeare's stage. The distant world of court and battlefield where historically based characters quarrel in blank verse and play out the scripts written by Tudor historiography comes from the chronicles; the vividly detailed contemporary world of Shallow's Gloucestershire from Shakespeare's own experience, remembered hearsay and local knowledge; the stagy atemporal world of Eastcheap from an old play.[89]

Taking its origins from the endlessly repeatable discourse of theatrical performance, the world of Eastcheap is set outside of time. This, in fact, is the first thing we learn about it. The first Eastcheap scene begins with Falstaff asking Hal the time of the day, thus providing the occasion for the Prince's witty (and Shakespeare's usefully expository) demonstration that Falstaff and his idle world have nothing to do with time:

What a devil hast thou to do with the time of the day? unless hours were cups of sack, and minutes capons, and clocks the tongues of bawds, and dials the signs of leaping-houses, and the blessed sun himself a fair hot wench in flame-color'd taffata; I

[88]Richard Helgerson, "The Land Speaks: Cartography, Chorography, and Subversion in Renaissance England," in *Representing the English Renaissance*, ed. Stephen Greenblatt (Berkeley: University of California Press, 1988), pp. 349–50.

[89]On the sources for the Gloucestershire scenes, see appendix III, "Local Color," in the Variorum edition of *The Second Part of Henry the Fourth*, ed. Matthias Shaaber (Philadelphia: Lippincott, 1940), pp. 600–603. On the relationship to *The Famous Victories of Henry the Fifth*, see the Arden edition of *1 Henry IV*, ed. A. R. Humphreys (London: Methuen, 1966), xxxii–xxxvi.

see no reason why thou shouldst be so superfluous to demand
the time of the day. (I.ii.6–12)

In the Boar's Head Tavern, the historical prince meets unhistorical characters who drink anachronistic cups of sack and wear
anachronistic ruffs and peach-colored silk stockings. There is
even a man called Pistol, a character whose very name is an
anachronism and whose speech is stitched together from scraps
of plays that were not written until the sixteenth century for a
theater that did not even exist at the time of Henry IV.[90]

Falstaff and his disorderly world have no place in history, but
they constitute the most vivid dramatic presence on Shakespeare's stage. Historically central, the king and his court are
dramatically remote. Henry IV is not really the hero of the plays
that bear his name. The king, and therefore the center, of the
represented historical world, he is decentered by a divided dramatic plot that assigns him a subsidiary role in the theatrical
performance. Dramatically inaccessible, enigmatic with the inscrutability of history itself, Shakespeare's Henry IV reveals no
motives or affections that are not directly involved with the
affairs of state (and very few of those). Even in his long soliloquy
in 2 *Henry IV* (III.i.1–31), alone on the stage in the middle of
the night and dressed in his nightgown, the closest Henry comes
to a personal reflection is to complain in generalized terms about
the cares of kingship.

The comic scenes provide the only bridge between the modern world of the audience and the historical world of Henry IV,
but the contact they provide is always compromised by the fact
of theatrical mediation. The historical world never takes on the
illusion of full presence. The double plot in the Henry IV plays,
in fact, can be seen as a kind of allegory of mediation, representing in dramatic structure the split between the historical
past that is represented and the theatrical mediation required
to make it present.

[90]On the sack, see the Variorum notes on p. 174; on the ruffs and peach-
colored silk stockings, see M. St. Clare Byrne, "The Social Background," in *A
Companion to Shakespeare Studies*, ed. Harley Granville-Barker and G. B. Harrison
(New York: Doubleday, 1960), pp. 191–92. For an excellent brief discussion of
Pistol, see Barton, *Shakespeare and the Idea of the Play*, pp. 140–43.

The only character who manages to operate in both worlds is the ambiguous and enigmatic Prince Hal, whose shadowy progress through the two parts of *Henry IV* marks the elusive track of their dramatic and historical agenda. As Henry IV says on his deathbed, all his reign has been a kind of prologue for Hal's (IV.v.197–99). Like the deposition of Richard II, the coronation of Henry V is the most anticipated dramatic event, as well as the most significant historical event, depicted in the play. Throughout the two Henry IV plays, the audience is led to anticipate the moment when Hal will abandon deception, throw off his loose behavior and shine forth in sunlike majesty as the mirror of all Christian kings celebrated by the English historians.

When that moment finally arrives, Falstaff, wasting time as usual, is off in Gloucestershire with an anachronistic Justice named Shallow in Shakespeare's play but identified by modern scholars with various actual justices who lived in Shakespeare's neighborhood in the second half of the sixteenth century.[91] Neither historical nor theatrical, the world of Shallow's Gloucestershire evokes the detailed material life of the Elizabethan present—the hade land to be sowed with red wheat, the pippin of Shallow's own grafting to be eaten with a dish of caraways (V.i.14–16; V.iii.2–3). It is a life particularized in terms of place as well as time. Shallow reminisces about "John Doit of Staffordshire" and "Will Squele, a Cotsole man" (III.ii.19–21); his servant Davy reveals that he has never been to London (V.iii.60); and he urges Shallow to favor his friend "William Visor of Woncote" in the legal action between him and "Clement Perkes a' th' Hill" (V.i.38–39).[92]

Shakespeare marks the separation between this world and the historical world of Henry IV by means of Shallow's nostalgic reminiscences about his own youth in the time of Thomas Mowbray, Duke of Norfolk (to whom he assigns Falstaff as a page) and "John a' Gaunt," with whom he associates "old Double" of his own town (III.ii.25, 40–45). Falstaff repudiates Shallow's recollections as lies (III.ii.302–326). Whatever the "truth" of the matter (Falstaff, the greatest liar of all, is clearly not a credible

[91]See Shaaber, pp. 637–44, for a good selection of excerpts from these arguments.

[92]For a more extended discussion of the Gloucestershire world, see Chapter 5, section II.

witness), Shallow's confused nostalgia, which mingles historical characters with the real (and therefore fictional) persons of
his own village, provides comic proof of his separation from
the great historical personages with whom he wishes to claim
contact.

The homely, familiar world of Gloucestershire—near in geography and near in its imaginative density to William Shakespeare's childhood home in Stratford-upon-Avon[93]—is as
remote from the theatrical world of Eastcheap as it is from the
historical world of the court. Shallow's servant Davy plaintively
declares, "I hope to see London once ere I die" (V.iii.60). When
Pistol rushes in, bursting with theatrical clichés and scraps of
dialogue from old plays and frantic to deliver a message, the
difficulty of communication between Eastcheap and Gloucestershire becomes the basis for an uproarious comedy of mis-
understanding. Falstaff urges Pistol to deliver his news "like a
man of this world" (V.iii.97–98); but, as his linguistic difference
indicates, Pistol really belongs to another world. None of the
other characters can tell what Pistol's message is because Pistol
will not speak "plain English." The inhabitants of Gloucestershire speak a plain, colloquial prose; but Falstaff, who, unlike
Davy, *has* been to London, finally breaks into a blank verse as
stagy as Pistol's own to demand, "O base Assyrian knight, what
is thy news? / Let King Cophetua know the truth thereof" (V.iii.101–02). Now, at last, having been questioned in the
unreal, mannered, anachronistic language of the sixteenth-
century stage, Pistol reveals his great historical message: Henry
IV is dead and Hal is now King Henry V.[94]

Just as Shallow's confused recollections discredit the nostalgia
that motivated the project of historical reproduction, Pistol's
confused message discredits its realization on Shakespeare's

[93]See C. Elliot Browne, "Master Robert Shallow: A Study of the Shakespeare
Country," *Fraser's* n.s. 15 (1877), 488–98: "The life described is not only the
provincial life of Gloucestershire, but of Gloucestershire within a few miles of
Stratford-upon-Avon." For excerpts from Browne's argument as well as a variety of other opinions on the exact location of the Gloucestershire scenes and
Shakespeare's personal acquaintance with the people and places named, see
appendix III, "Local Color," in the Variorum *2 Henry IV*, pp. 600–603.

[94]For suggestive discussions of Pistol's theatricality, see Barton, pp. 140–43,
and James Calderwood, *Metadrama in Shakespeare's Henriad: Richard II to Henry
V* (Berkeley: University of California Press, 1979), pp. 97–99.

stage. Throughout the two plays, Shakespeare has used the comic plot to comment upon the historical action and the East-cheap scenes to draw the audience into the historical world;[95] but at the very end of the second play he seems to imply the ludicrous impossibility of his project when he uses Pistol, the most fantastic and anachronistic character of all, to deliver the most important historical message in the play. Attempting to communicate the historical news of Henry's early fifteenth-century court to the inhabitants of a realistically conceived sixteenth-century Gloucestershire, Pistol repeatedly insists that he speaks nothing but the "truth (V.iii.117, 121), but the bombastic language in which he speaks obscures his true historical message with the taint of theatrical mediation; its echoes and quotations from sixteenth-century texts mark the temporal distance that separates Pistol from the event he reports. A character who has no place in the history he reports, Pistol is modeled on the braggart soldier who was a stock character in Renaissance drama.[96] His desperate efforts to communicate his message express the pathos of historical distance that undermines the ambitious project of presenting the glorious past on a modern stage.

— VI —

Beginning and ending in a sense of anachronism, the Renaissance revolution in historiography was impelled by a desire to recuperate an older, better world. Confronted with the destabilizing forces of rapid social change, Shakespeare's contemporaries took refuge in nostalgic historical myths of a stable, Edenic past. But those very efforts produced their own frustration in the perception of distance and difference that separated the history-writing present from the historical past and the con-

---

[95] This point has become a commonplace, but see the early and full demonstration by Cleanth Brooks and Robert B. Heilman in *Understanding Drama* (New York: Holt, Rinehart & Winston, 1948), pp. 376–87, and the provocative treatment by Calderwood in *Metadrama in Shakespeare's Henriad*, pp. 68–104.

[96] On Pistol's relation to the tradition of the *miles gloriosus*, see the Variorum *2 Henry IV*, pp. 629–30.

sequent awareness of the inadequacy of all historical representation. In *Richard II* Shakespeare manipulates the temporality of the action and invokes the tradition of medieval sacred drama to provide his audience with an analogue to the medieval vision of human history fully revealed under the aspect of eternity. In the fallen modern world of Henry IV, he uses a stock character from the sixteenth-century stage to mark the anachronistic distance that separates the historically specific site of his own theatrical representation from the lost past it can never truly present.

Writing at the beginning of the seventeenth century, Samuel Daniel expresses a similar recognition when he compares historical narratives to maps:

> Nor must we thinke, viewing the superficiall figure of a region in a Mappe, that wee know strait the fashion and place as it is. Or reading an Historie (which is but a Mappe of Men, and dooth no otherwise acquaint us with the true Substance of Circumstances then a superficiall Card dooth the Seaman with a Coast never seene, which alwayes prooves other to the eye than the imagination forecast it), that presently wee know all the world, and can distinctly iudge of times, men, and maners, iust as they were.[97]

Written from a distance, the historical narrative, like the inscrutable Henry IV or the enigmatic Henry V, could never recover the human motives and actual life that lay behind the events it recorded.

Daniel's response to this disillusioned recognition prefigures the now-familiar Johnsonian claims for the universality of human nature and poetic fiction. Defending Shakespeare against the charge of anachronism, Johnson wrote,

> His story requires Romans or kings, but he thinks only on men. He knew that Rome, like every other city, had men of all dispositions; and wanting a buffoon, he went into the senate house for that which the senate house would certainly have afforded him.[98]

[97]"A Defense of Rhyme," in *Elizabethan Critical Essays*, ed. Smith, 2:370–71.
[98]"Preface to Shakespeare," *Critical Theory*, p. 331.

Daniel anticipates Johnson's example as well as his premises:

> The distribution of giftes are universall, and all seasons have them
> in some sort. We must not thinke but that there were *Scipioes*,
> *Caesars*, *Catoes*, and *Pompeies* borne elsewhere then at *Rome*; the
> rest of the world hath ever had them in the same degree of nature,
> though not of state.[99]

As Daniel's argument suggests, the process of dehistoricizing
Shakespeare that culminates in nineteenth-century bardolotry
actually began in Shakespeare's own time. It can be seen in
the publication of the First Folio with Ben Jonson's dedicatory
celebration of the disembodied author as an enduring "Moni-
ment," "not of an age, but for all time" and even in Shakespeare's own self-presentation in the sonnets as the writer of
verses that "would outlive stones and monuments [and] last to
the 'edge of doome.' "[100]

The retreat from history exemplified in these texts displaces
the locus of stability and value from the pretemporal Edenic
past to the atemporal Universal present.[101] Despite this displacement, however, both forms of mystification represent attempts
to evade, suppress, or deny the scandal of anachronism that
compromises the historical project. A disreputable, unwelcome
guest at the scene of historical representation, Pistol embodies
that scandal. At the end of *2 Henry IV*, the new king banishes
Pistol along with Falstaff and the rest of his disorderly companions, but Pistol reappears in *Henry V* to discredit the king's
heroic enterprise by his shameless descriptions of the French
wars as opportunities for theft and lying (II.iii.55–56; V.i.87–90).
It is significant, I believe, that the same critical tradition that

[99]P. 371.

[100]For a facsimile of Jonson's dedicatory poem, see *The Riverside Shakespeare*,
pp. 65–66. For a brilliant and convincing demonstration of the ways the First
Folio constructs Shakespeare as the transcendent Bard, see Marcus, *Puzzling
Shakespeare*, chap. 1, "Localization," pp. 1–50. Marcus makes the point about
the sonnets on p. 40.

[101]Sidney, of course, has it both ways. The golden world of poetic imitation
is superior to history because "poesy deals with . . . the universal consideration,
and the history with . . . the particular." It also provides "no small argument
to the incredulous of that first accursed fall of Adam, since our erected wit
makes us know what perfection is and yet our infected will keeps us from
reaching unto it" (*Defense*, pp. 19, 10).

looked to Shakespeare for representations of universal human nature found Pistol a disappointment. To Brander Matthews, for instance, Pistol was "wearisome" because his characterization "was founded rather in fashion than in nature":

> [Pistol] has worn out his welcome today. . . . [He] no longer appeals to our risibilities, in spite of the fact that he probably evoked more laughter when he was first seen than any of his fellows. . . . When Pistol made his first appearance he was particularly up to date; but unfortunately what is up to date soon becomes out of date. . . . Pistol was contemporary, and therefore he has proved to be temporary only, as nearly always happens.[102]

But Pistol had already worn out his welcome when he first appeared. His language was always already outdated, his presence unwelcome from the beginning. Pistol's exploitation of the French wars for financial gain and his plans to misrepresent his role in them when he returns to Eastcheap might be construed as a parody of the players' own practice of rewriting the inspirational myths of English history for commercial gain. His uninvited, disruptive presence at the coronation and his refusal to stay banished insistently betray the taint of theatrical mediation and the scandal of anachronism that inevitably attend the scene of Shakespeare's historical representation.

[102]Brander Matthews, *Shakspere as a Playwright* (New York, 1913), p. 127, quoted in the Variorum 2 *Henry IV*, p. 630.

# —— 4 ——

# Patriarchal History and
# Female Subversion

The Epilogue to 2 *Henry IV* acknowledges the presence of a
woman on the English throne, kneeling, he says, "to pray for
the Queen." He also acknowledges the presence of women in
Shakespeare's theater audience: "All the gentlewomen here
have forgiven me," he says, and "if the gentlemen will not,
then the gentlemen do not agree with the gentlewomen, which
was never seen in such an assembly." Nonetheless, there is
nothing to mark the presence of women in the preceding
scene—the representation of the great historical moment that
Pistol interrupts.[1] The stage directions provide for the entrance
of "the king and his train." No female character is named, and
no female character has a speaking part in that scene. If female
characters did appear, they were restricted to the roles of silent
spectators. Pistol's anachronistic stagy language betrays the unwelcome presence of the common player in the scene of historical recuperation. The placement of women is equally
revealing. In the marginal space of the Epilogue's extradramatic
address to the audience, the players defer to the economic

[1] On the presence of women in the commercial playhouses, see Andrew Gurr,
*Playgoing in Shakespeare's London* (New York: Cambridge University Press, 1988),
pp. 59–64 and appendices I and II. On the implications of that presence, see
Jean Howard, "Crossdressing, the Theatre, and Gender Struggle in Early Modern England," *Shakespeare Quarterly* 39 (1988), 439–40, and Richard Levin,
"Women in the Renaissance Theatre Audience," *Shakespeare Quarterly* 40 (1989),
165–74.

power of their female customers and the authority of their queen, the present realities of female power and authority that hovered at the margins of their historical stage. In the central scene of historical representation, women have no place. The textual ambiguity that renders female characters either absent or silent within that scene is doubly determined; the same anxieties that excluded women from the company of players also repressed their roles in Shakespeare's historical sources. The cultural contradictions and discursive exclusions that determined the marginal location of women in the playhouse also marginalized their roles in the ideologically motivated discourse of Tudor history.

Renaissance historiography constituted a masculine tradition, written by men, devoted to the deeds of men, glorifying the masculine virtues of courage, honor, and patriotism, and dedicated to preserving the names of past heroes and recording their patriarchal genealogies. Within that historical record, women had no voice. Renaissance gender role definitions prescribed silence as a feminine virtue, and Renaissance sexual mythology associated the feminine with body and matter in contrast to masculine intellect and spirit. Depicted as blank pages awaiting the inscription of patriarchal texts, silenced by the discourse of patriarchal authority, the women could never tell their own stories.

No woman is the protagonist in a Shakespearean history play. Antagonists and consorts, queens and queans, witches and saints: women play almost every conceivable role on Shakespeare's historical stage. But there is one role that no woman can play, that of the hero. Aliens in the masculine world of history, women can threaten or validate the men's historical projects, but they can never take the center of history's stage or become the subjects of its stories. Taking their subjects from patriarchal history, Shakespeare's history plays marginalize the roles of the wives and mothers, centering instead on the heroic legacies of the fathers, the failures and triumphs of the sons.

Historiography is a major concern in Shakespeare's history plays. Characters repeatedly allude to history, past and future, and define their actions as attempts to inscribe their names in the historical record. Like their playwright, these characters show an obsessive concern with the work of the historian, the writing, reading, and preservation of historical texts. Shake-speare's historical protagonists, conceived both as subjects and as writers of history, were inevitably male. The women who do appear are typically defined as opponents and subverters of the historical and historiographic enterprise, in short, as antihis-torians.[2] But Shakespeare does give them a voice—a voice that challenges the logocentric, masculine historical record. For the most part, and especially in his earliest histories, Shakespeare depicts male protagonists defending masculine historical proj-ects against female characters who threaten to obstruct those projects and feminine appeals to the audience that threaten to discredit them. In his later history plays, but especially in *King John*, those feminine voices will become more insistent, threat-ening to invalidate the patriarchal myths that Shakespeare found in his historiographic sources and implying that before the masculine voice of history can be accepted as valid, it must come to terms with women and the subversive forces they rep-resent. However, as soon as Shakespeare attempts to incor-porate those feminine forces, marrying words and things, spirit and matter, historiography itself becomes problematic, no longer speaking with the clear, univocal voice of unquestioned tradition but re-presented as a dubious construct, always pro-visional, always subject to erasure and reconstruction, and never adequate to recover the past in full presence.[3]

In *1 Henry VI*, this pattern of masculine history-writing and

[2]Cf. Joan Kelly's argument in "Early Feminist Theory and the *Querelle des Femmes*, 1400–1789," *Signs* 8 (1982), 4–28, that early feminist writers, opposing their own experience to masculine texts, were "unremittingly critical of the authors—ancient, modern, even scriptural—at a time when the *auctores* were still *auctoritates* to many." The same discursive exclusions that required the oppositional postures of the real women Kelly described defined the roles of the female characters in Shakespeare's history plays. In both cases, the women were antihistorians because they had to be: this was the only part they could play in the story the men had written. See also Linda Woodbridge, *Women and the English Renaissance: Literature and the Nature of Womankind, 1540–1620* (Ur-bana: University of Illinois Press, 1984), p. 208. As Woodbridge points out, "Women's tongues are instruments of aggression or self-defense; men's are the tools of authority. In either case speech is an expression of authority; but male speech represents legitimate authority, while female speech attempts to usurp authority or rebel against it."

[3]Note, for instance, the ratification at the end of *Henry V* (discussed at the end of Chapter 2) of Joan's image in *1 Henry VI* of historical glory as a circle in the water that finally disperses to nought (I.ii.133–37).

feminine subversion can be seen in its simplest terms. Here Shakespeare contrives his action to subvert the subversive female voices and ratify the masculine version of the past. Defining the project of writing English history as an effort to preserve the legacy of English glory left by Henry V, he associates it with the masculine, military struggle to secure English power in France. Michel Foucault's observation that the Greek epic "was intended to perpetuate the immortality of the hero" aptly characterizes Shakespeare's conception of history at this point in his career. In Foucault's view, the hero's death represents a kind of trade-off between the hero and his story: "If he was willing to die young, it was so that his life, consecrated and magnified by death, might pass into immortality."[4]

The process by which human mortality is translated into textual immortality was a frequent theme for Renaissance theorists of historiography as well as for Shakespearean sonnets. However, a problem arises (as it did for historians during Shakespeare's own lifetime) when history, the second party to this trade, comes to be seen as itself subject to mutability. Faced with a growing consciousness that the historiographic text was not necessarily identical with the historical past, an increasing sense of alienation from the past, and repeated demonstrations that physical evidence could be more reliable than ancient texts, the authority of historical writing was breaking down.[5] Written accounts of the past were no longer accepted as authentic simply because they existed, and alternative accounts of historical events and opposed interpretations of their causes and significance now threatened each other's authority. Thus undermined, history loses its power to make the hero immortal.

This is the problem dramatized in *1 Henry VI*. The play begins as history itself begins, with (or immediately following) the death of the hero. The opening scene depicts the funeral of Henry V, the legendary warrior-king who was, we are told,

---

[4]"What Is an Author?" in *Textual Strategies: Perspectives in Post-Structuralist Criticism*, ed. Josué V. Harari (Ithaca: Cornell University Press, 1979), p. 142.

[5]Gabrielle M. Spiegel, "Genealogy: Form and Function in Medieval Historical Narrative," *History and Theory: Studies in the Philosophy of History* 22, no. 1 (1983), 43–53. See also Peter Burke, *The Renaissance Sense of the Past* (London: Edward Arnold, 1969), and F. J. Levy, *Tudor Historical Thought* (San Marino: Huntington Library, 1967).

"too famous to live long" (I.i.6); and the entire play can be seen as a series of attempts on the part of the English to write a history that will preserve Henry's fame. The struggle begins in the opening scene when the audience (along with their countrymen on stage) are confronted with reports of French victories that threaten to erase Henry's name from the historical record as surely as death has destroyed his body. Bedford's heroic invocation of Henry's ghost implies that the dead king will occupy a place in history even more glorious than Julius Caesar's, but Bedford's effort at prospective history-making is interrupted by a messenger who rushes in to announce that eight French cities have been lost:

> Henry the Fift, thy ghost I invocate:
> Prosper this realm, keep it from civil broils,
> Combat with adverse planets in the heavens!
> A far more glorious star thy soul will make
> Than Julius Caesar or bright—
>
> (I.i.52–56)

The Arden editor speculates that the Folio dash at the end of Bedford's speech "probably indicates illegibility of the copy or MS";[6] but the dash works very well as an indication that Bedford's speech is in fact interrupted, cut short in mid-sentence by the news of French victories that threaten to deny the English king a place in the historical record.

The French action—to erase the English record—operates at two levels. Within the represented action, the French fight to drive the English from their country. Moreover, at the rhetorical level, they attack both the English version of history and the values it expresses with an earthy iconoclasm that subverts the inherited notions of chivalric glory invoked by the English heroes. Talbot, the English champion, and Joan, his French antagonist, speak alternative languages.[7] His language reifies

---

[6] Andrew S. Cairncross, ed., William Shakespeare, *The First Part of King Henry VI*, Arden edition (London: Methuen, 1962), p. 7n.

[7] In *Henry V* the women will literally speak an alternative language. There Shakespeare departs from theatrical convention when he chooses to write the women's lines in French, excluding them from the linguistic community that includes virtually all of the male characters (French as well as English) along with his English-speaking audience. With its insistent physicality and bawdry,

glory, while hers is the language of physical objects. The play defines their conflict as a contest between English *words* and French *things*, between the historical record that Talbot wishes to preserve and the physical reality that Joan invokes to discredit it. Shakespeare departs from his sources when he has Talbot bury Salisbury, one of the last English heroes of the former age, in France. The real Salisbury was buried in England, but Shakespeare's Talbot announces that he will erect Salisbury's tomb in the "chiefest temple" of the French "upon the which, that every one may read, / Shall be engrav'd the sack of Orleance, / The treacherous manner of his mournful death, / And what a terror he had been to France" (II.ii.12–17). Talbot's effort here, as in his military campaign to secure Henry's French conquests, is a struggle to leave an English historical record in France.

Shakespeare repeatedly calls attention to the fact that the French champion is a woman, defining the conflict between England and France as a conflict between masculine and feminine values: chivalric virtue versus pragmatic craft, historical fame versus physical reality, patriarchal age versus subversive youth, high social rank versus low, self versus other. Representing the chivalric ideal that constituted an object of nostalgic longing for Shakespeare's Elizabethan audience, "English Talbot" is a venerable gentleman who fights according to the knightly code. Embodying the disorderly objects of present fears, the forces that threatened the patriarchal order, Joan is a youthful peasant whose army resorts to craft, subterfuge, and modern weapons (a French boy sniper shoots the great Salisbury, and Joan recaptures Rouen by sneaking in, disguised as the peasant she really is, to admit the French army).[8]

In addition to Joan, *1 Henry VI* includes two other female

---

the scene of Katherine's language lesson reiterates the French/female/physical/ illicit sexuality association that appears in Shakespeare's representation of Joan. For a brilliant exposition of these associations in contemporary language texts, see Juliet Fleming, "*The French Garden*: An Introduction to Women's French," *ELH* 56 (1989), 19–51.

[8]David Riggs, *Shakespeare's Heroical Histories: Henry VI and Its Literary Tradition* (Cambridge: Harvard University Press, 1971), pp. 22–23, 100–113, shows how the conventions of the funeral oration are used to characterize Talbot as well as Salisbury and Henry V. Riggs argues convincingly that Talbot exemplifies "the aristocratic ideal of military service and gentle blood" that was disappearing at the very time when *Henry VI* was written and that Joan "epitomizes the external forces that threaten[ed] that ideal."

characters, the Countess of Auvergne and Margaret of Anjou. All three are French, and all three represent threats to the English protagonists and to the heroic values associated with history as the preserver of masculine fame and glory.[9] Like Joan, the countess attacks Talbot; like Joan, she resorts to craft and stratagem; and like Joan she places her faith in physical reality over verbal report. The countess says she wants to verify the reports of Talbot's glory by seeing his person: "Fain would mine eyes be witness with mine ears / To give their censure of these rare reports." What she sees—"a child, a silly dwarf... this weak and writhled shrimp," in short, Talbot's physical appearance—convinces her that "report is fabulous and false" (II.iii.9–23).

The countess's preference for physical evidence over historical report associates her with the French and female forces in the play as a threat to the project of writing English history. We see this conflict in its purest form after Talbot's death when Sir William Lucy calls for him in heroic language:

> But where's the great Alcides of the field,
> Valiant Lord Talbot, Earl of Shrewsbury,
> Created, for his rare success in arms,
> Great Earl of Washford, Waterford, and Valence,
> Lord Talbot of Goodrig and Urchinfield,
> Lord Strange of Blackmere, Lord Verdon of Alton,
> Lord Cromwell of Wingfield, Lord Furnival of Sheffield,
> The thrice-victorious Lord of Falconbridge,
> Knight of the noble Order of Saint George,
> Worthy Saint Michael, and the Golden Fleece,
> Great marshal to Henry the Sixt
> Of all his wars within the realm of France?
>
> (IV.vii.60–71)

Rejecting the grandiose pretensions in the string of titles Lucy bestows on Talbot and relying on material fact to debunk the titles and attack Lucy's language, Joan replies:

[9]See David Bevington, "The Domineering Female in *1 Henry VI*," *Shakespeare Studies* 2 (1966), 51–58; Sigurd Burckhardt, "'I am But Shadow of Myself': Ceremony and Design in *1 Henry VI*," in *Shakespearean Meanings* (Princeton: Princeton University Press, 1968), pp. 47–77; and David Scott Kastan, "Shakespeare and 'The Way of Womenkind,'" *Daedalus* 111 (1982), 116.

Here's a silly stately style indeed!
The Turk, that two and fifty kingdoms hath,
Writes not so tedious a style as this.
Him that thou magnifi'st with all these titles
Stinking and fly-blown lies here at our feet.
(IV.vii.72–76)

Lucy describes Talbot as history was to describe him, decked in the titles that designate his patriarchal lineage and heroic military achievements. Joan, like the countess, insists on physical fact, rejecting the masculine historical ideals and significance that Lucy's glorious names invoke.

Joan's reductive, nominalistic attack has an obvious appeal for an audience: her vigorous language, tied to the material facts of earth, threatens to topple the imposing formal edifice Lucy has constructed with his tower of names. But in this play the subversive female voice is never allowed to prevail for more than a moment. It is tempting to speculate that at least some in Shakespeare's audience may have realized that the glorious words of Lucy, unlike Joan's fictitious speech, take their authority from an enduring historical monument, Talbot's tomb at Rouen, where they were inscribed. Reciting the words of the inscription, Lucy invokes a historical authority more permanent and less mediated than the narratives of Shakespeare's chronicle sources. And although Lucy is barely mentioned in Shakespeare's chronicle sources, he himself possesses a similar authority; a man named Sir William Lucy did in fact live in Shakespeare's neighborhood at the time of Henry VI, and it has been suggested that Shakespeare knew of him from local oral tradition. If these speculations are correct, then Lucy represents Shakespeare's attempt to invoke a historical authority beyond historiographic mediation in order to refute Joan's appeal to physical presence.[10]

In the case of the countess, no such speculation is required. Shakespeare contrives Talbot's encounter with the countess so

[10]On Sir William Lucy, see Matthias A. Shaaber, ed. *A New Variorum Edition of The Second Part of Henry the Fourth* (Philadelphia: Lippincott, 1940), pp. 639, 640; F. E. Halliday, *A Shakespeare Companion 1564–1964* (Baltimore: Penguin, 1964), p. 292; and Norman Sanders, ed., *The First Part of King Henry the Sixth* (Harmondsworth, England: Penguin, 1981), p. 214. On the titles taken from the inscription on Talbot's tomb, see Sanders, p. 220.

that she, and the audience along with her, will be clearly instructed in the superiority of report over physical fact. Just before Talbot summons the hidden soldiers who will free him from her trap, he announces, "I am but shadow of myself. You are deceiv'd, my substance is not here" (II.iii.50–51). A minute later the countess acknowledges that the verbal reports she doubted were really true. For the audience, Talbot's lines were doubly significant. A "shadow" was a common term for an actor, and in that sense the man who spoke those lines was quite literally "but a shadow" of the elusive Talbot, the emblem of a lost historical presence celebrated by historiographer and playwright but never present in substance even to the countess who thinks she has him captured in her castle. Relying as it does on physical presence, the reductive, French, female version of Talbot is always vulnerable to metadramatic attack, which invokes the ultimate fact of theatrical occasion to remind the audience that no actual physical presence is involved.

This reminder is important because, as I argued in Chapter 3, the issue of physical presence versus historical record, dramatized in *1 Henry VI* as a conflict between English men and French women, is central, not only to this particular play, but to the history play genre itself. Nashe's reference to Talbot raised from the tomb of historical writing to "triumph again on the stage, and have his bones new embalmed with the tears of ten thousand spectators who . . . imagine they behold him fresh bleeding" describes an audience that went to the history play hoping to see those historical records brought to life and to make direct contact with the living reality that was celebrated but also obscured by the "worme-eaten" books of history.[11]

For Shakespeare's audience, as for the characters in the play, Talbot's "glory [still] fill[ed] the world with loud report" (II.ii.43). His mere name, like the name of God, is sufficient to rout the French soldiers (I.iv.50; II.i.79–81); and although Talbot is finally killed, his glory survives his physical death. Like the countess, Shakespeare's audience wanted to *see* the renowned Talbot, and like her, they were likely to be disappointed. Exploiting the inadequacies of theatrical representation to validate the historical record, Shakespeare instructs his audience along

[11]See Chapter 3, section III.

with the countess that what they see on stage is only a "shadow" of Talbot, that history and renown portrayed him more truly than physical presence ever could do. The masculine authority of history is thus sustained against the feminine challenge of physical presence as the play is revealed as a re-presentation. Presence remains ineluctably absent—the elusive Other, that, like the feminine principle itself, must be suppressed in order to sustain the masculine historiographic narrative. The nominalist challenge posed by the women's appeals to physical fact is discredited by reminders that the drama contains no physical facts, and the verbal construction of Talbot's glory survives.

In this context the scene of Talbot's death is instructive. A long contention between Talbot and his son (a son repeatedly addressed by his father as "Talbot," the father's own name) in which each urges the other to save his life by fleeing from battle and in which neither, of course, will flee ends with the death of both. Despite Talbot's paternal solicitude, the boy refuses to leave because "flight" would "abuse" his father's "renowned name" (IV.v.41): "Is my name Talbot? and am I your son? / And shall I fly?" (IV.v.12–13). Shakespeare departs from history to make the boy Talbot's only son. As a result, young Talbot's filial devotion, along with both Talbots' devotion to honor, ensures that there will be no survivor to carry their name into the future. In Shakespeare's construction, only the name will survive, stripped now of any human referent but immortalized by heroic sacrifice.

The argument that finally convinces Talbot to allow his son to stay with him and die in battle is the boy's claim that if he runs away, he will lose his patriarchal English title and become "like . . . the peasant boys of France": "if I fly, I am not Talbot's son. . . . If son to Talbot, die at Talbot's foot" (IV.vi.48, 51–53). Talbot and his son both make the heroic choice described by Foucault, sacrificing their lives to preserve their honor and their heroic titles. In direct contrast, Shakespeare contrives Joan's final interview with her father to show her placing life above patriarchal lineage and personal honor. We see her rejecting her father, revealed as a bastard, and finally claiming to be pregnant with yet another bastard in a futile effort to save her life (V.iv).

This final schematic contrast between the strong bond that

unites the male Talbots and Joan's denial of her peasant father completes Shakespeare's picture of Talbot and Joan as opposites and connects the various terms in which their opposition has been defined: historian versus anti-historian, noble man versus peasant woman, realist versus nominalist. Realists, the Talbots die to preserve the disembodied name of a great medieval family. To the nominalist Joan, her individual physical life is all that matters. As Kenneth Burke has pointed out, the medieval realist conception of language had strong affinities with the medieval feudal conception of the family, for both realism and feudalism treat "individuals as members of a group" or "tribe." In direct contrast, nominalism, the subversive movement in medieval philosophy, is "linguistically individualistic or atomistic," because it treats "groups as aggregates of individuals." Realism and feudalism both imply history because both involve what Burke calls "an *ancestral* notion." A realist conception of language holds that universals precede things and "give birth" to them.[12] Nominalism, like Joan, denies history because it denies the diachronic links that unite meaning and word like the successive generations of a great feudal family (the kind of family whose name the Talbots die to preserve). Drawing the same kind of connections, R. Howard Bloch associates the story of Abelard's castration with the fact of Abelard's nominalism: just as Abelard's intellectual position disrupted the "intellectual genealogy" of words, so too is his own physical genealogy represented as disrupted.[13] Moreover, although Bloch does not mention it, the castration, like the nominalism, also associates Abelard with the feminine.

Joan's sexual promiscuity and her association with bastardy are hinted at even in her first appearance, when she is introduced to the Dauphin (and to Shakespeare's audience) by the Bastard of Orleans and quickly becomes the object of the courtiers' lascivious jokes (I.ii). The suggestion of illicit sexuality that

[12]Kenneth Burke, "Realist Family and Nominalist Aggregate" and "Familial Definition," both in *A Grammar of Motives* (Cleveland: Meridian, 1962), pp. 247–52 and 26–27.

[13]R. Howard Bloch, *Etymologies and Genealogies: A Literary Anthropology of the French Middle Ages* (Chicago: University of Chicago Press, 1983), p. 149. Bloch also cites a fourteenth-century Provençal author who developed an elaborate system of analogies between modes of paternity and modes of lexical derivation (p. 42).

always surrounds Joan is less obviously connected than her nominalism to her role as antihistorian, but it is connected none-theless. Just as her nominalism associates her with the Countess of Auvergne, her sexual promiscuity associates her with the third French woman in the play, Margaret of Anjou, soon to become the adulterous queen of Henry VI. Immediately linked to Joan in the audience's eyes, Margaret is introduced as a cap-tive led onto the stage at the same time that Joan is led off after her final capture.[14] Moreover, as we quickly learn in 2 *Henry VI*, the marriage between Margaret and Henry threatens to erase history itself:

> Fatal this marriage, cancelling your fame,
> Blotting your names from books of memory,
> Rasing the characters of your renown
> Defacing monuments of conquer'd France,
> Undoing all as all had never been!
>
> (I.i.99–103)

Besides Joan, Margaret is the only woman who plays a major part in the *Henry VI* plays and the only character of either sex who appears in all four plays of the first tetralogy. Margaret's disruptive role becomes increasingly prominent as the story progresses and the world of the plays sinks into chaos. A virago who defies her husband, leads armies into battle, and gloats at the murder of an innocent child, Shakespeare's Margaret has a "tiger's heart wrapp'd in a woman's hide" (3 *Henry VI*: I.iv.137).[15] Shakespeare follows Hall, who makes Margaret "a

---

[14]It is interesting that even in Margaret's own time, she was asssociated with Joan. Patricia-Ann Lee in "Reflections of Power: Margaret of Anjou and the Dark Side of Queenship," *Renaissance Quarterly* 39 (1986), 198–99, quotes from *The Commentaries of Pius II* both a speech in which Margaret is reported to have enjoined her French captains, "You who once followed a peasant girl, follow now a queen" and a report that those who heard the speech "said that the spirit of the Maid, who had raised Charles to the throne, was renewed in the queen." Although Lee questions the veracity of Pius's account, what is sig-nificant, I believe, is that his fiction draws the same connection between Joan and Margaret that Shakespeare's does.

[15]Robert Greene's famous attack on Shakespeare as a *"Tygers heart wrapt in a Players hyde"* (*Greens Groats-worth of Wit*, 1596, reprinted in Chambers, 4:241) offers a tantalizing suggestion of identity between the gentle playwright de-scribed in Ben Jonson's *Discoveries* ("honest, and of an open, and free nature") and the wicked queen. Stephen Orgel, in "Prospero's Wife," *Representations* 8

manly woman, usyng to rule not to be ruled," and he also exploits the old Yorkist slander that she was an adulteress.[16]

Like Joan's sexual promiscuity, Margaret's adultery has no real impact on the action of the *Henry VI* plays. In both cases, the women's sexual transgressions are dramatically unnecessary: Apparently added to underscore the women's characterization as threats to masculine honor, they recall the gratuitous slanders by which a Renaissance woman who transgressed in any way, even by excessive gossip and railing, was commonly characterized as a whore.

Shakespeare does not elaborate the relationship between sexual transgression and historical subversion until he comes to *King John*, but the relationship is always there, even though in the first tetralogy it is only implicit. For there is a very important sense in which women's sexual autonomy can always subvert the central objects of Renaissance history—the celebration of men's honor and perpetuation of men's names. In considering the power of women to undermine the masculine historical project, it is important to remember that Renaissance historiography was not only a masculine project; it was also patriarchal. More than a record of heroic names and glorious deeds or an aggregate of individual biographies, the Tudor histories told a connected story, authorizing present power in genealogical myths of patriarchal succession.

Genealogical explanations appear in virtually every area of Renaissance thought, saturating the discourse with the structures that validated the social order.[17] Invoking the legendary

---

(1984), suggests that Prospero (who is generally recognized as a Shakespearean self-representation), in his claim to have raised the dead, "has incorporated Ovid's witch [Medea], . . . the wicked mother" (p. 11). Nowhere is Shakespeare/ Prospero's claim more applicable than in the English history plays, and nowhere is Orgel's observation more suggestive. In those plays, Shakespeare incorporates the women and raises the dead in order to confute the historical record. He does so with women's own weapons: lies (fictitious characters, dialogues, events) and materiality (stage spectacle), both of which he uses to oppose the written historiographic text.

[16] Edward Hall, *The Union of the Two Noble and Illustre Famelies of Lancastre & Yorke* (1548; rpt. London: J. Johnson et al. 1809), p. 249. For an excellent account of the historical myths that grew up around Margaret, see Lee, "Reflections of Power," pp. 183–217.

[17] Cf. Thomas Hyde, "Boccaccio: The Genealogies of Myth," *PMLA* 100 (1985),

names of Brut and Arthur, Tudor historians produced fables of ancient descent and providential purpose to validate the new dynasty's claim to the English throne. Living in a time of unprecedented social mobility, Shakespeare and his contemporaries provided a thriving business for the heralds who constructed the genealogies by which they attempted to secure their places in an unstable social hierarchy.[18] Confronted by rapid linguistic change, humanists developed the new science of philology, using etymology to define the meanings of words by tracing their historical ancestry.[19] Renaissance histories were organized by the same principle of genealogical succession. Divided into chronological segments that represented the reigns of successive kings and tracing the passing down of land and titles from one man to another, the historical narratives were structured by the same principles of patriarchal genealogy that the heralds used, and they served the same purpose—to provide a historical rationale for the social order of their own time.[20]

---

744. Citing Boccaccio's illegitimate birth, his obsessive recounting of tales of foundlings recovering their birthrights, and his use of a genealogical structure to organize his great encyclopedia of ancient mythology, Hyde speculates that Boccaccio generalized "his personal burden into an image for the new age he helped to inaugurate. An illegitimate and upstart age, cast loose from historical succession, at sea, attempting with an uneasy combination of aggression and filial piety to adopt a foster parent, wishing for legitimacy but unwilling to accept its imaginative restraints, struggling greedily and guiltily to inherit."

[18]Lawrence Stone, "Social Mobility in England, 1500–1700," *Past and Present* 33 (1966), 16–55, and *The Crisis of the Aristocracy, 1558–1641* (Oxford: Clarendon Press, 1965). As Stone points out (*Crisis*, p. 23), "One of the most striking features of the age was a pride of ancestry which now reached new heights of fantasy and elaboration. . . . Genuine genealogy was cultivated by the older gentry to reassure themselves of their innate superiority over the upstarts; bogus genealogy was cultivated by the new gentry in an effort to clothe their social nakedness, and by the old gentry in the internal jockeying for position in the ancestral pecking order." For an account of Shakespeare's own family's efforts, over a period of thirty years, to acquire and retain their coat of arms, see Samuel Schoenbaum, *William Shakespeare: A Compact Documentary Life* (Oxford: Oxford University Press, 1978), pp. 227–32.

[19]A. Bartlett Giamatti, *Exile and Change in Renaissance Literature* (New Haven: Yale University Press, 1984), pp. 14–15.

[20]Cf. Spiegel, "Genealogy: Form and Function," p. 47. Spiegel writes about late medieval French historiography, but, as scholars have long recognized, the Tudor sponsorship of historiography was clearly motivated by Tudor genealogical anxiety. David Riggs's observations about Elizabethan nostalgia for the fast-vanishing ideal of the hereditary feudal aristocrat are also relevant

The patrilineal genealogy that organized the structure of Renaissance history and rationalized the structure of Renaissance society required the repression of women for the same reason that it could never do without them.[21] Authorized by the principle of patrilineal inheritance, patriarchal society depended for its very existence on the wives and mothers within whose bodies that inheritance was transmitted from father to son. As a result, the women signify a constant source of anxiety; for—as Shakespeare's cuckold jokes endlessly insist—no man could truly know that he was the father of the boy who was destined to inherit his name and property. The only custodians of that most important and most dangerous of all knowledge, the women embodied the truth that threatened to dishonor the heroes and disinherit their sons, and in so doing, subvert the entire project of patriarchal history.

Because an adulterous woman at any point could make a mockery of the whole story of patriarchal succession, women were inevitably threatening to the patriarchal historiographic enterprise. The written historiographic narrative suppressed women because it had to suppress the knowledge that all men and women have of the physical impossibility of ever discovering a sure biological basis for patriarchal succession. Hence the association of women with nominalism and their characterization as subverters of the historiographic record.[22] In a very

---

here, as is the fact that Queen Elizabeth, whose refusal to marry had always provoked anxiety about the succession, was now well past the age of marriage and childbearing.

[21]Coppélia Kahn explores the psychological dimensions of this paradox in *Man's Estate: Masculine Identity in Shakespeare* (Berkeley: University of California Press, 1981). As Kahn points out, giving "men control over women," patriarchy also made "them dependent on women indirectly and covertly for the validation of their manhood. Paradoxically, their power over women also [made] them vulnerable to women" (p. 17). "The willingness of women to be married to husbands of their fathers' choice, and to be sexually faithful to their husbands in bearing legitimate male heirs—in both ways serving the continuation of patriarchy—is the invisible heart of the whole structure" (p. 13).

[22]Gayle Rubin ("The Traffic in Women: Notes on the 'Political Economy' of Sex," in *Towards an Anthropology of Women*, ed. R. Reiter [New York: Monthly Review Press, 1975], p. 188) quotes Lacan discussing Lévi-Strauss's argument that the structures of language are implicated "with that part of the social laws which regulate marriage and kinship," i.e., with legitimacy and patriarchal succession, mythologies that serve male interests. Jacques Derrida, in *Of Gram-*

important sense, Tudor history was not simply written without women; it was also written *against* them. Patriarchal history is designed to construct a verbal substitute for the visible physical connection between a mother and her children, to authenticate the always dubious relationships between fathers and sons, and to suppress and supplant the role of the mother.

Such is the story told by Renaissance historians, and such is the story Shakespeare told in most of his English history plays. A number of Shakespeare's history plays offer positive images of women in subsidiary roles, but none of them attempts to represent female authority, even though (or perhaps because) all but the last were written during the reign of Queen Elizabeth.[23] Female authority, a complicated, troubling presence in the patriarchal world that Elizabeth ruled, is always absent in Shakespeare's histories. A dream of ultimate validation, an object of yearning as well as fear, it inevitably escapes the historiographic narrative. The possession of women is necessary to validate patriarchal authority, and women are needed to serve as its conduits from father to son; but female authority can never be acknowledged in patriarchal history except at the moment of its appropriation by men. Essential to the exercise and transmission of patriarchal authority, women can never exercise authority in their own right. Some of the women have power, but authority—the *right* to exercise power—is always defined in patriarchal terms, so whatever power the women exercise is defined in terms of menace to the patriarchy that contains them and opposition to its historical project. Serving as grounds and evidence of patriarchal authority, the women remain curiously voiceless and disembodied. Once they become speaking sub-

*matology*, trans. Gayatri Spivak (Baltimore: Johns Hopkins University Press, 1974), pp. 124–25, also argues that "the birth of writing (in the colloquial sense) was nearly everywhere and most often linked to genealogical anxiety" and "the genealogical relation and social classification are the stitched seam of arche-writing. . . ." Also see Bloch, passim, especially chapters 1 and 2 and the association of literacy with patrilineal legitimacy in the dialog between Launce and Speed in III.i. of *The Two Gentlemen of Verona*, a play probably written at the same time as Shakespeare's early histories.

[23]For a good account of Elizabethan anxieties and ambivalence about the queen's authority, see Louis Adrian Montrose, "'Shaping Fantasies': Figurations of Gender and Power in Elizabethan Culture," *Representations* 2 (1983), 61–94.

jects, they can only subvert the mythology in which their representation plays an essential role.

Within that mythology, marriage constitutes the great image of patriarchal political order. Both Elizabeth and James repeatedly likened their relationships to their countries to that of a husband to his wife. Eliding, as Elizabeth did, the troubled question of female patriarchal authority, Shakespeare uses the husband-sovereign analogy in a number of places, most notably, perhaps, in Kate's long speech (V.ii.146–79) at the end of *The Taming of the Shrew*, which describes a husband as his wife's "sovereign" and compares her duty to him to the "duty . . . the subject owes the prince." Richard II uses the analogy when he attacks the enemies who forcibly separate him from both wife and kingdom: "Doubly divorc'd! Bad men, you violate a twofold marriage—'twixt my crown and me, and then betwixt me and my married wife" (V.i.71–73). It also forms the basis for the imagery of the "troubled family" that appears throughout act V of *Richard II* and both parts of *Henry IV*, constructing a series of analogies, both implicit and explicit, between the disorder of Bullingbrook's kingdom and that of a family in discord. Edward Hall, a major source for Shakespeare's English histories, titled his history of all the kings from Henry IV to Henry VIII "The Union of the Two Noble and Illustre Fameiles of Lancastre and Yorke," emphasizing the dynastic marriage that marks the end of his long chronicle and explaining that "the union of man and woman in the holy sacrament of matrimony" symbolizes political peace and unity.[24]

All of Shakespeare's legitimate kings are equipped with wives. Lacking patriarchal authority, Shakespeare's usurping Henry IV, like his King John, also lacks a wife, even though both have sons. Except for the subversive Margaret, however, none of the queens plays a major role on Shakespeare's stage. In *Richard II*, where the king has both loyal wife and patriarchal

[24]I am indebted to Peter L. Rudnytsky, who kindly shared with me his unpublished paper "'Th' Offending Adam': Patriarchal Structure and the Fall in the *Henriad* and *Paradise Lost*," for bringing the reference from Hall to my attention. For an excellent account, documented by extensive references to Renaissance texts, of the ways the analogy pervaded political and social discourse, see Susan D. Amussen, "Gender, Family and the Social Order, 1560–1725," in *Order and Disorder in Early Modern England*, ed. Anthony Fletcher and John Stevenson (Cambridge: Cambridge University Press, 1985), pp. 196–205.

legitimacy, we see very little of the queen, who, unlike her loquacious husband, has very little to say. She has the intuitive power to foresee Richard's fall (II.i.), the loyalty that makes her grieve for it, and the fortitude to reprove his passive submission to Bullingbrook (V.i.26–33). At the end of the play, it is she who receives Richard's charge to tell his sad story (V.i.40–50).[25] Nonetheless, she is isolated from the historical action. As long as her husband remains king, she is never shown in dialogue with him. Isolated from the arena of power, she can foresee the outcome of the historical action before it occurs, and she can report it after it is complete, but she can do nothing at all to affect its course. The warrant of Richard's patriarchal authority, the queen herself has neither authority nor power, not even a name in the dramatic text. Unlike Margaret and Joan and the unruly women who play such important parts in the chaotic world of *King John*, she never comes into sharp focus as a dramatic presence.

Insofar as Shakespeare's English histories tell a connected story, they describe a long struggle to restore legitimacy to the throne and peace to the nation by resolving the crisis of patriarchal authority that begins with the deposition of Richard II. Henry IV spends two plays trying to expiate his crime and put down the rebellious forces it unleashed. "No king of England, if not king of France" (II.ii.193), Henry V conceives his French wars as an enormous trial by combat to win the right to the English throne that he could not inherit from his usurping father. The first tetralogy traces the long, disastrous reign of Henry VI, a story of battles and bloodshed as Yorkists and Lancastrians press their equally and incurably defective claims to the crown. But the problem of legitimacy is never fully resolved until the end of *Richard III*, when the Lancastrian Henry VII turns to a woman to secure a crown he has won in battle, announcing that he will unite the warring factions by marrying the Yorkist princess Elizabeth. The best efforts of three generations of kings and their suffering subjects and the struggles of three generations of men killing each other in battle can never

---

[25]Note, however, that he wants her to tell it as a winter's tale, the sort of melancholy oral narrative that, as Mary Ellen Lamb demonstrated in a paper presented at the 1989 annual meeting of the Shakespeare Association of America, was specifically associated with women.

resolve the problem of royal legitimacy. It can only be resolved in marriage, with the incorporation of the necessary female ground of all patriarchal authority—in this case, the Princess Elizabeth. With the murder of her brothers, the princess has become the sole heir to the legacy of Edward IV and a crucial object of contention between the future Henry VII and his rival, Richard III, both seeking possession of her (and her claim to the throne) in marriage. Significantly, however, the princess never advances this claim in her own right, and she never appears on stage in Shakespeare's play.[26]

A similar pattern can be seen in *Henry VIII*, when the troubles and ambiguities of a painful reign are finally resolved in the birth of the infant Elizabeth, the baby who will become the last and best of the Tudor monarchs, the queen who ruled the world in which all but this last of Shakespeare's history plays were produced. Elizabeth as an authoritative voice is never allowed on Shakespeare's stage even though her authority as queen constituted an ineluctable present reality in his world and a pressing absence in the plays. Shakespeare does not bring Elizabeth onto the stage until *Henry VIII*, a play written during the reign of her successor. Moreover, she comes in only at the end and only as a newborn baby, the object of the characters' hopes for the future, the audience's nostalgia for the past. No doubt the baby was represented by some sort of doll or effigy, but even as he displays the effigy, Shakespeare insists upon the absence of the living queen. He accompanies the brief, tantalizing representation of the babe with reminders that the real Elizabeth is already dead, as inaccessible to Shakespeare's nostalgic Jacobean audience as she had been to the Henrician subjects represented on stage who marvel at Cranmer's prophecies of her future greatness.

The king who most resembles Elizabeth as an image of benevolent royal authority is Henry V, and he is also the king who most bases his authority on women. Henry's position in the two tetralogies is analogous to that of Elizabeth in *Henry VIII*. A memory of lost glory throughout the first tetralogy, an anticipation of future greatness in the second, Henry is "the mirror of all Christian kings" (II.Chorus, 6). As the image of

---

[26]Cf. Kastan, "Shakespeare and 'The Way of Womenkind,'" p. 116.

the mirror suggests, Henry's glory is not so much an immediate dramatic presence as an iconic image, set apart from the world of time and change to measure the deficiencies of the troubled reigns of his predecessors and successors. Cranmer describes Elizabeth in similar terms: "She shall be (but few now living can behold that goodness) a pattern to all princes living with her and all that shall succeed" (V.iv.20–23). Like the fleeting apparition of Elizabeth at the end of *Henry VIII*, the brief time of Henry's glory is a transcendent moment, no sooner achieved than snatched away into the inaccessible treasure-house of history, the chronicle of praise that Canterbury compares to "the ooze and bottom of the sea," the repository of "sunken wrack and sumless treasuries" (I.ii.164–65).

Characterized in terms of absence and deferral, Elizabeth and Henry both represent the transcendent ideal of perfect authority that eludes dramatic representation. Cranmer's prophecy elides Elizabeth's mortal life: even at the moment of her birth, he foretells her death in order to insist upon her immortality:

> as when
> The bird of wonder dies, this maiden phoenix,
> Her ashes new create another heir
>
> . . . . . . . . . . . . . . . . . . . . . . . . . . . . . . . .
>
> Who from the sacred ashes of her honor
> Shall star-like rise as great in fame as she was,
> And so stand fix'd.
>
> (V.iv.39–47)

The image of the maiden phoenix declares Elizabeth's transcendence of the linked bonds of procreation and death that circumscribe earthly life. The fixed star—the image, *par excellence*, of transcendence—recalls the final chorus of *Henry V*: "Small time; but in that small most greatly lived / This star of England" (lines 5–6). Emphasizing the brevity of Henry's triumphant reign, the final chorus reminded Shakespeare's audience of his impending death. Like Cranmer's prophecy, the chorus represents a movement beyond drama. Cast in the form of a sonnet, it abandons theatrical representation to invoke a higher discourse, that of an elite genre, purely textual, associated with the celebration of transcendent ideals and the translation of human mortality into textual immortality. Like Elizabeth, Henry is finally characterized as a lost presence, a fleeting moment of perfection that cannot be represented on stage because it transcends the limitations of sublunary life.[27]

Although Shakespeare makes Henry the protagonist of three plays, he manages to depict his greatness as a brief flash of glory by repeatedly deferring the moment of his apotheosis. Hal promises at the beginning of *1 Henry IV* that after "a while" he will shine forth in sunlike majesty, showing his true self and "redeeming time when men think least I will" (I.ii.195–217), but the redemption is constantly postponed. At the beginning of *Henry V*, Canterbury proclaims,

> The breath no sooner left his father's body
> But that his wildness, mortified in him,
> Seem'd to die too; yea at that very moment,
> Consideration like an angel came
> And whipt th' offending Adam out of him,
> Leaving his body as a paradise
> T' envelop and contain celestial spirits.
>
> (I.i.25–31)

But here again the redemption is deferred. The Henry we actually see, unlike the image of prelapsarian perfection described by Canterbury or the invulnerable icon of royal authority constructed by the chorus, suffers from human failings and human doubts about the legitimacy of his actions and his reign. The Henry who speaks for himself on Shakespeare's stage repeatedly demands assurance that his invasion of France is justified, that the guilt for the horrors of war is not his. He suffers terrible remorse for his father's offense against Richard, and he prays

[27]This conception of Henry appears as early as the opening scene of *1 Henry VI*, where Bedford says that he was "too famous to live long" (I.i.6), Gloucester declares that "his deeds exceed all speech" (I.i.15), and Bedford likens his soul to a "glorious star" (I.i.55). Moreover, the same complex of images and concepts associated with Henry V and Elizabeth also marks the Talbots' heroic choice to exchange earthly life for eternal fame. Cf. Talbot's declaration that he and his son, "winged through the lither sky, / In [Death's] despite shall scape mortality" (IV.vii.21–22) and Lucy's prophecy that "from their ashes shall be rear'd / A phoenix" (IV.vii.92–93). As the scene with the Countess of Auvergne insists, Talbot, like Elizabeth and Henry, finally eludes dramatic representation.

anxiously before the battle of Agincourt, "Not to-day, O Lord, O, not to-day, think not upon the fault my father made in compassing the crown," describing the many acts of penance he has undertaken to expiate his father's crime, and finally admitting that "all that I can do is nothing worth, since that my penitence comes after all, imploring pardon" (IV.i.292–305).

The Henry who acts on Shakespeare's stage, unlike the image of perfection already completed and in the past evoked by the words of the chorus, is a Henry engaged in the process of acquiring his authority and his place in history. If he fails to conquer France, he says, he will "lay these bones in an unworthy urn":

> Tombless, with no remembrance over them.
> Either our history shall with full mouth
> Speak freely of our acts, or else our grave,
> Like Turkish mute, shall have a tongueless mouth,
> Not worshipp'd with a waxen epitaph.
>
> (I.ii.228–33)

As Henry's curious simile of the tongueless Turkish mute suggests, he identifies both his Englishness and his manhood with his place in history. Ironically, however, he can secure that place only by turning to women, in fact, to *French* women. Henry must win his legitimacy in battle, conquering France to prove his right to the English throne, but first he must prove his right to France. In the first act, he turns to the Archbishop of Canterbury to justify his claim to the French throne. Canterbury responds with a long, comically involuted rationalization (I.ii.35–100), in which only one thing is perfectly clear: the question turns on the issue of inheritance through the female line. Not everyone in Shakespeare's audience is likely to have remembered that Henry claimed the French throne by descent from his great-grandmother Isabella, the mother of Edward III. Few, however, could have missed Canterbury's comically reiterated efforts to explain away the French argument that disallowed it: "*In terram Salicam mulieres ne succedant*, 'No woman shall succeed in Salic land'." Tracing his right to France through the female line, Henry ratifies it in battle, but at the end of the play he feels compelled to secure it once again. In the last act, he makes his last, best effort to inscribe his name in a royal genealogy. Relying once again on the principle of female succession, he courts the French princess for his wife in order to appropriate her place in the French royal line. Like Henry VII's marriage to Elizabeth of York, Henry V's marriage to the French princess represents the last and best of all his conquests: the appropriation of the indispensable female ground of patriarchal authority.

In the end, Henry's efforts do not succeed. Winning a temporary authority for himself, he fails to bequeath it to his son, who is tormented throughout his long reign by a headstrong, disloyal wife and Yorkist claimants to his crown, both powerful threats to the patriarchal authority Henry's son never manages to assume. In *Henry V*, the Yorkist claim is never voiced on stage. Shakespeare seems to collude in Henry's repression, depicting the rebels in act II as mercenary traitors motivated by French bribery. Only Cambridge's cryptic statement, "For me, the gold of France did not seduce, although I did admit it as a motive the sooner to effect what I intended" (II.ii.155–57) hints at the repressed threat that will finally invalidate Henry's efforts, the offstage existence of another, alternate line of would-be kings who undermine every Lancastrian claim to legitimacy. Nonetheless, although the Yorkist claim is never expressed in *Henry V*, it hovers at the edge of consciousness, lending a suppressed irony to Henry's reliance on female inheritance to justify his claims to France. For the Yorkists, unlike Henry, trace their claim to the English throne through the female line.[28]

That irony approaches the surface of the text in the final chorus when Shakespeare reminds his audience of the Henry VI plays, "which oft our stage hath shown," a disturbing reminder of the futility of Henry's efforts. The Henry VI plays had ended in the victory of the Yorkists; and the Yorkist claim to the throne, utterly repressed in *Henry V*, is an ever-present

---

[28]Although the Lancastrians base their claim on an unbroken male line to John of Gaunt, the fourth son of Edward III, the Yorkist claim (arguably better, since it is based on descent from Lionel Duke of Clarence, Gaunt's older brother) depends at crucial points upon women (Lionel's daughter Philippa as well as Anne Mortimer). In this connection, it is interesting to note that Mary Queen of Scots, who represented a powerful genealogical threat to Queen Elizabeth (who had been declared a bastard), was descended from the sister of Henry VIII, thus tracing her claim to the Tudor heritage through the female line.

reality in the world of his son, undermining the authority of Henry's heir from the very beginning of his reign. Edmund Mortimer, the legitimate heir of Richard II, who never appears on stage in *Henry V*, intrudes (unhistorically) into the world of Henry VI to transmit the legacy of Richard II to the Yorkists and describe the female line of descent that supports his claim. Mortimer's appearance is confined to a single, isolated scene; an ancient vestige of another world, characterized in terms of repression, he erupts briefly into a time two generations beyond his own to transmit the royal legacy usurped by Henry V's father to the family that will finally take the crown from Henry V's son. As Mortimer explains from his prison cell, a "loathesome sequestration" that he (unlike his historical prototype) has suffered ever "since Henry Monmouth [i.e., Henry V] first began to reign" (II.v.23–25),

> I was the next by birth and parentage;
> For by my mother I derived am
> From Lionel Duke of Clarence, third son
> To King Edward the Third; whereas he
> From John of Gaunt doth bring his pedigree,
> Being but fourth of that heroic line.
>
> (II.v.73–78)

Dying, he bequeaths his claim to York, again transmitting it through the female line: since York's father has no claim on the legacy, it is York's mother, Mortimer's sister, who provides the crucial link (II.v.86).

Constrained by both past and future, by the anticipated failures of Henry VI no less than the remembered crime of Henry IV, Henry V can never win the patriarchal authority he desires. Without the necessary female ground, the best efforts of this best of Shakespeare's English kings can never secure a place in the royal line that led, in the fullness of time, to the Tudors. The closest he comes, ironically, is through his marriage to the French princess Katherine who, after Henry's early death, married the Welsh gentleman Owen Tudor and became, by that marriage, the grandmother of Henry VII.[29]

[29]It is worth noting here that Henry VII inherited his own share in the blood of John of Gaunt through Margaret Beaufort, his mother.

Shakespeare never mentions Katherine's Welsh marriage, not in *Henry V*, and not in *1 Henry VI*, the play that depicts the early years of her son's life. The matter of Wales, like the matter of the women, haunts the borders of the historical world that Shakespeare constructed in his Lancastrian histories, and for good reason. If the question of female authority evoked powerful anxieties for the genealogically obsessed patriarchal culture ruled by Elizabeth I, so did the question of Wales; and the two were connected in the person of the female monarch who traced her patriarchal right to a Welsh grandfather who had incorporated the red dragon of Cadwallader in the royal arms and invoked the name of King Arthur to buttress his tenuous genealogical authority. The Welsh troops, mentioned but never seen in *Richard II*, mark the transmission of royal power when they desert Richard's army, "gone to Bullingbrook, dispers'd and fled" (III.ii.74). Throughout the two parts of *Henry IV*, we are reminded of Hal's title as Prince of Wales, and even in *Henry V*, the king's Welsh origins are a subject of repeated emphasis. Nonetheless, the only history play in which Shakespeare actually takes his audience to the wild country just beyond the English border is *1 Henry IV*. The country of the Others, a world of witchcraft and magic, of mysterious music, and also of unspeakable atrocity that horrifies the English imagination, Wales is defined in terms very much like those that define the woman. In addition to the liminal location at England's geographical borders that makes Wales a constant military threat and the liminal attributes that make it psychologically disturbing, Wales also acts as the repository of true legitimacy, in the person of Edmund Mortimer.[30]

Owen Glendower's castle in Wales is the setting for Edmund Mortimer's only appearance in the second tetralogy, even

[30]The same construction of Wales reappears in *Cymbeline*, a play based on Holinshed and taking the name of its heroine from Innogen, the wife of the legendary Trojan founder of the British royal line. A land of miracles and music and also of mortal danger, the Wales in *Cymbeline* is also the place where the true heirs to the British throne (disguised with the historically resonant names of Polydore and Cadwal) are sequestered. For the mythic-historical associations of the Welsh material in *Cymbeline*, see Frances Yates, *Majesty and Magic in Shakespeare's Last Plays: A New Approach to Cymbeline, Henry VIII and the Tempest* (Boulder, Colo.: Shambhala, 1975), pp. 39–62; and Emrys Jones, "Stuart Cymbeline," *Essays in Criticism* 11 (1961), 84–99.

though his name in the mouths of rebels represents an ever-present danger to the Lancastrian kings who rule the English world of Shakespeare's historical action. In 1 *Henry IV*, Mortimer is still a young man, and the Percys use his right to the throne to justify their rebellion. From the very beginning of the play, Mortimer's name represents a potent threat to the king's authority. Hotspur's initial quarrel with the king centers on the question of Mortimer's ransom; and Hotspur quickly recognizes the power of Mortimer's name as a weapon against the king: "His cheek look'd pale, and on my face he turn'd an eye of death, trembling even at the name of Mortimer" (I.iii.142–44). Nonetheless, Mortimer the man plays no part in the confrontations and battles that constitute the political action of the play. He appears onstage only in the scene in Wales and there has very little to say until the ladies come in.

When Glendower and Hotspur haggle over their proposed division of the English kingdom, Mortimer remains mostly silent, entering the dialogue only to act as a peacemaker between them. But once the women make their entrance and the conversation turns to love, Mortimer is the first to speak. Completely absorbed in his wife, Mortimer plays only one role on Shakespeare's stage, that of a lover. Like the lascivious Edward IV in 3 *Henry VI* who sacrifices Warwick's support and endangers his throne to make a disastrous marriage to a woman he desires, Mortimer is totally absorbed in his sensuality and his wife.[31] His manhood lost to female enchantment, the heir of Richard II never appears on the fields of battle where English history is made.

Mortimer can speak no Welsh, his wife no English, but Glendower translates for his daughter:

> She bids you on the wanton rushes lay you down,
> And rest your gentle head upon her lap,
> And she will sing the song that pleaseth you,
> And on your eyelids crown the god of sleep,
> Charming your blood with pleasing heaviness,
> Making such difference 'twixt wake and sleep

[31]For a perceptive discussion of the Welsh scenes, see Matthew Wikander, *The Play of Truth and State: Historical Drama from Shakespeare to Brecht* (Baltimore: Johns Hopkins University Press, 1986), pp. 14–25.

As is the difference betwixt day and night
The hour before the heavenly-harness'd team
Begins his golden progress in the east.

(III.i.211–19)

Here, in the twilight world of Welsh sorcery, the gender divisions that separate the warrior from the woman break down. Unwilling to part with her amorous companion, Mortimer's wife has resolved that "she'll be a soldier too, she'll to the wars" (III.i.193). Preferring the "feeling disputation" of kisses with his wife to military war with men, Mortimer is "as slow as hot Lord Percy is on fire to go" to join the battle that will decide the future of the English kingdom (III.i.203, 263–64).

Renaissance sexual mythology condemned masculine sensuality and uxoriousness as effeminate; and, as Matthew Wikander observes, "the pastoral bower in which Mortimer is invited to repose is the same abode of sensual self-abandonment that Guyon must destroy in Book II of *The Faerie Queen.*"[32] From the very beginning of the play, Wales is identified as the scene of emasculation and female power, and also as the site of a repression in the historical narrative. Immediately following the king's exposition of the initial historical situation, Westmerland reports Mortimer's capture, the Welsh victory over his army, and "the beastly shameless transformation" performed by Welsh women upon the corpses of the English dead, an act "as may not be without much shame retold or spoken of" (I.i.44–46).[33] The scene in Glendower's castle replaces the repellent

[32] *The Play of Truth and State*, p. 24. Stephen Greenblatt's exposition of the ways the allurements of the Bower of Bliss threaten the "civilization—which for Spenser is achieved only through renunciation and the constant exercise of power" is also relevant here, as are his analogies to European responses to the natives of Africa and North America and the English colonial struggles in Ireland. See his *Renaissance Self-Fashioning: From More to Shakespeare* (Chicago: University of Chicago Press, 1980), pp. 173–74, 179–92.

[33] Cf. Raphael Holinshed, *Chronicles of England, Scotland and Ireland* (1587; rpt. London: J. Johnson et al., 1808), 3:20: "The shamefull villanie used by the Welshwomen towards the dead carcasses, was such, as honest eares would be ashamed to heare, and continent toongs to speake thereof." Cf. p. 34, where in the account of another battle three years later, Abraham Fleming adds a detailed account, marginally identified as coming from Thomas Walsingham's *Ypodigma Neustriae*, of the "shamefull villanie executed upon the carcasses of the dead men by the Welshwomen," who "cut off their privities, and put one part thereof into the mouthes of everie dead man, in such sort that the cullions

literal emasculation of Westmerland's report with the seductive allure of a world that is feminine, effeminating, and also theatrical. Endlessly repeated in antitheatrical polemics, the charge that theatrical performance corrupted its audiences with incitements to sexual lust (often accompanied by supporting anecdotes) attests to an attraction as powerful as the anxiety it produced.[34] The lush, theatrical scene that depicts Mortimer's Welsh idyll has a similar ambivalence.[35] Replacing historical narrative with dramatic enactment and Westmerland's horrified report with the sensual beauty of Glendower's poetry and his daughter's singing, it moves the audience from the austere English court to a seductive, outlandish world of idleness and dangerous, irrational pleasure. It calls on the power of theatrical performance to disrupt the historical narrative with a fleeting glimpse of all that must be excluded to preserve its coherence.[36]

---

hoong downe to their chins; and not so contented, they did cut off their noses and thrust them into their tailes as they laie on the ground mangled and defaced." It is significant, I believe, that even though Fleming seems delighted with the grisly story, introducing it with numerous descriptions of gory atrocities committed by women against men in classical times, he also feels constrained to defend his decision to write the problematic material into the English historical record: "Though it make the reader to read it, and the hearer to heare it, ashamed: yet bicause it was a thing doone in open sight, and left testified in historie; I see little reason whie it should not be imparted in our mother toong to the knowledge of our owne countrimen, as well as unto strangers in a language unknowne."

[34]Ann Jennalie Cook, "'Bargaines of Incontinencie': Bawdy Behavior in the Playhouses," *Shakespeare Studies* 10 (1977), 271–90. On the anxieties about effeminating effects of the theater, see Laura Levine, "Men in Women's Clothing: Anti-theatricality and Effeminization from 1579 to 1642," *Criticism* 28 (1986), 131–37.

[35]The bickering between Hotspur and Glendower, in fact, recalls the terms if not the earnestness of the debates about the theater. Hotspur is impatient at the waste of time in Wales. Glendower identifies himself as a magician. Hotspur calls Glendower a liar and associates his magic with the work of the devil. Shakespeare, however, seems in this scene to be complicit with Glendower. Together they entertain—and detain—their guests with an idyllic interlude that interrupts and retards the progress of the historical plot. When Glendower declares that he will summon musicians who "hang in the air a thousand leagues from hence" to play for his guests, Shakespeare's text supports Glendower's project, and his claim to magical power, with the stage direction "*The music plays*" (III.i.17–68, 221–31).

[36]Similar oppositional moments occur as early as *2 Henry VI* in the leave-taking scenes between Gloucester and Eleanor and between Suffolk and Margaret. Defined in terms of misogynist stereotypes—extravagant ostentation in dress, excessive ambition, disloyalty, disobedience, and witchcraft—Eleanor's

The relentless progress of that narrative resumes in the following scene, returning the audience to the English court, the site where history is written. But Mortimer remains behind. Bewitched and enthralled in Wales, the heir to the English throne is willing to abandon the King's English, the discourse of patriarchal authority, for the wordless language of love. When his lady cries, Mortimer responds that he is "too perfect in" the language of her tears, and "but for shame, in such a parley should I answer thee" (III.i.200–201). "The deadly spite that angers" him is not his usurped right to the throne (a right we never hear him mention in this play) but the fact that his "wife can speak no English, I no Welsh" (III.i.190–91). He looks beyond language to communicate with his lady ("I understand thy looks . . . I understand thy kisses, and thou mine") and he resolves to learn Welsh (III.i.198–205), the language of England's barbarous enemies, the incomprehensible language of the alien world that lies beyond the bounds of English historical narration.[37]

Mortimer's wife speaks only Welsh on stage, meaningless sounds that Shakespeare represents by repeated stage directions: "*The lady speaks in Welsh*" or "*Glendower speaks to her in*

---

role in the historical plot is entirely negative. She provides the means by which Margaret and Suffolk can advance their plots against her virtuous husband, the last representative of the generation of Henry V and of justice and good government in the corrupt court of Henry VI. Nonetheless, the extended dramatization of the pathetic leave-taking between Eleanor and her husband (II.iv), which is unnecessary to the historical plot, anticipates the leave-taking scene in *Richard II* and complicates the conventional lesson in the dangers of uxoriousness. Even Suffolk and Margaret are granted a pathetic scene of parting (III.ii.329–412), also unnecessary to the historical plot and also likely to elicit at least a momentary sympathy for the wicked adulterous lovers. For the argument about these oppositional moments, I am indebted to Scott McMillin. For his suggestive discussion of the role of the queen in *Richard II*, see "Shakespeare's *Richard II*: Eyes of Sorrow, Eyes of Desire," *Shakespeare Quarterly* 35 (1984), 40–52.

[37]Stephen Mullaney points out in *The Place of the Stage: License, Play and Power in Renaissance England* (Chicago: University of Chicago Press, 1988), pp. 77, 162, that although Henry VIII had outlawed Welsh in 1535, the alien language ("nothing like, nor consonant to the natural Mother Tongue within this realm") consistently defied English efforts "to control or outlaw it." Resisting repeated "pressures of assimilation and suppression . . . Welsh remained a strange tongue, a discomfiting reminder that Wales continued to be a foreign and hostile colony, ruled and to an extent subjected but never quite controlled by Tudor power."

*Welsh, and she answers him in the same."* Like the French that Katherine speaks in *Henry V*, the lady's language requires constant translation, and like Katherine's French, it is doubly the language of the other, the language of England's enemies and also the language of women and of love. The difference, however, is that while Katherine must learn English in order to communicate with Henry, Mortimer proposes to enter the alien discourse. Appropriating Katherine's French right for his English purposes, Henry also assimilates her into the discourse of English history. Mortimer remains curiously isolated from that discourse, a hovering threat that never comes to fruition. Serving only to transmit Richard II's right to York's heirs, he functions very much as the women do, as a name and a conduit for a patriarchal authority he can never exercise in his own right. Henry V, who cannot transmit that authority, manages nonetheless to exercise it for one brief glorious moment. He domesticates the savage Welsh in the form of the comically adoring Welsh captain Fluellen, a great student of history, who is also Henry's greatest admirer. He also learns French, but not so well as Katherine learns English, the language in which their bilingual courtship finally ends when Katherine agrees, in broken English, to become Henry's wife. The essential ritual of patriarchal appropriation, the marriage will make Katherine's country, as well as herself, the property of the English king.

Showing us Henry's bilingual courtship of Katherine, Shakespeare assimilates the discourse of the other into his historical representation. Unlike Richmond's briefly noted acquisition of Elizabeth of York (a character reduced to a name for genealogical authority, who never even appears on stage), Henry's courtship of Katherine is arguably the climactic episode in his play. Moving beyond the limits of authoritative historical discourse, colonizing the discourse of the other, Shakespeare, at the end of his last Elizabethan history, abandons stage convention to depict the courtship of Henry and Katherine as a difficult, bilingual dialogue. Here, an audience might suppose, is the thing itself—no official representation, but the world of the other in full presence. Nonetheless, the play ends with the courtship. Despite the enormous significance invested in the wedding of Henry and Katherine, we never see it, or any other wedding, on Shakespeare's historical stage. Shakespeare satisfies historical drama's appetite for spectacle with battles and coronations, not with royal weddings, regardless of the importance the marriages had in determining the course of future events and regardless (or perhaps because) of the extraordinary pressure that patriarchal ideology brought to bear upon the concept of marriage. Representing, through its own theatrical machinery, the patriarchal incorporation of female genealogical authority, a wedding is a dangerous moment when that authority cannot be denied. The weddings, like female authority itself, are endlessly deferred, pushed into the margins of Shakespeare's historical scripts.

At the ends of the two tetralogies and in *Henry VIII*, the last of his English history plays, Shakespeare transvalues the feminine and suggests its incorporation into his historical project. In *Richard III*, Margaret is transformed from a destructive French interloper whose marriage to the English king threatens to "cancel" English fame and blot English "names from books of memory" to the voice of divine vengeance, descending upon the guilty Yorkists to purge England and make it ready for the glorious Tudor accession. At the end of that play, it is the marriage of Richmond and Elizabeth that finally resolves the problems of the past and enables the prosperity of the future. Similarly, *Henry V*, the last play in the second tetralogy, culminates in the arrangements for the marriage of Henry to the French princess; and *Henry VIII*, the last play of all, culminates in the birth of the Princess Elizabeth. In all these cases, however, the incorporation of the feminine represents the end of the historical process, a movement beyond the limits of the historiographic narrative. The marriages are announced, but they will not take place until after the plays have ended. Their announcements, like the announcement of Elizabeth's birth, are accompanied by prayers for future prosperity that go beyond the known facts of history, looking forward to the present time of the audience and even beyond it to an unknown future. The incorporation of the feminine can only take place at the point where history stops.[38] A world that truly includes the feminine is a world in which history cannot be written.

[38]In *1 Henry VI*, the beginning of the historiographic project is represented as a struggle against French women to preserve the memory of Henry V; in

Shakespeare's only attempt to depict such a world is *King John*. Female characters, for once, are sharply individualized, and they play more important and more varied roles here than in any of Shakespeare's other English histories. In the first tetralogy, the female characters fall neatly into groups, and their generic gender characteristics always transcend and subsume their individual identities. In *1 Henry VI*, although Joan is a peasant and the Countess of Auvergne and Margaret of Anjou are noblewomen, all three are united in nationality and in their roles as enemies to the English, male protagonists' struggle to preserve the legacy of Henry V. In *2 Henry VI*, Margaret and Eleanor are bitter enemies, but Shakespeare characterizes them in similar terms and uses them for similar purposes: self-willed and ambitious, both women defy their husbands' authority and threaten the peace of the realm, exposing the weakness of patriarchal authority in an increasingly disordered world. In *Richard III*, Margaret is a vengeful Lancastrian widow and Elizabeth a Yorkist Queen, but before the play ends they too will be united with each other and with the Duchess of York in a chorus of distinctively female lamentation: all victimized and bereaved, all gifted with the power to prophesy and curse and articulate the will of providence.

The *Henry VI* plays depict a world where male right is threatened by female wrong; in the wicked world ruled by Richard III, the women line up on the side of heaven and the Earl of Richmond. But no such simple moral equations are possible in *King John*. Its female characters will not reduce to a single class or category. Like the ambiguous ethos of the play itself, the female characters here are deeply divided, as is the feminine spirit. Elinor is a soldier queen, a tough, Machiavellian dowager;

---

*Henry V*, the end of Henry's own historiographic project is represented as his marriage to the French princess. The other who threatens the project of English history making at its beginning, the French woman is married and incorporated at its end. This same association between the incorporation of the feminine and the end of history is also implicit in the elegiac scene when Richard II and his queen make their final farewell (V.i). The only scene in the play that represents Richard united with his queen, it is also the scene in which both prepare for their departure from the stage of history. See also McMillin's argument that "the Queen's role is designed to insist on [the] invisible presence" of what lies "beyond representation, or perhaps behind representation" ("Eyes of Sorrow," p. 43).

Constance an outraged, lamenting mother; Blanch a compliant, helpless victim. Elinor and Constance back rival claimants for the English throne, and they wrangle openly on stage, adroitly subverting each other's claims and arguments (II.i.120–94). Blanch and Constance are both depicted as suffering victims, but neither can be consoled without wronging the other; when they kneel together before the Dauphin (III.i.308–10) they do so to plead for opposite decisions.

In a well-ordered patriarchal world, women are silent or invisible. First as daughters, then as wives, they are subject to male control, and their men speak and act on their behalf. But in *King John*, the fathers and husbands are dead, reduced to the status of names in history books, and the mothers survive on Shakespeare's stage to dispute the fathers' wills and threaten their patriarchal legacies. Elinor and Constance interrupt the parley between the two kings to accuse each other of adultery and each other's sons of bastardy (II.i.120–33). Elinor impugns her grandson's birth in order to deny him the patriarchal right she knows is his (I.i.39–43). Constance, in the name of that right, impugns the legitimacy of her husband, subverting the patriarchal lineage that authorizes her son's claim to the throne. She proposes an alternate, female genealogical chain, deriving from Elinor and conveying a heritage of sin and suffering:"Thy sins are visited in this poor child,/ The canon of the law is laid on him,/ Being but the second generation/ Removed from thy sin-conceiving womb" (II.i.179–82). And she refuses to hold her tongue, despite the men's commands.

Speaking with strong, irreverent voices, these mothers claim a place in the historical narrative and challenge the myths of patriarchal authority that the men invoke to justify their actions. When John answers the French threat with the conventional boast, "Our strong possession and our right for us," Elinor wittily and irreverently reminds him, "Your strong possession much more than your right, / Or else it must go wrong with you and me" (I.i.39–40). When Pandulph claims that Constance lacks the "law and warrant" that give him, the papal legate, the authority to curse John, Constance replies by challenging the law itself:

> ... when law can do no right,
> Let it be lawful that law bar no wrong;
> Law cannot give my child his kingdom here,
> For he that holds his kingdom holds the law;
> Therefore since law itself is perfect wrong,
> How can the law forbid my tongue to curse?
> (III.i.185–90)

In *King John*, Shakespeare subjects the masculine voices of patriarchal authority to skeptical feminine interrogation. No longer
speaking with the clear, univocal voice of unquestioned tradition, the history he represents becomes problematic, an arena
for contending interests rather than an authoritative voice to
resolve their differences.

Like Margaret and Joan, the disorderly women in the first
tetralogy, women in *King John* usurp masculine prerogatives.
Elinor announces in the opening scene that she is "a soldier"
(I.i.150), and her role is no anomaly in a play where "ladies and
pale-visag'd maids, / Like Amazons come tripping after drums,"
changing "their thimbles into armed gauntlets ... their needl's
to lances, and their gentle hearts / To fierce and bloody incli-
nation" (V.ii.154–58). Unlike Talbot, the men in *King John* seem
to accept the blurring of the gender distinctions that excluded
women from the battlefields that constituted a privileged arena
of patriarchal history, becoming unmanned (as Mortimer was
to become) by the presence of powerful women.[39] The English
soldiers have "ladies' faces" (II.i.68); when the Earl of Salisbury
weeps, the Dauphin declares that he values those "manly
drops" above the "lady's tears" that have "melted" his heart
in the past (V.ii.47–49). Both contenders for the English crown—
the bold and warlike John no less than his infant rival—compromise their patriarchal authority by subjection to the domi-

[39]The reciprocal nature of the binary opposition that defined the difference
between masculine and feminine gender was well understood in the Renaissance. Anxieties about masculine women inevitably involved the feminization
of men. Cf. Caesar's accusation (*Antony and Cleopatra*: I.iv.5–7) that Antony "is
not more manlike / Than Cleopatra; nor the queen of Ptolomy / More womanly
than he" and Linda Woodbridge's observation about the *"hic-mulier"* controversy of the early seventeenth century: "Whether praising or damning, comment on women in masculine attire was almost always accompanied by remarks
on male effeminacy" (*Women and the English Renaissance*, p. 141).

nation of powerful, vociferous mothers. The king of France bows to the threats of a mother church. Unwilling to break his truce with John lest they "make . . . unconstant children" of themselves (III.i.243), he finally agrees to do both after Pandulph threatens that "the Church, our mother, [will] breathe her curse, / A mother's curse, on her revolting son" (III.i. 256–57).

Blanch is the only woman in the play who is cast in the traditional feminine mold. Imported into the plot (as John, apparently, imports her into France) only for her ill-fated marriage to the Dauphin, she is placed in the archetypically feminine role of a medium of exchange between men.⁴⁰ Blanch is perfectly docile: "My uncle's will in this respect [i.e. the marriage] is mine. / If he see aught in you that makes him like, / That any thing he sees, which moves his liking, I can with ease translate it to my will"(II.i.510–13). With no will or agenda of her own, Blanch is ready to be used as an instrument of kinship arrangements, political alliance, and patriarchal succession. Perhaps taking his cue from the name of the historical character, Shakespeare depicts his Blanch as a blank page awaiting the inscription of masculine texts.⁴¹ To the Dauphin, Blanch is a "table" where his own image is "drawn" (II.i.503). To the two kings, she is the medium in which they will write their peace treaty. And to all three men, she represents a site for the inscription of a patriarchal historical narrative.

Exercising a traditional patriarchal right by marrying his son to the blank and docile Blanch, the French king makes his strongest claim to historical authority: "The yearly course that brings this day about," he declares, "shall never see it but a holy day" (III.i.81–82). Like Elizabeth of York in *Richard III* and Katherine of France in *Henry V*, Blanch will serve as the inert

---

⁴⁰See Rubin, "Traffic in Women."

⁴¹See Susan Gubar, "'The Blank Page' and Female Creativity," in *Writing and Sexual Difference*, ed. Elizabeth Abel (Chicago: University of Chicago Press, 1982), pp. 73–93, for a discussion of this traditional construction of women as blank pages awaiting the inscription of men's writing. See especially p. 75, where Gubar cites a number of examples of this trope, ranging from Henry James's *Portrait of a Lady*, with its description of "the ideal *jeune fille* . . . as 'a sheet of blank paper,'" to Shakespeare's Othello, who asks whether his Desdemona, "this fair paper, this most goodly book, / [was] Made to write 'whore' upon" (IV.ii.71–72).

female material of masculine history-making. But in *King John* that female material also includes the recalcitrant and self-willed Elinor and Constance. Rejecting the French king's effort at prospective history-making, Constance demands,

> What hath this day deserv'd? what hath it done,
> That it in golden letters should be set
> Among the high tides in the calendar?
> Nay, rather turn this day out of the week.
> (III.i.84–87)

Constance's own appeal to the heavens—"Let not the hours of this ungodly day / Wear out the day in peace; but ere sunset, / Set armed discord 'twixt these perjur'd kings!" (III.i.109–111)— seems to be answered. Refusing to allow the marriage a place in the historical record, Constance rejects the news of it as a "tale" "misspoke, misheard" (III.i.4–10) and demands to have the day on which it took place removed from the calendar. Denying the men's story and demanding the literal erasure of the date, she speaks for the forces that make the writing of patriarchal history impossible in the world of this play.

Inverted by a world turned upside down, the traditional bases for order and unity become in *King John* sources of disorder and conflict. The natural bonds that unite mother and child serve to divide Elinor and Constance. The marriage of Blanch to the Dauphin, which momentarily promises to unite the rival forces after their inconclusive battle for Angiers, is immediately contravened by the intervention of the papal legate Pandulph, a spokesman for a religious power as ambiguous as every other source of authority in this play.[42] In fact, the marriage becomes

[42]Sigurd Burckhardt argues in "*King John*: The Ordering of This Present Time," *Shakespearean Meanings*, pp. 116–43, that every source of authority fails in *King John* except the ties of blood and the simple human decency that prevents Hubert from murdering Arthur. Burckhardt's demonstration of the ways the play subverts religious and political authority is thoroughly convincing, but I find it difficult to accept his claims about Hubert. In the world of this play, no actions are conclusive, neither marriages nor battles nor the human kindness that finally persuades Hubert to spare Arthur. In the chronicles, the reports of Arthur's death were ambiguous, and although Shakespeare provides his audience with eyewitness knowledge of the scene that no one but Arthur ever saw, he also shows the false reports that kept even Arthur's contemporaries from true knowledge of the circumstances of his death. Shake-

a source of further conflict when the Dauphin uses it as an excuse to claim the English throne. Blanch, the conventional compliant woman, allows herself to be used as an instrument of kinship arrangements, political alliance, and patriarchal succession. But Constance's immediate, outraged rejection of the news of Blanch's marriage as a "tale" "misspoke, misheard" and her hyperbolic demand to have the day on which it took place removed from the calendar remind an audience that the political alliance the marriage is designed to effect would still leave Constance and Arthur and the hereditary rights they urge upon us unincorporated and unappeased and that the marriage will have no impact upon history.

Failing in her traditional feminine role as a medium to unite the warring kings, Blanch becomes the embodiment of their divisions. Niece to the English king, wife to the French Dauphin, she pleads desperately for the peace her marriage was designed to secure. Having failed in her plea, she cries,

> Which is the side that I must go withal?
> I am with both; each army hath a hand,
> And in their rage, I having hold of both,
> They whirl asunder and dismember me.
> (III.i.327–30)

This image of dismemberment makes Blanch the human embodiment of the many divisions that characterize this play: of the divisions among the female characters, of the division of the English throne between John's possession and Arthur's right, and especially of the divided allegiances that perplex the audience as they struggle with the ethical and political ambivalences that make *King John* the most disturbing of all Shakespeare's English histories.[43]

---

speare also shows the political and military effects of their ignorance in the nobles' defection from John. The truth of Hubert's mercy has no impact upon the plot of the play or the course of history.

[43]In *King John*, Shakespeare exposes the inadequacy of all explanatory schemes: law, *Realpolitik*, providential order, natural-humanistic right. Constance reminds the audience that law can be "perfect wrong" (III.i.189). John reminds sixteenth-century Englishmen that the pope's authority is "usurped" (III.i.160), and he trades charges of usurpation with the King of France (II.i.118–20). Elinor reads the Bastard's face aright to find him Coeur-de-lion's son, but

Separated from the temporal and genealogical chain that unites the two tetralogies, *King John* depicts a world in which no actions are conclusive, neither the wills of fathers, nor the marriages of children, nor the French king's repeated efforts at prospective history-making. Philip swears that he will put John down "Or add a royal number to the dead, / Gracing the scroll that tells of this war's loss / With slaughter coupled to the name of kings" (II.i.347–49). But the historical scroll he foresees will never be written, for he, no less than his English enemy, lives in a world where history-making is impossible. Only at the end, and only when he is about to die, does John associate himself with a historical text; but the text he imagines is as fragile and mutable as he now sees his own life to be: "a scribbled form, drawn with a pen / Upon a parchment," shrinking up against the fire that will destroy it (V.vii.32–34).

The image of the burning parchment completes Shakespeare's picture of John's estrangement from the tradition of Renaissance historiography. Tudor accounts of John's reign tended to emphasize his quarrel with the Pope, collapsing the distance between John's world and their own to depict John as a heroic prototype of Henry VIII, a patriotic English king defying the foreign power of the papacy. Compared to his predecessors, Shakespeare makes very little use of the antipapal material, and his John is a much less sympathetic figure than theirs. Constructed in terms of difference and distance, Shakespeare's amoral portrait of John resists the patriotic appropriations of humanist historiography. John envisions his history as a fragile manuscript, the kind of text that was produced in his own medieval time, not as the kind of enduring monument that the Renaissance humanists found in their classical sources and tried to emulate in the printed books that they produced and that Shakespeare associated with Henry V. Moreover, when John envisions the manuscript shrinking up in flames, he anticipates what would happen when the monasteries were destroyed in the time of Henry VIII. In this construction, Henry VIII becomes not the heir and fulfillment of John's historical legacy, but its destroyer.

---

Pembroke and Salisbury (IV.ii.70–81) and John (IV.ii.221–22) all misread Hubert's face to mistake him as Arthur's murderer.

Critics have called *King John* the "most unhistorical" of Shake-speare's English histories, an "incoherent patchwork" where "the action is wandering and uncertain."[44] This incoherence is moral as well as structural, and it relates closely to the crisis in patriarchal authority the play depicts. In *King John*, Shakespeare leaves his audience, like the Bastard, "amaz'd" and lost "among the thorns and dangers" of an incomprehensible world (IV.iii. 140–41) where every source of authority fails and legitimacy is reduced to a legal fiction. For the characters within the play, there is no clear royal authority. For the audience watching it, there is no unblemished cause and no unquestioned authority to claim their allegiance. None of these dilemmas is resolved until the end of the play when John's death ends the crisis of patriarchal authority and the Bastard adopts the idiom of his-torical faith and English patriotism. The accession of Prince Henry, we are promised, will "set a form upon that indigest, which [John] hath left so shapeless and so rude" (V.vii.26–27). It is significant, I believe, that before this reconstruction can take place, the women's voices must be stilled.[45] Blanch is removed from the stage, reduced to a genealogical pretext for the Dau-phin's claim to the English throne. Elinor and Constance die, offstage and unhistorically, their deaths three days apart re-ported in a single speech of six lines (IV.ii.119–24), as if to suggest the containment of these bitter enemies within a single, genderically determined category, their reduction from vocif-erous actors to the silent objects of male narration.

As long as the women live and speak, however, they set the subversive keynote for the other characters. John and the French king trade charges of usurpation (II.i.118–20), matching the women's mutual charges of adultery. Pandulph shares their

---

[44]Noted by E. A. J. Honigmann, ed., *King John*, Arden edition (London: Methuen, 1967), p. xxxi.

[45]I am indebted for the point about the women's silencing as a necessary condition for the restoration of patriarchal historical discourse to Virginia Ma-son Vaughan's comments on an earlier version of my discussion of *King John*, presented at the seminar on *King John* led by Deborah Curren-Aquino at the 1985 meeting of the Shakespeare Association of America; and to Lisa Sigler, a student in my graduate seminar on Shakespeare's history plays and Renais-sance historiography at the University of Pennsylvania. For a fuller discussion, see Vaughan's article, "*King John*: A Study in Subversion and Containment," in Aquino's anthology *King John: New Perspectives* (Newark: University of Del-aware Press, 1989), pp. 62–75.

distrustful vision of political process, embracing *Realpolitik* with a cynicism that matches their own. The Bastard shares their iconoclastic idiom, satirizing the heroic language that "talks as familiarly of roaring lions / As maids of thirteen do of puppy-dogs," and linking it to the patriarchal authority it claims to represent when he protests, "I was never so bethump'd with words / Since I first call'd my brother's father dad" (II.i.459–67). The demystification of patriarchal authority in *King John* is so pervasive that it extends beyond the temporal limits of the represented action, reaching back into the past to undermine the heroic image of Coeur-de-lion. Like *1 Henry VI*, *King John* looks back to a dead, heroic king; but while the legacy of Henry V was opposed and endangered in the world his infant son inherited but could not rule, it remained an intact and clearly defined, if increasingly remote, ideal. In *King John*, the legacy of the great Coeur-de-lion is discredited and dispersed. The audience sees his lion's skin adorning the back of the dishonorable Archduke of Austria, "little valiant, great in villainy . . . ever strong upon the stronger side" (III.i.116–17), and the same scene that describes his "honor-giving hand" bestowing knighthood upon Robert Faulconbridge (I.i.53) also reveals that he dishonored Faulconbridge by seducing his wife. Coeur-de-lion has left no clear successor. His only biological son is a bastard. His heir by law of primogeniture is his nephew Arthur. The Bastard has "a trick of Cordelion's face" and "the accent of his tongue" (I.i.85–86). Arthur, a dispossessed and defenseless child, has his lineal right to the throne. And John, who has neither, sits upon that throne.

The dispersion of Coeur-de-lion's legacy among three defective heirs makes it impossible even to know who is the rightful king of England, and it gives rise to the crucial issue in *King John*: the problem of legitimacy. As Herbert Lindenberger has pointed out, "The action of historical drama is more precisely a struggle for legitimacy than a struggle for power as such. Dramas that depict a hereditary throne generally present sharply divergent readings of genealogies to justify the rights of various contenders for the throne."[46] Although Richard II is

---

[46]*Historical Drama: The Relation of Literature and Reality* (Chicago: University of Chicago Press, 1975), p. 160.

the undoubted heir of Edward III, his enemies invoke the law of primogeniture (II.iii.122–24) and the rituals of royalty (IV.i) to justify his deposition.[47] Genealogical anxiety haunts Shakespeare's Lancastrian kings, and genealogical arguments rationalize the rebellions that plague them. Richard III follows what Robert Ornstein has called the "time-honored custom for usurpers to bastardize those they overthrow" when he orders Buckingham to "infer [i.e., assert] the bastardy of Edward's children" (III.v.75).[48] Imputations of bastardy provide potent weapons in all the plays. In 1 *Henry VI*, for instance, Gloucester uses them against Winchester, and even the threat of being thought a bastard is sufficient to persuade Burgundy to change sides in the middle of a war (III.iii.60–61). Young Talbot refuses to leave the battlefield where he faces certain death because he fears even more the prospect of being thought a bastard:

> Is my name Talbot? and am I your son?
> And shall I fly? O, if you love my mother,
> Dishonor not her honorable name
> To make a bastard and a slave of me!
> The world will say, he is not Talbot's blood,
> That basely fled when noble Talbot stood.
> (IV.v.12–17)

Although legitimacy is always the issue in Shakespeare's history plays, it is nowhere else so central as it is in *King John*. The entire action hangs on the unanswerable question: "Who is the legitimate heir of Coeur-de-lion?"; and the presiding spirit of this play is not the king who gives it its name but the human embodiment of every kind of illegitimacy, the Bastard. The Bastard's literal illegitimacy characterizes the status of the king (who relies on "strong possession" rather than "right" for his throne), the issues the play explores, and the curious nature of Shakespeare's creation. Failures of authority—that is, problems of legitimacy—take a variety of forms in and around *King John*. For the characters within the play, these range from specific, literal accusations of bastardy (brought against Arthur and John as

[47]See Phyllis Rackin, "The Role of the Audience in Shakespeare's *Richard II*," *Shakespeare Quarterly* 36 (1985), 262–81.

[48]*A Kingdom for a Stage: The Achievement of Shakespeare's History Plays* (Cambridge: Harvard University Press, 1972), p. 26n.

well as Philip Faulconbridge) to the general absence of any clear royal authority. For the audience watching the play, there is no unblemished cause and no unquestioned authority to claim their allegiance. For scholarly editors, the play has a confused text and a clouded authorial genealogy. Not only does it include an abundance of fictional material not found in the historiographic sources, but there is no way to know whether Shakespeare is the original author of that fictional material, since much of it is also found in a roughly contemporary play, *The Troublesome Raigne of Iohn King of England* (London, 1591), and no one has been able to determine which play was written first (although, of course, many arguments have been advanced on both sides of the question).[49]

The most powerful and dramatically compelling of the characters, the Bastard is also the one to whom John assigns "the ordering of this present time" (V.i.77) and Shakespeare gives the last word in the play. Nonetheless, the Bastard has no real place in history, neither in the chain of patriarchal succession, where he can never inherit his father's throne, nor in the historical record Shakespeare found in Holinshed. And he dominates a play unique among Shakespeare's English histories for its own lack of historical authority. *King John* has the flimsiest of relationships to its historiographic sources, compressing and marginalizing John's dispute with Rome and the revolt of his nobles, centering instead on a historically insignificant character invented for the sixteenth-century stage.[50]

A curious episode, which serves to introduce the Bastard, takes up most of the first act in *King John* and exposes, like nothing else in any of Shakespeare's histories, the arbitrary and conjectural nature of patriarchal succession and the suppressed centrality of women to it. The Bastard, here called Philip Faulconbridge, and his younger brother Robert come before the king to dispute the Faulconbridge legacy, Robert claiming that his

[49]Estimates of the date of Shakespeare's composition range from 1591 to 1598. For a detailed account of the problems concerning the sources, the text, and the dating, see Honigmann's introduction to the Arden edition.

[50]If the *Troublesome Raigne* was a source for Shakespeare's play, the Bastard has a dramatic source there, but the historical basis for the Bastard is confined to one sentence in Holinshed on "Philip bastard sonne to king Richard, to whome his father had given the castell and honor of Coinacke, [who] killed the vicount of Limoges, in revenge of his fathers death" (Holinshed, 2:278).

older brother is not really their father's son and should not inherit the Faulconbridge lands and title. The Faulconbridge quarrel, like the war between Arthur and John over the English throne, hinges on ambiguities and ruptures in the relationship between legal and biological inheritance. In both families, that of the king and that of the Faulconbridges, the patriarchal succession has been interrupted. John has taken the throne that belongs by law of primogeniture to Arthur, a fact that Shakespeare emphasizes by suppressing Holinshed's record of Richard I's bequest of the throne to John, by inventing Elinor's unequivocal assertion that John's claim is based on "strong possession much more than . . . right," and even by implying that Arthur is Coeur-de-lion's son (as he does by ambiguous wording when France describes Coeur-de-lion as the "great forerunner" of Arthur's "blood" [II.i.2] and again when Constance says that Arthur is Elinor's "eldest son's son" [II.i.177]). Like the controversy over the crown, the Faulconbridge controversy involves a disputed will and rival claimants to patriarchal succession, and both quarrels involve the mothers—but not the fathers— of the contending heirs. John's mother, Elinor, and Arthur's mother, Constance, play important roles in the historical contest between their sons, but neither is the chief actor. The fictional Faulconbridge quarrel, on the other hand, centers on a woman. Lady Faulconbridge's infidelity has created the nightmare situation that haunts the patriarchal imagination, a son not of her husband's getting destined to inherit her husband's lands and title. Like Shakespeare's ubiquitous cuckold jokes, the Faulconbridge episode bespeaks the anxiety that motivates the stridency of patriarchal claims and repressions, the repressed knowledge of women's subversive power.

John's attempt to arbitrate the Faulconbridge quarrel exposes a deep contradiction in patriarchal law. He says to Robert:

> Sirrah, your brother is legitimate,
> Your father's wife did after wedlock bear him;
> And if she did play false, the fault was hers,
> Which fault lies on the hazards of all husbands
> That marry wives. Tell me, how if my brother,
> Who, as you say, took pains to get this son,
> Had of your father claim'd this son for his?
> In sooth, good friend, your father might have kept

This calf, bred from his cow, from all the world;
In sooth he might; then if he were my brother's,
My brother might not claim him, nor your father,
Being none of his, refuse him. This concludes:
My mother's son did get your father's heir;
Your father's heir must have your father's land.

(I.i.116–29)

According to the laws of patriarchy as expounded by John (and according to good English law in Shakespeare's time), the woman, like a cow, is mere chattel, possession of the man. All her actions, even an act so radical as betrayal of the marriage bond, are totally irrelevant, powerless to affect her son's name, possession, legal status, or identity. Only the man's entitlement has significance under law. She is his possession, and any child she bears is his, even if he is not the biological father.[51] Thus, the very absoluteness of patriarchal right provides for its own subversion.

By admitting that the relationship between father and son is finally no more than a legal fiction, John attacks the very basis of patriarchal history. Relying on "strong possession" rather than "right" for his throne (I.i.40), John opposes the patriarchal authority that would legitimate Arthur. Having himself crowned a second time, he denies the permanence and efficacy of the ritual that made him king (IV.ii.1–34). Everything, even the supreme ritual by which patriarchal authority is passed down in temporal succession from one hand to another, is now endlessly repeatable and reversible. In this play, it is not John but the King of France who values history and wants to write it. The French king supports Arthur's lineal right to the English throne and describes Arthur as a "little abstract" of what "died in" Arthur's father, which "the hand of time shall draw . . . into as huge a volume" (II.i.101–3). With this description of father and son as "volume" and "abstract," the French king grounds the historical record in nature. But John's verdict on the Faulconbridge controversy demythologizes that record, depriving it

[51]In the Arden *King John*, Honigmann glosses John's verdict on the Faulconbridge quarrel with a similar judgment from H. Swinburne's *Briefe Treatise of Testaments* (1590): "he which maried the woman, shall bee saide to bee the father of the childe, and not hee which did beget the same . . . for whose the cow is, as it is commonly said, his is the calfe also."

of the natural status implied by the French king's metaphor of man as volume and boy as abstract and exposing it as a social construct designed to shore up the flimsy (and always necessarily putative) connections between fathers and sons.

Elinor is the first to guess the Bastard's true paternity, for she can read the wordless text of his physical nature:

> He hath a trick of Cordelion's face;
> The accent of his tongue affecteth him.
> Do you not read some tokens of my son
> In the large composition of this man?
>                                         (I.i.85–88)

But without Lady Faulconbridge's testimony, the Bastard's paternity would remain conjectural, and his name and title would belie the biological truth of the paternity they purported to represent. It takes one woman to guess the truth and another to verify it. In Holinshed, Coeur-de-lion recognizes his bastard son, giving him "the castell and honor of Coinacke." In the *Troublesome Raigne*, the Bastard guesses his true paternity even before he asks his mother.[52] Only in Shakespeare is he required to receive his paternity from the hands of women.

Lady Faulconbridge is an unhistorical character, but she is the only one who knows the truth about the Bastard's paternity. The Bastard's words are significant: "But for the certain knowledge of that truth / I put you o'er to heaven and to my mother" (I.i.61–62). The Bastard's ironic coupling of his adulterous mother with heaven as the only sources of the elusive truth that no man can know on earth suggests a deep affinity between them as keepers of the unwritten and unknowable truth never directly accessible to the knowledge of men, the others who delineate the boundaries of the male self's territory of knowledge and control. To incorporate women in the story, as Shake-

---

[52]In fact, he gets the news from Nature herself: "Methinks I hear a hollow echo sound," he says, "That *Philip* is the son unto a King: / The whistling leaves upon the trembling trees, / Whistle in concert I am *Richard's* son; / The bubbling murmur of the water's fall, / Records *Phillipus Regis filius*; / Birds in their flight make music with their wings, / Filling the air with glory of my birth; / Birds, bubbles, leaves and mountains, echo, all / Ring in mine ears, that I am *Richard's* son." See *The Troublesome Raigne of John, King of England* (London: Sampson Clarke, 1591), Part 1:i.242–51.

speare does in *King John*, is to go beyond the patriarchal historical narrative into the realm of the unwritten and the conjectural, the inaccessible domain (the no-man's-land) of the true paternity of a child and the actual life that can never be fully represented in the words of the historical text.

Renaissance historiography constructed a patriarchal mythology, delineating a chain of inheritance passed down from father to son. Like the strings of "begats" in the Old Testament, it suppressed the role of women. The son's name and entitlement and legitimacy all derived from the father,[53] and only the father was included in the historiographic text. But only the mother could guarantee that legitimacy. As bearers of the life that names, titles, and historical records could never fully represent, the women were keepers of the unspoken and unspeakable reality that always threatened to belie the words that pretended to describe it.

The Bastard's mother is a fictitious English lady, and Joan is a historical French peasant, but both perform analogous acts of subversion. Like Joan's nominalism, Lady Faulconbridge's adultery belies the men's words and subverts their claims to authority. The women in Shakespeare's English history plays differ in virtue, strength, nationality, and social rank; and they speak with a variety of voices. Despite their many roles, however, they are never the central actors, and they differ only as the masculine project of writing history is conceived differently. In the historical world that Shakespeare constructed, women were inevitably alien, representatives of the unarticulated residue that eluded the men's historiographic texts and threatened their historical myths.

Our own history tells us that women in Shakespeare's England—not only Queen Elizabeth but also her female subjects—had considerable power and more authority than patriarchal

---

[53]For a striking expression of this fact, see Lee, "Reflections of Power," p. 191n. Lee quotes from an anonymous fifteenth-century chronicle, *An English Chronicle of the Reigns of Richard II., Henry IV., Henry V., and Henry VI., written before the year 1471 . . .* , ed. John Silvester Davies (Camden Society Publication No. 64 [London]: 1856), p. 79: "The quene [Margaret] was defamed and desclaundered, that he that was called Prince, was nat hir sone, but a bastard goten in avoutry." Confusing to modern eyes, the sentence assumes that the child of Margaret's body would not be her "sone" unless he was also the legitimate child of her husband.

ideology could accommodate. Women could and did inherit and bequeath property of every kind, including land, and they exercised substantial social and economic power, even after their marriages. The difference between prescription and practice was apparent even at the time. Smith's *De Republica Anglorum*, first published in 1583, acknowledges that "although our lawe may seeme somewhat rigorous toward the wives, yet for the most part they can handle their husbandes so well and so doulcely, and specially when their husbands be sicke: that where the lawe giveth them nothing, their husbandes at their death of their good will give them all."[54] In the aristocracy, land was inherited by daughters about one-third of the time. Among villagers significant numbers of women, wives as well as daughters, not only inherited property but also served as executors for their husbands' and parents' wills. Women also bequeathed property in their own right, and, like their husbands, they bequeathed it to daughters as well as to sons.

As Susan Amussen has observed, "The behaviour of women in writing their wills opens a small crack in the patriarchal facade of early modern England."[55] That patriarchal facade, constructed in historiographic accounts of the medieval past as well as in sermons and advice manuals directed to the Elizabethan present, was not so much a description of as a response to the conditions of actual Elizabethan life. In a world where marriages were economic partnerships, it was difficult to enforce patriar-

[54]Sir Thomas Smith, *De Republica Anglorum*, ed. Mary Dewar (Cambridge: Cambridge University Press, 1982), Book III, chap. 6, p. 133. Smith goes on to point out that except in London, "where a peculiar order is taken by the citie much after the fashion of the civill lawe," "fewe there be that be not made at the death of their husbandes either sole or chiefe executrixes of his last wil and testament, and have for the most part the government of the children and their portions." Cf. Pearl Hogrefe, "Legal Rights of Tudor Women and the Circumvention by Men and Women," *Sixteenth Century Journal* 3 (1972), 97–105.

[55]"Families, Property, and Family Economies," in *An Ordered Society: Gender and Class in Early Modern England* (Oxford: Blackwell, 1988), p. 93. Keith Wrightson, *English Society, 1580–1680* (New Brunswick, N.J.: Rutgers University Press, 1982), p. 94, points out that "the naming of a wife as executor and the granting to her of full control of the family patrimony . . . was not merely frequent in the wills of the period, it was normal." Amussen, pp. 66–94, presents detailed statistical evidence of this fact. On p. 87, for example, she shows that in the village of Cawston over fifty percent of the estates were divided equally among all children, daughters as well as sons.

chal injunctions of absolute and universal wifely submission. Examining personal diaries from the period, Keith Wrightson concludes "that quarrels were not uncommon, that the wife very often seems to have taken the initiative in asserting herself, and that marital bickering was not usually cut short promptly by assertions of the husband's patriarchal authority." "Conventional definitions of roles and the actual performance of them in life can be quite different things."[56] Examining wills, Amussen reaches a similar conclusion: "the descriptions we have of experience in household manuals are inadequate guides to reality: life was lived in tension with prescription."[57]

What that life was, we can never fully know. But the repressions and elisions of patriarchal discourse betray deep anxieties about female power and authority. The validating object of men's desires, the deepest threat to their fulfillment, the specter of the woman hovers at the margins of the patriarchal text, constructed as a paradox that exposes the contradictions in patriarchal history, a truth that eludes expression in authoritative patriarchal discourse. Never present in patriarchal history, women could only be represented, and what they represented was the material physical life that patriarchal discourse could never completely capture or control. This ambivalence was actualized in Shakespeare's theater: the same patriarchal ideology that marginalized the women in Shakespeare's historical sources also excluded women from his company of actors, but the presence of women in the audience prevented their total erasure from the scene of theatrical performance. Portrayed by boy actors, Shakespeare's female characters could only represent a reality that they could never truly embody. Nonetheless, they performed those representations in the presence of real women who were paying customers in the theater, and the presence of the boy's body beneath the woman's dress destabilized the connection between physical sex and social gender that rationalized women's inferior social status in natural difference.[58]

Within this ambivalent context, it is not surprising that Shakespeare's female characters often come to the stage trailing clouds

[56]*English Society, 1580–1608*, pp. 95, 92.
[57]"Families, Property, and Family Economies," p. 93.
[58]Phyllis Rackin, "Androgyny, Mimesis, and the Marriage of the Boy Heroine on the English Renaissance Stage," *PMLA* 102 (1987), 29–41.

of supernatural power. Excluded from Shakespeare's stage and denied by the logic of patriarchal discourse, incomprehensible within the categories of patriarchal thought, the inconceivable reality of female authority and the intolerable fact of female power could be rationalized only in terms of the supernatural. In the comedies and romances, those supernatural forces are benevolent. Shakespeare's comic heroines are valued as representatives of a transcendent reality. They inhabit golden worlds like Portia's Belmont and Rosalind's Forest of Arden, which promise to resolve the problems of the realistically conceived marketplace of Shylock's Venice and the troubled households at the beginning of *As You Like It*. In the romances, as in *Henry VIII*, which shares many of the generic features of romance, women are associated with a benevolent, redemptive providence.[59] The saintly Katherine is granted a vision of a blessed troop, accompanied by celestial music, who promise her eternal happiness in heaven (*Henry VIII*: IV.ii.83–90), and the newborn babe Elizabeth will bring "a thousand thousand blessings" on the land (V.iv.19).

Looking beyond the world of history for heavenly redemption of troubled human worlds and heavenly redress of wrongs that cannot be righted by human means, Katherine in *Henry VIII* is associated with the divine providence that governs the action of romance. *Richard III*, the most providential of the earlier history plays, delineates a similar relationship between the feminine and the supernatural when the women invoke God's curses on the wicked king and foresee his coming destruction. But in the plays where the perspective is confined to the historical level, the women who invoke supernatural powers derive them from the devil. Joan claims at first to derive her inexplicable martial power from "Heaven and our Lady" (I.ii); but she finally turns out to be a witch, consorting with evil spirits. Of the four women in *2 Henry VI*, all but Margaret are associated with negative forms of supernatural power. Margery Jordan is a witch; Eleanor, the unruly wife of the good Duke Humphrey, consorts with witches and solicits their spells and prophecies; and the

---

[59]In this, as in many other respects, *The Tempest* is the exception. Appropriating the feminine role of nurturing parent, Prospero also appropriates the feminine powers of theatrical illusion and benevolent magic. The woman with supernatural powers in Prospero's world is Sycorax, an evil witch.

wife of Simpcox collaborates in the bogus miracle by which he attempts to deceive the naive but virtuous king.

Although generic differences transvalue the associations between the feminine and the supernatural, the relationship itself persists, reformulated as the objects of desire and loathing are reconstituted from genre to genre. In Shakespeare's romantic comedies, the object of desire is the prelapsarian golden world of neoplatonic mythology; in his late romances, it is the benevolent providence that can forgive human sins and redeem human sufferings. In the world of the Elizabethan histories, however, the object of nostalgic yearning is the anachronistic image of patriarchal order and pure chivalry that the Elizabethans projected onto the Middle Ages. The histories rewrite the past and reenact its rituals just as Elizabeth's ambitious courtiers put on feudal costumes to engage in nostalgic reconstructions of medieval tournaments and newly prosperous commoners purchased coats of arms to claim an ancient lineage. Shakespeare represents this nostalgic ideal in *1 Henry VI* in the form of Talbot, but he expresses it most powerfully in the great set speech delivered by John of Gaunt just before he dies in *Richard II*:

> This royal throne of kings, this sceptred isle,
> This earth of majesty, this seat of Mars,
> This other Eden, demi-paradise,
> This fortress built by Nature for herself
> Against infection and the hand of war,
> This happy breed of men, this little world,
> This precious stone set in the silver sea,
> Which serves it in the office of a wall,
> Or as a moat defensive to a house,
> Against the envy of less happier lands;
> This blessed plot, this earth, this realm, this England,
> This nurse, this teeming womb of royal kings,
> Fear'd by their breed, and famous by their birth,
> Renowned for their deeds as far from home,
> For Christian service and true chivalry,
> As is the sepulchre in stubborn Jewry
> Of the world's ransom, blessed Mary's Son.
>
> (II.i.40–56)

The ideal country Gaunt describes is a "royal throne of kings" who are "renowned . . . for Christian service and true chivalry," a "fortress" surrounded by a sea that serves it as a "moat"—in short, an idealized medieval landscape. Characterized as a "nurse," a "teeming womb of royal kings" (II.i.51), it also anticipates the feminine qualities of the golden worlds in Shakespeare's romantic comedies. But there is a very important difference. Inhabited only by a "happy breed of men," Gaunt's demi-paradise has no place for women. The object of Gaunt's nostalgic longing is an Eden inhabited exclusively by men; the deeds that prove its worth are the deeds of warfare.

Gaunt invokes an ideal past in order to rebuke a degenerate present: the degraded world of an effeminate young king who wastes the land's wealth and honor on luxurious pleasures rather than augmenting them in manly wars against the French. More complicated than Gaunt's simple binary opposition, Shakespeare's vision of the medieval past is, nonetheless, colored by a similar nostalgia. Written in the time of Elizabeth—a queen frequently compared to Richard II—Shakespeare's English histories depict a warlike, masculine historical world that represses the present realities of female power and authority.[60] Thomas Nashe, in fact, suggests that this opposition is actually the purpose of the English histories. The plays, he wrote, revive "our forefathers valiant acts . . . than which, what can be a sharper reproofe to these degenerate effeminate dayes of ours?"[61] Nashe, like Gaunt, constructs a heroic past that asso-

---

[60]Queen Elizabeth's often-quoted comment, "I am Richard II, know ye not that?," the absence of the deposition scene in quartos printed during her lifetime, and the fact that Essex's followers sponsored a performance of the play on the eve of their rebellion all attest to the strength of the association between the fourteenth-century king and the Tudor queen. The problematic union of patriarchal authority and female sex embodied in Queen Elizabeth (who had herself been declared a bastard) provides a crucial contemporary context for Shakespeare's practice in all his English history plays, in *King John* no less than *Richard II*. On the complicated relation between dramatic representation and the subversion of royal authority, masculine as well as feminine, see David Scott Kastan, "Proud Majesty Made a Subject: Shakespeare and the Spectacle of Rule," *Shakespeare Quarterly* 37 (1986), 459–75.

[61]*Pierce Penilesse his Supplication to the Divell* (1592), in Chambers, *The Elizabethan Stage*, 4:238. The same association between English patriotism and masculine purity recurs when Nashe asserts the superiority of the English theater on the basis of its exclusion of women from the stage: "Our Players are not as the players beyond Sea . . . that have whores and common Curtizens to playe womens partes" (p. 239).

ciates English patriotism with masculine purity in order to reprove a degenerate, effeminate present.

Although scholars are still debating whether female power and authority increased or contracted during the reign of Elizabeth, some have argued that it was actually decreasing.[62] Nonetheless, the proliferation of antifeminist invective clearly indicates a high level of masculine anxiety.[63] Court records from the period tell a similar story, reporting an intensified level of prosecution of women for scolding, witchcraft, and other activities that threatened patriarchal order.[64]

This same anxiety informs Nashe's nostalgic longing for the masculine world of the forefathers, a world he seems to have found in Shakespeare's history plays. Nashe's admiring description of "brave *Talbot* (the terror of the French)" revived from his tomb to "triumphe againe on the Stage" appears to be a direct reference to *1 Henry VI*.[65] Celebrating Shakespeare's creation in jingoistic, masculinist terms, Nashe marks its place in the discourse of patriarchal history. Staging "our forefathers valiant acts," Shakespeare, no less than his chronicle sources, participated in the construction of genealogical myths of martial valor that repressed the reality of female authority and discredited expressions of female power.

The privileged site of patriarchal history, the battlefield has no place for women. Those who seek to invade it are invariably stigmatized. Usurping masculine prerogatives, Joan and Margaret and the "soldier" queen Elinor pollute the masculine purity of war by depriving the men of the victories that are their due and using dishonorable tactics and modern weapons that

[62]See, e.g., Joan Kelly, "Did Women Have a Renaissance?" in *Becoming Visible: Women in European History*, ed. Renate Bridenthal and Claudia Koonz (Boston: Houghton Mifflin, 1977), pp. 137–63; Merry E. Wiesner, "Women's Defense of Their Public Role," in *Women in the Middle Ages and the Renaissance: Literary and Historical Perspectives*, ed. Mary Beth Rose (Syracuse: Syracuse University Press, 1986), pp. 1–28; and Rackin, "Androgyny," pp. 29–41.

[63]See especially Woodbridge, pp. 13–73; and Katherine Usher Henderson and Barbara F. McManus, *Half Humankind: Contexts and Texts of the Controversy about Women in England, 1540–1640* (Urbana: University of Illinois Press, 1985).

[64]David Underdown, "The Taming of the Scold: the Enforcement of Patriarchal Authority in Early Modern England," *Order and Disorder in Early Modern England*, ed. Anthony Fletcher and John Stevenson (Cambridge: Cambridge University Press, 1985), pp. 116–65.

[65]Pp. 238–39.

violate the men's chivalric code. The most powerful of these female warriors, Joan, is also the most demonic. Initially portrayed in positive terms (as "Deborah" [I.2.105] and "Astraea's daughter" [I.vi.4]) that associate her with Queen Elizabeth, Joan is finally degraded to resolve the ideological paradox of female power.[66] By the end of 1 Henry VI, her shocking military success is explained as the product of witchcraft, the illicit supernatural power of a disorderly woman who has refused to abide by the limits of her natural role.

Joan's witchcraft is closely related to her appropriation of masculine dress and masculine behavior. Edward Hall, Shakespeare's chief historiographic source for 1 Henry VI, links Joan's masculinity with her demonic power when he describes her as "this wytch or manly woman."[67] Using the two terms as if they were synonymous and interchangeable, Hall suggests an unexamined connection between them in Renaissance ideology. Sexual difference constituted the necessary ground of patriarchal order and the essential categories of patriarchal thought. Inconceivable in terms of those categories, female transgression of the gender divisions that organized Renaissance society and thought was literally unspeakable.[68] When the Welsh women intrude on the battlefield in 1 Henry IV to mutilate the corpses of the fallen warriors, they commit an act that "may not be / Without much shame retold or spoken of"(I.i.45–46). The single combat between Joan and Talbot (an encounter that Shakespeare invented) is characterized in similar terms—as emasculating,

[66]Gabriele Bernhard Jackson made this point in a paper entitled "Ideological Paradox: The Prototypes of Shakespeare's Joan of Arc," delivered at the section on Feminist Shakespeare Criticism at the 1987 annual meeting of the Northeast Modern Language Association, and published in an expanded version entitled "Topical Ideology: Witches, Amazons, and Shakespeare's Joan of Arc" in ELR 18 (1988), 40–65. Jackson traces a number of associations between positive aspects of Shakespeare's representation of Joan (as an Amazon, as Deborah, as Astraea's daughter) and contemporary representations of Queen Elizabeth (including her self-representation at Tilbury, buskined, plumed, and equipped with truncheon, gauntlet, and gorget).

[67]Jackson, "Topical Ideology," 64; Hall, Union, p.157.

[68]As Catherine Belsey points out, female characters who transgress "the system of differences which gives meaning to social relations . . . are defined as extra-human, demonic," a demonization that "places them beyond meaning, beyond the limits of what is intelligible." See The Subject of Tragedy: Identity and Difference in Renaissance Drama (London: Methuen, 1985), pp. 184–85.

shameful, and indescribable. Deprived of his "strength," "valor," and "force," Talbot cannot understand the female power that makes him impotent: "My thoughts are whirled like a potter's wheel, / I know not where I am, nor what I do" (*1 Henry VI*: I.v.1, 19–20). All he can do is lament the "shame" of his defeat at Joan's hands and, ascribing it to supernatural forces, conclude that Joan is a witch.

The emblem of social and spiritual transgression, Joan's transvestite costume associates her with Queen Elizabeth's triumphant appearance at Tilbury, dressed in armor and declaring her androgyny; but it also prepares for her final association with the demonic.[69] As Leah Marcus points out, "The figure of Joan airs a wide range of anxious fantasies which had eddied about the English queen in the years leading up to the Armada victory and in the Armada year itself, fantasies which could be allowed to surface only after the worst of the Catholic threat had receded."[70] In Shakespeare's later romantic comedies, when the vogue for transvestite heroines was well established and real women in Shakespeare's London had also taken to wearing masculine dress,[71] fashion collaborated with generic convention

---

[69]Jackson, "Ideological Paradox." For a perceptive analysis of Elizabeth's androgynous self-presentation and her often-quoted statement at Tilbury ("I have the body of a weak and feeble woman, but I have the heart and stomach of a king, and of a king of England too"), see Leah Marcus, "Shakespeare's Comic Heroines, Elizabeth I, and the Political Uses of Androgyny," in *Women in the Middle Ages and the Renaissance*, pp. 135–41.

[70]*Puzzling Shakespeare: Local Reading and Its Discontents* (Berkeley: University of California Press, 1988), p. 66. See also chapter 2, "Elizabeth," passim. Among many illuminating observations about the connections between Joan and Elizabeth, Marcus points out that the two Frenchmen Joan claims to have been her lovers—the Duke of Alençon and the Duke of Anjou—have the same names as the two Frenchmen Elizabeth "had come closest to marrying" in the previous decades (p. 68).

[71]Jackson ("Topical Ideology," pp. 53–54) suggests that Joan may have been the first female character to appear on stage in masculine attire. For a discussion of the Elizabethan fashion of women wearing masculine dress, see Woodbridge, pp. 139–53. Although Woodbridge points out that "the real-life fashion of masculine attire for women was a recurrent phenomenon in Elizabethan times," she infers that it was "quiescent" during the 1590s and early 1600s, the period of Shakespeare's transvestite comedies, because it received "almost no literary attention" during those years. I believe it is equally easy to derive the opposite inference: to conclude that the lack of literary attention to the fashion during those years may very well indicate that it was so widespread and so generally accepted that it became unremarkable.

to produce a positive response to cross-dressed heroines. In these plays, transvestite costume associates the heroines with the figure of the androgyne, an idealized image of prelapsarian perfection and human self-completion.[72] In the masculine world of the histories, however, it serves as the mark of forbidden transgression. In both cases, cross-dressing is the sign of supernatural power; in the histories, however, the power is demonic, and the sign stigmatizes its wearer as a witch.[73] Joan's masculine dress, like the beards of the witches in *Macbeth*, is the sign of the uncanny. It associates sexual ambiguity with the dangers that lurk at the boundaries of the known, rationalized world of sexual difference and exclusion constructed by patriarchal discourse, the inconceivable realities of female power and authority that threatened the idealized world of masculine longing constructed by Shakespeare's historical myths.[74]

[72]Rackin, "Androgyny," pp. 29–41.

[73]For an especially perceptive discussion of the ways witchcraft beliefs served to construct and legitimate patriarchal hegemony, see Peter Stallybrass, "*Macbeth* and Witchcraft," in *Focus on Macbeth*, ed. John Russell Brown (London: Routledge and Kegan Paul, 1982), pp. 189–209.

[74]Portions of this chapter were presented at the University of Pennsylvania's Mellon Seminar on the Diversity of Language and the Structure of Power. I am indebted to the members of that seminar, especially to Lucienne Frappier-Mazur, Gwynne Kennedy, Maureen Quilligan, and Carroll Smith-Rosenberg, for their stimulating questions and suggestions. Other portions were presented at the 1988 Shakespeare Association seminar, "Shakespeare and History: Theorizing Practice." I am indebted to Susan Dwyer Amussen for her helpful commentary on that occasion.

# 5

# Historical Kings/Theatrical Clowns

Captured by her English enemies, Joan is condemned to die at the end of 1 *Henry VI*, despite her (probably false) claims to be pregnant with an illegitimate child. Nonetheless, there is a sense in which her fictitious bastard progeny survive, reappearing in various forms in Shakespeare's remaining history plays, continuing and developing her antihistorical project. The women in the succeeding *Henry VI* plays preserve Joan's illicit legacy of witchcraft and adultery, but most of the characters who take up her agenda will be men. Women were not the only persons whose existence was effaced by patriarchal history. Not only a masculine enterprise, Renaissance historiography was also aristocratic. Its heroic subject matter, its genealogical purpose, and its status as written text all served to exclude common men as well as women from the elite province its discourse constructed.

Shakespeare defines the antihistorical forces that Joan represents as much by status and class[1] as by gender; her opposition

---

[1]Although the use of the word "class" in connection with a pre-capitalist society can be challenged, Shakespeare's representations of rebellious commoners seem to me to involve issues of class as well as status. The traditional view that despite its "sharply delineated system of status," pre-industrial England was "a one-class society" is emphatically stated by Peter Laslett in *The World We Have Lost*, 2d ed. (New York: Charles Scribner's Sons, 1971), pp. 23–54. However, as Jean Howard has recently argued, conceptions of class are also relevant: "Social historians of the period increasingly speak of the clash in the late sixteenth and early seventeenth centuries between emergent capitalistic social relations and older modes of social organization based on status or degree." She also cites the emergence of an entrepreneurial middle class in

to Talbot pits peasant against aristocrat as well as woman against man, and the two forms of subversion were closely related in Renaissance thought. Their connection is explicit, for instance, in Hall's account of a letter sent from the King of England to the Duke of Burgundy and other princes to justify the English execution of Joan and to refute French claims for her sanctity. Along with charges of blasphemy and disobedience, the letter emphasizes Joan's usurpation of status and gender insignia to which she had no right:

> It is commonly renoumed, and in every place published, that the woman, commonly called the Puzell, hath by the space of twoo yeres and more, contrary to Goddes lawe, and the estate of womanhed, been clothed in a mannes apparell, a thyng in the sight of God abhominable. . . . Beside this, she usurped a cote of armes, and displaid a standard, whiche thynges, be apperteinyng only to knightes and esquiers: and of a greate outrage, and more pride and presumpcion, she demaunded to beare the noble and excellent Armes of Fraunce, whiche she in part obteined, the whiche she bare in many skirmishes and assautes, and her brethren also (as men report) that is to say: the feld azure, a swerd, the poynt upward in pale silver, set betwene two flower deluces, firmed with a croune of gold.[2]

Assuming masculine dress, Joan has violated biblical prohibition and the gender regulations that governed women's "estate" in society. Assuming a coat of arms, she represents a threat to the entire social order.

Conflating the two forms of subversion, Hall's account implies that distinctions that separated aristocrats from peasants and those that divided men from women were homologous. In Shakespeare's history plays, this same homology informs the

London and the enclosure movement, the new agricultural practices, and the putting-out system of cloth production that were "creating a rural proleteriat dependent on wage labor for subsistence" as well as the "'vagabonds and masterless men' so feared by the Elizabethan authorities." See her "Cross-dressing, the Theatre, and Gender Struggle in Early Modern England," *Shakespeare Quarterly* 39 (1988), 421n. See also the studies to which she refers, especially David Underdown, *Revel, Riot, and Rebellion: Popular Politics and Culture in England, 1603–1660* (Oxford: Clarendon Press, 1985), and Keith Wrightson, *English Society 1580–1680* (New Brunswick, N.J.: Rutgers University Press, 1982).

[2]Edward Hall, *The Union of the Two Noble and Illustre Famelies of Lancastre and Yorke* (1548; rpt. London: J. Johnson et al., 1809), p. 157.

representations of common men, who occupy a discursive position similar to the one that defines the roles of women. Silenced and marginalized by Shakespeare's historiographic
sources, the common men, like the women, speak for the unarticulated residue of experience that eluded expression in the
ideologically motivated discourse of historiography. Like the
women, they represent a constant challenge to the mystifications of a historiographic tradition that was not only masculine
but also elite.

Despite individual variations in characterization, the essential
paradigm remains the same. Usually illiterate, these characters
always distrust words. Excluded, disempowered, or represented as demonic others by historiographic writing, they derive
their subversive authority from the present, material reality of
theatrical performance. Joan and Jack Cade have real historical
prototypes, and Falstaff, the chief inheritor in the second tetralogy of Joan's antihistorical legacy, is both literate and a
knight; but all are inscribed within the same binary opposition
that opposes historiographic writing to theatrical speech and
present, corporeal life. Falstaff's response to the noble corpse
of Sir Walter Blunt at the Battle of Shrewsbury—"I like not such
grinning honor as Sir Walter hath. Give me life" (*1 Henry IV*:
V.iii.58–59)—and his demystification of chivalric honor recall
Joan's contemptuous description of Talbot's corpse (*1 Henry VI*:
IV.vii.72–76). Both express the same nominalism, the same con-
tempt for empty titles and historical renown, and the same
conviction that material, physical life is the ultimate reality and
*summum bonum*. To Falstaff, honor is worthless because it has
no physical efficacy: it cannot "set to a leg. . . . Or an arm. . . .
Or take away the grief of a wound":

> What is honor? A word. What is in that word honor? What is
> that honor? Air. A trim reckoning! Who hath it? He that died a'
> Wednesday. Doth he feel it? No. Doth he hear it? No. 'Tis insen-
> sible then? Yea, to the dead. But will't not live with the living?
> No. Why? Detraction will not suffer it. Therefore I'll none of it,
> honor is a mere scutcheon. And so ends my catechism. (*1 Henry
> IV*: V.i.133–41)

Shakespeare's characterization of Falstaff, in fact, repeats
many of the features that Renaissance misogyny attributed to

women. Not only his lack of military valor but also his lying, his inconstancy, and his outrageous incontinence locate him on the wrong side of the binary opposition that divided man from woman, spirit from matter, aristocrat from commoner. *1 Henry IV* ends with Falstaff's mutilation of Hotspur's corpse (V.v.128). Wounding the dead hero's thigh, he reenacts the female threat to manhood and military honor symbolized in the opening scene by the report of the Welshwomen's mutilation of the corpses of English soldiers (I.i.43–46). Neither female nor plebeian, Falstaff is nonetheless the most fully developed embodiment of the disorderly conduct and subversive speech that express the threat both women and commoners represented in Shakespeare's historical world.[3]

There is, however, at least one crucial difference between the two groups: The women, like Falstaff, *symbolize* the dangers of disorder. The plebeian men in the first tetralogy *literalize* them. It is significant, I believe, that there are no women among the "ragged multitude of hinds and peasants" (IV.iv.32–33) that follows Jack Cade in *2 Henry VI* even though Cade's rebellious agenda reflects the deeply embedded cultural anxieties that conflated fears of the loss of property and status with fears of unconstrained female sexuality. "All things shall be in common" (IV.vii.19), not only property and money, but women as well: "wives [shall] be as free as heart can wish or tongue can tell" (IV.vii.124–25).[4] Nonetheless, despite the fact that women

---

[3]On the discursive homologies that associated masterless women with masterless plebeians see Jean Howard, "Crossdressing, the Theatre, and Gender Struggle," 424–27. On Falstaff's female characteristics, see Valerie Traub, "Prince Hal's Falstaff: Positioning Psychoanalysis and the Female Reproductive Body," *Shakespeare Quarterly* 40 (1989), 456–74.

[4]Peter Stallybrass, in "Patriarchal Territories: The Body Enclosed," in *Rewriting the Renaissance: The Discourses of Sexual Difference in Early Modern Europe*, ed. Margaret W. Ferguson, Maureen Quilligan, and Nancy J. Vickers (Chicago: University of Chicago Press, 1986), pp. 126–29, draws the connection between transforming private enclosures to common land and having an unchaste wife. Cf. *2 Henry VI* (I.iii.16–22) where a poor petitioner brings a complaint "against John Goodman, my Lord Cardinal's man, for keeping my house, and lands, and wife and all, from me" and Suffolk replies, "Thy wife too? that's some wrong indeed." Suffolk's unsympathetic response is in character, since he himself is an adulterer, but it also serves to emphasize the connection between wife and land. On the roles of women in early modern riots and rebellions, see Stallybrass, "'Drunk with the cup of liberty': Robin Hood, the Carnival-

played prominent roles in the riots and rebellions that troubled the peace in early modern England, they are as absent from Cade's company of rebels as they were from Shakespeare's company of actors.

The absence points to the essential difference between the subversive roles of women and the equally, but differently, subversive roles of common men in Shakespeare's historiographic representation. Impersonated by male actors, female characters could only appear on Shakespeare's stage as the objects of theatrical representation. Common men, by contrast, could appear in their own persons. The stage directions that mark the first entrance of Cade's followers on Shakespeare's stage are revealing. Act IV, scene ii begins, *"Enter Bevis and John Holland,"* and the speech headings for the first thirty lines use the same two names. Explained by editors as a mistake or a "convenience" on Shakespeare's part,[5] the use of the actors' names rather than those of the characters reminds us not only that the names of common men rarely appeared in Renaissance historical writing but also that their bodies constituted a real presence on Shakespeare's stage.

The restrictions that excluded women from the profession of acting collaborated with the exclusions of patriarchal history to marginalize the roles of female characters in Shakespeare's representations of the English past. This doubly determined repression was relieved only by the presence of women in Shakespeare's theater audience and their economic power as paying customers.[6] Despite that presence and that power, however, women could never speak for themselves from the public platform of the stage. Represented by male actors, speaking lines written by a male playwright, Shakespeare's female characters are always, in some measure, the instruments of male ventriloquism. In the case of the common men, however, the conditions of theatrical production opposed the repressions of

esque, and the Rhetoric of Violence in Early Modern England," *Semiotica* 54 (1985), 122–27.

[5]See, e.g., Andrew S. Cairncross, ed., William Shakespeare, *The Second Part of King Henry VI*, Arden edition (London: Methuen, 1962), p. 109n.

[6]On the implications of that presence and that power, see Howard, "Crossdressing, the Theatre, and Gender Struggle in Early Modern England," pp. 439–40.

the dominant culture and its authoritative and authorizing historiography. Profound differences, both in status and in gender, separated the actors from every other object of their representation. Only in the case of the common men could they speak from their own social location. Impersonated by actors who occupied the same social location as the characters they portrayed, the common men constituted a material presence within the scene of performance. They spoke with their own voices and appeared in their own bodies. Their lines, moreover, were written by one of their own, a common player who was also the son of a bankrupt glover from Stratford.

Dissolving the barriers of representation and historical distance, the plebeian clowns who joined the audience at the *platea* of theatrical presence subverted the authority of historical representation and the ideological repressions it required.[7] Grounded in the contemporary material reality of the playhouse, they undermined the authority of the imagined historical action, and with it the authority of history.[8] The historical characters and plots derived their authority from the ideologically constructed facts of the history they represented and the received truths it revealed, that is, from fidelity to the past. The players derived theirs from the approval and pleasure of the audience in the present scene of performance—the open-roofed

[7]See Robert Weimann, *Shakespeare and the Popular Tradition in the Theater: Studies in the Social Dimension of Dramatic Form and Function*, ed. Robert Schwartz (Baltimore: Johns Hopkins University Press, 1987), pp. 73–85, 224–26, and "Bifold Authority in Shakespeare's Theatre," *Shakespeare Quarterly* 39 (1988), 409–10. Weimann argues that the upstage *locus* of mimetic illusion, the site of "decorum, aloofness from the audience, and representational closure," privileged the authority of "what and who was *represented*," while the *platea*, the forestage where clowns performed their antics and actors addressed their audiences, challenged that authority by calling attention to the immediate theatrical occasion, with all its subversive potential.

[8]See my discussion of Pistol in Chapter 3. See also the scene of Falstaff's counterfeit death *1 Henry IV* (V.iv) and the discussions of it in Sigurd Burckhardt's *Shakespearean Meanings* (Princeton: Princeton University Press, 1968), pp. 146–48; and James Calderwood's "*1 Henry IV* : Art's Gilded Lie," *English Literary Renaissance* 3 (1973) and *Metadrama in Shakespeare's Henriad: Richard II to Henry V* (Berkeley: University of California Press, 1979), pp. 68–75. As these critics point out, the entire scene serves to undermine dramatic illusion; and Falstaff's terrified response to the sight of Hotspur's corpse—"How if he should counterfeit too and rise?"—functions in context to remind the audience of the living actor ("counterfeit") who portrayed the dead Percy and thus of the unreality of the theatrical representation.

playhouse that made the audience as visible as the actors, the thrust stage that brought them together, and the "neutral materiality" of the bare stage, which, as Robert Weimann has argued, tended to authorize the representing actor and undermine the authority of the objects he represented.[9] The physical site and material conditions of theatrical production made the playhouse a site of subversion because they opposed theatrical presence to a past that was only represented, the actuality of low social status to the theatrical costumes that symbolized elite privilege, and the real presence of actors and audience to the mediated authority of the written script.

Because that audience was socially heterogeneous and disorderly, any authority they were given constituted a threat to established order. Assembled to hear the public speech of actors who lacked both status and institutional power, the theater audience constituted a cultural and political anomaly, the object of profound anxieties. These anxieties can be seen in the censorship of *Sir Thomas More*. The playscript opened with a disorderly mob of citizens protesting their grievances, but the Master of the Revels ordered the players to "leave out the insurrection wholy and the Cause ther off and begin with Sir Thomas Moore att the mayors sessions with a reportt afterwards off his good service don being Shrive off London uppon a mutiny Agaynst the Lumbards only by A short reportt and nott otherwise att your own perilles."[10] Substituting historical narrative ("A short reportt") for present dramatic enactment, the prescribed censorship interposed the barrier of narrative mediation to contain the rebels within the dramatic fiction and separate them from their dangerous present counterparts in the unruly theater audience.

The eruption of Jack Cade's rebellious followers on Shakespeare's stage constitutes a similar moment of danger. Rupturing the conceptual barriers that insulated the represented world of the play from the actual world of the audience, it opened a breach for the licensed disorder of fictional theatrical representation to invade the actual world of the audience, where it was

[9]Weimann, "Bifold Authority," p. 409.

[10]E. Tyllney, quoted by Janet Clare in "'Greater Themes for Insurrection's Arguing': Political Censorship of the Elizabethan and Jacobean Stage," *Review of English Studies* n.s. 38 (1987), 171.

clearly illicit. Giving public voice to the grievances they shared
with actual rebels in Shakespeare's England, the actors threatened to produce in the real time of the audience the same disorder they enacted in the fictive time represented on stage.
"Inspir'd with the spirit of putting down kings and princes"
(IV.ii.35–36), the rebels who materialize on Shakespeare's stage
evoke the anxieties that disorderly women and commoners,
actors and audiences in the public theaters could all evoke in
Shakespeare's world: the nightmare prospect of a world turned
upside down that was the only conceivable alternative (and
therefore the justifying antithesis) to the existing social hierarchy. Like actors, the rebels are most "in order when . . . most
out of order" (IV.ii.189). Putting on the discarded clothes of
aristocrats to impersonate their betters, actors violated the
sumptuary laws that stabilized the emblems of status in the real
world.[11] George Bevis and John Holland propose an even more
dangerous inversion when they complain that the nobility
"scorn to go in leather aprons" (IV.ii.12–13). Projecting a universal leveling—"it was never merry world in England since
gentlemen came up"; "let the magistrates be laboring men; and
therefore should we be magistrates" (IV.ii.8–9, 17–18)—the rebels' political program addresses the same issues and expresses
the same utopian dreams that animated popular riots and rebellions in early modern England.[12] Cade even echoes John
Ball's famous and often-repeated slogan from the fourteenth-
century Peasants' Revolt: "When Adam delv'd and Eve span; /
Who was then a gentleman?" (IV.ii.134).[13]

[11]Wilfred Hooper, "The Tudor Sumptuary Laws," *English Historical Review*
30 (1915), 433–49, points out (p. 436) that "The reign of Elizabeth marks an era
of unprecedented activity in the history of restraints on apparel." At the same
time, Thomas Platter noted that "the comedians are most expensively and
elegantly apparelled, since it is customary in England, when distinguished
gentlemen or knights die, for nearly the finest of their clothes to be made over
and given to their servants, and as it is not proper for them to wear such
clothes but only to imitate them, they give them to the comedians to purchase
for a small sum." The passage comes from Platter's description of his travels
1595–1600, the translation by E. K. Chambers in *The Elizabethan Stage* (Oxford:
Clarendon Press, 1923), 2:365.

[12]Michael Bristol, *Carnival and Theater: Plebeian Culture and the Structure of
Authority in Renaissance England* (London: Methuen, 1985), pp. 89–90.

[13]Cf. Raphael Holinshed, *Chronicles of England, Scotland and Ireland* (1587; rpt.
London: J. Johnson et al., 1808), 2:749.

In 1 *Henry VI*, the threat of contemporary domestic disorder is displaced onto historical French women. The plebeian men in 2 *Henry VI* bring the threat home to sixteenth-century England when they literalize and specify the objects of the anxieties that the women symbolically represent. When Bedford complains that Margaret's marriage to Henry VI will blot noble English "names from books of memory," raze "the characters of [their] renown," and deface the "monuments of conquer'd France" (2 *Henry VI*: I.i.100–102), he speaks metaphorically. Cade literalizes the threat when he commands, "Burn all the records of the realm, my mouth shall be the parliament of England" (IV.vii.12–14). Unlike the metaphorical erasure that Bedford describes, Cade's burning is a material act of destruction: if Cade has his way, the historical records will literally burn, and so will London Bridge and the Tower (IV.vi.13–15).[14]

Joan's nominalism and her earthy, skeptical speech consituted a discursive antithesis to the patriarchal historographic tradition whose mystifications she threatened to discredit. In the hands of Cade and his followers, Joan's subversive, antihistorical project takes the literal form of a class rebellion. Cade's command to burn the historical records and tear down the historical monuments not only specifies the literal objects he wishes to destroy; it also specifies the present political significance of his antihistorical project and recognizes the function of historical writing in the world of the Tudors as a basis for an oppressive present authority. The collection and systematizing of legal records supplied a crucial instrument for the Tudor effort to construct an absolutist state. Collected, translated into English, and printed, the "Great Boke of Statutes" with its forty-six page "chronological register by chapters of the statutes 1327 to 1523" not only provided a systematic review of parliamentary history; it also produced an authoritative source for legal reference. Royal proclamations, "no longer merely fixed to walls and doors and other

---

[14]All the objects of Cade's destruction—the ancient monuments and the learned men, no less than the written records—are preservers of the history that Cade sets out to obliterate. Holinshed's complaint about the 1381 rebels makes this connection explicit: "Could they have a more mischeefous meaning, than to burne and destroie all old and ancient monuments, and to murther and dispatch out of the waie all such as were able to commit to memorie, either any new or old records?"(2:746).

public places," were for the first time brought together in "a convenient octavo volume and furnished with a table of contents." Codifying and making systematic previously scattered and contradictory records, sixteenth-century legal history was more than an academic exercise; it constituted a powerful instrument of control.[15]

The list of Cade's intended victims—"all scholars, lawyers, courtiers, gentlemen" (IV.iv.36)—makes explicit the association between learning, law, and privilege. The rebels attack lawyers, the literate, and the elite with equal enthusiasm. The "first thing" they plan to do is "kill all the lawyers" (IV.ii.76–77). Their first victim is the clerk of Chartam, accused of knowing how to "write and read and cast accompt," of having "a book in his pocket," and, worst of all, of possessing the ability to "make obligations, and write court-hand." The clerk confesses only that he knows how to write his own name, but that is enough to condemn him. Inverting the elite privilege of "benefit of clergy" which allowed literate prisoners who could recite a Latin "neck-verse" to escape hanging, Cade orders his followers to hang the clerk "with his pen and inkhorn about his neck" (IV.ii.85–110).[16]

The fullest expression of the rebels' fury is reserved for Lord Say, the most aristocratic of their victims and also the one most fully identified with language and learning. Initially condemned because he can speak French (IV.ii.166), Lord Say is later charged by Cade with a full spectrum of offenses against illiteracy:

> Thou hast most traitorously corrupted the youth of the realm in erecting a grammar school; and whereas, before, our forefathers had no other books but the score and the tally, thou hast caus'd

[15]Elizabeth L. Eisenstein, *The Printing Press as an Agent of Change: Communications and Cultural Transformations in Early-Modern Europe* (Cambridge: Cambridge University Press, 1979; paperback reprint, 1982), pp. 104–5. Cf. Jack Goody's argument, in *The Logic of Writing and the Organization of Society* (Cambridge: Cambridge University Press, 1986), p. 167, that "while customary law is local, written law generalizes." See also Benedict Anderson's analysis, in *Imagined Communities: Reflections on the Origin and Spread of Nationalism* (London: Verso, 1983), of the role of print culture in the creation of nation-states.

[16]Cf. act IV, scene vii, lines 43–46, where Cade charges that the Lord Say has put poor men "in prison, and because they could not read, [has] hang'd them, when, indeed, only for that cause they have been most worthy to live."

printing to be us'd, and, contrary to the King, his crown, and
dignity, thou hast built a paper-mill. It will be prov'd to thy face
that thou hast men about thee that usually talk of a noun and a
verb, and such abominable words as no Christian ear can endure
to hear. (IV.vii.32–41).

Cade's anachronistic references to the paper-mill and printing
identify the historical treasurer of Henry VI with the emergent
culture of printing and literacy. The appropriately named Say
answers eloquently, but Say's use of a Latin phrase (the mark
of his identification with humanist learning) increases Cade's
fury, and his citation of Caesar's *Commentaries* does nothing to
allay it. Cade is momentarily stirred by Say's words, but he
bridles his own remorse and orders, "He shall die, and it be
but for pleading so well for his life" (IV.vii.106–07).

The rebels are finally routed, appropriately, by a word. When
Clifford invokes history—the English conquest of France under
Henry V—Cade's followers desert him for the king. As Cade
says, "The name of Henry the Fift hales them to an hundred
mischiefs, and makes them leave me desolate" (IV.viii.56–58).
But Cade's own death is complicated by another kind of oral
deprivation, the lack of food. A starving fugitive, Cade dies in
a final act of transgression when he steals into Alexander Iden's
garden to look for food. Caught and killed by the landowner,
he declares, "Famine and no other hath slain me" (IV.x.60).

There is no reference to famine in Hall, who describes Iden's
exploit as a lesson to rebels and traitors: "One Alexander Iden,
esquire of Kent found hym in a garden, and there in his defence,
manfully slewe the caitife Cade, & brought his ded body to
London, whose hed was set on London bridge. This is the
successe of all rebelles, and this fortune chaunceth ever to tray-
tors.''[17] Shakespeare's expanded representation of the incident
exhibits the same moral valences, but with significant compli-
cations. Iden enters announcing himself as an emblematic representation of a virtuous country gentleman, content with "this
small inheritance my father left me," never seeking "to wax
great by others' waning, / Or gather wealth," always ready to
send "the poor well pleased from my gate" (IV.x.18–23). Un-
aware of Cade's identity, he refuses at first to fight with the

---

[17]Hall, *Union*, p. 222.

poor, starving vagabond he finds in his garden, but when Cade insists, Iden easily kills the belligerent trespasser.

No sooner does Iden learn that the man he has killed is "that monstrous traitor" Cade (IV.x.66), than he reconceives his act in terms consistent with Hall's ideological history, transforming his deed from a defense of private property to a heroic victory in defense of his king and defining it in traditional chivalric terms, the sword that won it as a historical monument and a heraldic emblem of honor:

> Sword, I will hallow thee for this thy deed,
> And hang thee o'er my tomb when I am dead.
> Ne'er shall this blood be wiped from thy point,
> But thou shalt wear it as a herald's coat,
> To emblaze the honor that thy master got.
>
> (IV.x.67–71)

Cade, by contrast, insists that he has been "vanquish'd by famine, not by valor" (IV.x.75), invoking the present material reality of hunger to demystify the historical account.

The alternative explanations for Iden's victory oppose the material effects of hunger to the emblematic language of heraldry. Iden mystifies his victory as an acquisition of chivalric honor, but Cade dies reaffirming his commoner's faith in the power of things and distrust for the validity of noble words. His last speech is an exhortation to "all the world to be cowards; for I, that never fear'd any, am vanquish'd by famine, not by valor" (IV.x.74–75). This opposition between eating, food, and cowardice on the one hand and the historical record of military valor on the other is deeply embedded in Shakespeare's historiographic discourse. It appears, for instance, in the second scene of *1 Henry VI* when Alanson doubts that the English will win at Orleans because "They want their porridge and their fat bull-beeves"(I.ii.9). When the English do win, he invokes the historical record to account for their victory: "Froissard, a countryman of ours, records / England all Olivers and Rolands bred / During the time Edward the Third did reign. / More truly now may this be verified" (I.ii.29–32). Froissart's historical account is verified not simply by the heroism of the English soldiers but by their ability to do without food: "Lean raw-bon'd rascals!

who would e'er suppose / They had such courage and audacity?" (I.ii.35–36).

The antithesis that sets aristocratic military valor and historical validity in opposition to plebeian hunger mystifies class conflict even as it points to its material roots.[18] It has an ideological basis in the system of analogies that rationalized the social hierarchy. The aristocracy, like the lofty, immaterial soul, has no need for earthly food; the plebeians, like the base, material body, cannot live without it.[19] The antithesis also has a material basis in the food riots that repeatedly erupted in early modern England.[20] Like the rebellious mob inspired by Jack Cade's promises of "seven halfpenny loaves sold for a penny," "three-hoop'd" pots with "ten hoops" (IV.ii.65–67), and "the pissing-conduit run[ning] nothing but claret wine" (IV.vi.3–4), real peasants who rebelled in early modern England were motivated by famine. Cade's ruthless demands for universal leveling expressed the fears of the ruling elite, but his promises of abundant food, low prices, and the abolition of enclosures (IV.ii.68–70) address genuine grievances that created actual hunger among the poor.

Cade's promise of lower prices addresses the horror of infla-

[18]Consistently invoked as a proof of aristocratic valor, the ability to do without food also distinguishes noble warriors from cowardly plebeians in *Coriolanus*, where, as Janet Adelman has pointed out, the issue of food forms the basis of the class conflict, and "nobility consists precisely in *not* eating." See her "Feeding, Dependency, and Aggression in *Coriolanus*," in *Representing Shakespeare: New Psychoanalytic Essays*, ed. Murray M. Schwartz and Coppélia Kahn (Baltimore: Johns Hopkins University Press, 1980), p. 132. See also Maurice Charney, "The Imagery of Food and Eating in *Coriolanus*," *Essays in Literary History*, ed. Rudolf Kirk and C. F. Main (New Brunswick: Rutgers University Press, 1960), pp. 37–55.

[19]As David Kastan reminds me, the plebeians' need for food associates them with the Bakhtinian grotesque body. See Mikhail Bakhtin, *Rabelais and His World*, trans. Hélène Iswolsky (Bloomington: Indiana University Press, 1984), pp. 278–367. And as Frank Whigham points out: "The gentleman cares more about the reified tangibles of reputation than about material needs. . . . The gentleman is materially ascetic; any such 'pleasures' are merely instrumental to governance. At the same time, he is as ferocious in defense (and pursuit) of reputation as the starveling is in search of food." *Ambition and Privilege: The Social Tropes of Elizabethan Courtesy Theory* (Berkeley: University of California Press, 1984), p. 77.

[20]For an account of food riots in sixteenth- and seventeenth-century England, see Wrightson, *English Society 1580–1680*, pp.173–82. Wrightson points out (pp. 173–74) that government records indicate "some forty outbreaks of [food riots] in the period 1585–1660."

tion in an era of rising population, which produced an over-supply of labor and a scarcity of food. Keith Wrightson points out that the "average prices of foodstuffs in southern England, which had remained fairly stable throughout the later fifteenth century, had trebled by the 1570s, and by the early decades of the seventeenth century they had risen sixfold." This rapid inflation of food prices, most pronounced in the case of the cheaper foods (that is, in the sustenance of the poor), was coupled with a steady decline in real wages, which, by the first quarter of the seventeenth century were half what they had been a hundred years earlier.[21] Enclosure of common land, another grievance to the poor, took away traditional grazing and hunting rights and dispossessed tenant farmers in order to provide pastures for wealthy sheepfarmers.[22]

Despite the present reality of the grievances that Cade's rebellion expresses, Shakespeare's London audience is not very likely to have sympathized with his plans. He threatens to destroy their city's famous monuments: "First go and set London Bridge on fire, and if you can, burn down the Tower too . . . the Savoy . . . the Inns of Court; down with them all" (IV.vi.14–15; vii.1–2). When Cade promises that "all the realm shall be in common, and in Cheapside shall my palfrey go to grass" (IV.ii.68–69), he opposes the process of enclosure that oppressed the rural poor, but he also threatens to transform the chief commercial street of Shakespeare's London audience into a common pasture.[23]

Cade's rebellion took place in 1450, and Shakespeare's representation of it draws heavily on accounts of the even earlier Peasants' Revolt led by Wat Tyler in 1381. Nonetheless, Shakespeare loads the rebels' speeches with anachronistic references to current grievances and literal places that serve to localize the

[21]*English Society 1580–1680*, p. 125.

[22]On Shakespeare's own involvement in the enclosure of land near Stratford, see Terence Hawkes, *That Shakespeherian Rag: Essays on a Critical Process* (London: Methuen, 1986), pp. 7–10. On the enclosure riots, see Wrightson, pp. 173–80, and Underdown, *Revel, Riot and Rebellion*, pp. 107–16.

[23]Cf. Alexander Leggatt, *Shakespeare's Political Drama: The History Plays and the Roman Plays* (London: Routledge, 1988), p. 17. Arguing that Shakespeare's representation of Cade's rebellion foregrounds "the anarchy that is the dark side of carnival," Leggatt points out that "the first London audiences must have felt the threat more sharply as it crept toward familiar places."

action in sixteenth-century England; and his representation of the struggle between Cade and Iden focuses on an issue that produced real suffering and real social unrest in his own time: the conflict between the traditional right of the starving poor to be fed and the emergent ethos of private property that gave the rich an absolute right to enclose and defend their own land. As Christopher Hill has shown, a world where "the employment of industrious laborers" was replacing "the maintenance of loyal dependants" as the way to prosperity could no longer sustain the older ideal of hospitality which was increasingly supplanted by poor laws designed as much to discourage idleness and dependency as to succor the needy.[24] The old distributive justice, which required that in cases of famine or extreme need the human right to sustain life must take precedence over private property rights, gave way to a new justice of *suum cuique*, which gave property owners an unconditional right to defend what was theirs, even by force.[25]

Iden's initial declaration that he "sends the poor well pleased from my gate" associates him with the old, benevolent tradition, but Cade's final statement that he was "vanquish'd by famine, not by valor" associates him with the starving victims of a changing economy and a harsh new ideology of private property (IV.x.23, 75). As Stephen Greenblatt points out, the "aristocrat has given way to the man of property," the contest "between an aristocrat and a churl" to a contest between "a well-fed owner of property and a 'poor famished man.'"[26] Nonetheless, Shakespeare contrives his representation of the incident to vindicate Iden's act and obscure the novelty of the ethos it represents.[27]

---

[24]"The Poor and the Parish," in *Society and Puritanism in Pre-Revolutionary England* (New York: Penguin Books, 1986), pp. 263–65.

[25]Istvan Hont and Michael Ignatieff, eds., *Wealth and Virtue: The Shaping of Political Economy in the Scottish Enlightenment* (Cambridge: Cambridge University Press, 1983), pp. 27–29.

[26]"Murdering Peasants: Status, Genre, and the Representation of Rebellion," in *Representing the English Renaissance* (Berkeley: University of California Press, 1988; originally published in *Representations* 1 [1983]), p. 25. See also pp. 23–25 for a provocative reading of the encounter between Iden and Cade as a transformation of status relations into property relations.

[27]Iden's self-characterization as a virtuous, hospitable country gentleman, content with his small patrimony and disdainful of worldly ambition, anticipates the construction and ideological functions of the ideal of civic humanism described by J. G. A. Pocock in *The Machiavellian Moment: Florentine Political*

Like the English gentleman he repeatedly declares himself to be, Iden refuses at first to fight with the starving vagabond: "Nay, it shall ne'er be said, while England stands, / That Alexander Iden, an esquire of Kent, / Took odds to combat a poor famish'd man" (IV.x.42–44).[28] He fights only when Cade insists. Moreover, Iden never describes his act as a defense of his own private property; instead, he defines it in the old feudal terms as service to his king and the killing of a "monstrous traitor."

Shakespeare's representation of Iden's act and his character rationalizes a new source of status, the ownership of private property, in the emblems of an older world: the "inheritance my father left me" (IV.x.18), the hospitality that fed the poor, and the "herald's coat" to which Iden likens the bloody sword with which he killed Cade (IV.x.70).[29] Thus, despite the vividness of Cade's characterization and the real social ills his rebellion addresses, Cade is finally reduced to a mechanism for ideological containment. Shakespeare's representation of Cade invokes the stereotypes of murdering thief and comic villain,

---

*Thought and the Atlantic Republican Tradition* (Princeton: Princeton University Press, 1975) and *The Ancient Constitution and the Feudal Law* (Cambridge: Cambridge University Press, 1957) and celebrated by Alexander Pope in his "Ode on Solitude."

[28]The fact that both Cade and Iden are Kentishmen, so designated in the chronicles and so named in Shakespeare's script, provides an especially resonant setting for their contest. "Gavelkind," the Kentish custom of inheritance by equal shares, and the absence of villeinage in Kent both associated it with the new economic order. Even in the fifteenth century, Paul Murray Kendall reports, "Kent was famous for its heavy cloth," and the forests were thinned, their wood providing "fuel for iron and glass works. . . . Beer supposedly came into England with the Reformation, but it was already being brewed in Kent. . . . Situated on the route from London to the Continent, Kentishmen were an efficient and progressive race. . . . [Instead of] the manorial tradition of tilling open fields . . . [Kent had] enclosed holdings . . . the land so tightly hedged and ditched . . . that travellers afoot or on horseback could not cut across fields but had to keep strictly to the highways." *The Yorkist Age: Daily Life during the Wars of the Roses* (New York: Doubleday, 1962), pp. 2–3.

[29]See Lawrence Stone, *The Crisis of the Aristocracy, 1558–1641* (Oxford: Clarendon Press, 1965), pp. 22–23, where he discusses Coke's project of "making radical political notions respectable by dressing them up in garbled medieval precedents: "Because of [the] crushing burden of belief in the need for social stability, all change had to be interpreted as the maintenance of tradition. In religion the reformation was defended as a return to the early church; in politics, parliamentary sovereignty was defended as the enforcement of fourteenth-century customs; in society the rise of new men was disguised by forged genealogies and the grant of titles of honour."

the first to project and the second to defuse the anxieties of privileged property owners who could find a flattering portrait of themselves in Alexander Iden, the virtuous country gentleman. Like the historical English kings and noblemen of the first tetralogy, and unlike Cade and the other commoners, Shakespeare's Iden is never comic. Among the wellborn characters in the first tetralogy, only the French and the villainous Richard III are tainted by the comedy that marks the commoners and contains their subversive power.

The ethical distinction between the "noble" and the "ignoble" and the generic distinctions between comedy and tragedy were deeply implicated in the divisions that separated "gentlemen" of high birth and good character from the "clowns" and "villains" who, because they lacked the first, were required by the principles of dramatic decorum to be represented as lacking the second as well. When Sidney objected to the "mongrel tragicomedy" that mingled "kings and clowns," he was objecting at least as much to the social transgression involved in thrusting in a clown "to play a part in majestical matters" as he was to the violation of the divisions that separated dramatic genres. The two, in fact, could hardly be separated.[30] From the time of Aristotle, the generic divisions that separated comedy from both tragedy and history were bound up with the social divisions that separated high from low. Like history, tragedy dealt with great deeds and great men. Comedy was the medium for representing the base, in both senses of the word. When Aristotle wrote, "Comedy aims at representing men as worse, Tragedy as better than in actual life," the terms he used, *kheirous* ("worse") and *beltious* ("better") referred as much to differences

---

[30]*Sir Philip Sidney's Defense of Poesy*, ed. Lewis Soens (Lincoln: University of Nebraska Press, 1970), p. 49. Sidney's argument, although expressed in terms of dramatic decorum, is obviously based on the requirements of social decorum: "But besides these gross absurdities, how all their plays be neither right tragedies nor right comedies, mingling kings and clowns, not because the matter so carries it but thrust in the clown by head and shoulders to play a part in majestical matters with neither decency nor discretion." See also Dympna Callaghan, *Women and Gender in Renaissance Tragedy: A Study of "King Lear," "Othello," "The Duchess of Malfi" and "The White Devil"* (Atlantic Highlands, N.J.: Humanities Press International, 1989), p. 37: "Tragedy was privileged over comedy by the likes of Sidney and Puttenham precisely because of an identification of genre with class."

in social status as they did to differences in ethical character.[31] In English no less than in Greek the ethical distinctions between better and worse, the social distinctions between high and low, and the categories of dramatic decorum are all conflated in words like "villain" and "clown."

The same discursive oppositions that separated tragedy from comedy associated it with history. For Aristotle, the tragic protagonist "must be one who is highly renowned and prosperous—a personage like Oedipus, Thyestes, or other illustrious men of such families" (*Poetics* XIII). He must also be historical: unlike comic poets, who first construct their plots and then insert "characteristic names," "tragedians still keep to real names" (*Poetics* IX). The same contrast between tragic history and comic fiction appears in Lope de Vega's distinction: "For a subject tragedy has history and comedy has feigning."[32] In *The Arte of English Poesie* (1589) the conflation of social status with ethical value that marks the difference between comedy and tragedy is used to explain the absence of "meane & base personages" from historical writing:

> Now because the actions of meane & base personages tend in very few cases to any great good example; for who passeth to follow the steps and maner of life of a craftes man, shepheard, or sailer, though he were his father or dearest frend? yea how almost is it possible that such maner of men should be of any vertue other than their profession requireth? therefore was nothing committed to historie but matters of great and excellent persons & things.[33]

Shakespeare's representations of plebeian characters in the first tetralogy tend, in the last analysis, to reproduce the aristocratic bias he found in historical source and dramatic convention alike. Plebeian characters constitute a significant presence

---

[31]*Poetics* II.4 in *Aristotle's Theory of Poetry and Fine Art*, ed. S. H. Butcher, 4th ed. (New York: Dover, 1951), pp. 12–13.

[32]*The New Art of Making Comedies* (1609), in *Literary Criticism: Plato to Dryden*, ed. Allen H. Gilbert (Detroit: Wayne State University Press, 1962), p. 543.

[33]*The Arte of English Poesie. Contrived into three Bookes: The first of Poets and Poesie, the second of Proportion, the third of Ornament* (London: Richard Field, 1589), Book I, chap. 19, in *Elizabethan Critical Essays*, ed. G. Gregory Smith (London: Oxford University Press, 1904), 2:43. Although the text was published anonymously, it is usually attributed to George Puttenham.

in 2 *Henry VI*, but their characterization, their roles, and their interests are finally determined by the requirements of the historical plot and the conventions of dramatic representation, subsumed under hegemonic structures that expressed the interests of the elite. Shakespeare's management of the enclosure issue provides a good illustration of this process. The issue is introduced for the first time in act I, scene iii, when the poor petitioners attempt to protest the enclosure of the Melford commons. Designated only as "1 *Petit.*" and "2 *Petit.*," the petitioners have no names and only a few lines to speak (I.iii.1–24). The dramatic purpose of the episode is to display the vices and virtues of the elite characters, who are also the leading actors in the dramatic plot; its ideological purpose is to drive home a moral lesson that has nothing to do with the rights and needs of the oppressed villagers. Suffolk, the corrupt and haughty courtier responsible for the enclosure, intercepts their petition. The equally corrupt and haughty queen, Suffolk's adulterous lover, destroys it. The dramatic purpose of the episode is to raise the audience's antipathy toward Suffolk and Margaret. Its ideological purpose is to absolve the older aristocracy, represented by the good Duke of Gloucester (to whom the petition is addressed) of blame for the unpopular enclosures and to fix it on parvenu courtiers like Suffolk.

The last we hear about the issue of enclosure is Cade's preposterous demand that "all the realm shall be in common, and in Cheapside shall my palfrey go to grass" (IV.ii.68–69), a proposal so outrageous as to discredit the real grievances it addressed. Even Cade does not finally or fully speak for himself. As York's pawn and alter ego, he follows a scenario of York's devising, a plot laid out in soliloquy by York before Cade ever reaches the stage (III.i.355–81). As Shakespeare's, he proposes a revolution so radical and so ludicrous that it discredits the just grievances it addresses.

Unlike the rebellion scenes in *Sir Thomas More*, the ones in 2 *Henry VI* appear to have escaped censorship.[34] Potentially subversive, they seem finally designed to justify oppression. Dissident sentiments are first evoked, then discredited and demonized as sources of anxiety, and finally defused in comic

[34]Clare, p. 173.

ridicule and brutal comic violence. The first representation of popular protest—the appearance of the humble petitioners in act I, scene iii—is fully sympathetic. In act II, scene i., initial sympathy gives way to comic debasement. Simpcox and his wife, (like Joan before them), enter the stage of history, an assembly of royalty and nobles, claiming to be the recipients of heavenly grace; and even after their hoax is exposed, Simpcox's wife, like the starving Cade, is allowed a moment of self-justification when she explains, "Alas, sir, we did it for pure need" (II.i.153). Nonetheless, it is the just and admirable Duke of Gloucester who exposes the hoax, first by the clever questions that disprove Simpcox's claim to have been born blind, then by the simple expedient of having him whipped until he leaps and runs to disprove his claim to be lame. Apparently designed to dissipate in brutal comedy whatever sympathy Simpcox has managed to elicit, the violence that removes Simpcox from the stage also anticipates Jack Cade's onstage slaughter at the hands of Iden, the only other character in the play as unequivocally virtuous as Gloucester.[35]

In the first tetralogy, the subversive potential of these characters is finally contained, but it is never fully effaced. The real presence of common men on Shakespeare's stage gave them a

---

[35]The same design can be seen in the transformation of Joan's character in 1 *Henry VI*. Hall had described Joan as a "wytch" who told such "visions, traunses and fables, full of blasphemy, supersticion and hypocrisy, that I marvell much that wise men did beleve her, and lerned clerkes would write suche phantasies" and reported with indignant skepticism, "What should I reherse, how they saie, she knewe and called hym her kyng, whom she never saw before. What should I speake how she had by reuelacion a swerde, to her appoynted in the churche of saincte Katheryn . . . in Torayne where she neuer had been" (*Union*, p. 148). Shakespeare's initial representation of Joan (I.ii.) subverts the received judgment of English history: he validates the story of the sword by having Joan use it to defeat the Dauphin in single combat to prove her claim to divine inspiration. He also validates the story of Joan's miraculous recognition of the Dauphin, dramatizing it as present action on stage, embellishing it and making Joan's task more difficult by having the Dauphin attempt to conceal his identity. At the end of the play, however, he shows his Joan consorting with evil spirits, attempting to escape death by claiming she is pregnant, and generally vindicating all the worst charges that the English chroniclers and the English characters in the play have brought against her, thus coming to terms with a historiographic tradition that was at once masculine, elite, and English.

uniquely privileged status in dramatic performance. Opposing the transgressions of theatrical practice to the repressions of official discourse, the roles of common men in dramatic production provided the basis for the most radical challenge to those repressions. This challenge is implicit even in the opening lines in the first rebellion scene in 2 *Henry VI*—"Come and get thee a sword, though made of a lath" (IV.ii.1–2)—which allude to the strip of lath used by the Vice in the morality plays, thus reducing the sword represented within the frame of dramatic illusion to the stage property that represented it. The sword of lath, like the speech heading that assigned those lines to George Bevis, undermines dramatic illusion and with it historical representation to insist on the material reality of theatrical performance.

Like Joan, Cade was based on a historical prototype; like hers, his identity as a demonic other who threatened the established order was probably too firmly implicated in English historical mythology to be altered. For the three plays of the *Henriad*, however, Shakespeare invented a series of fictional commoners who challenge the dominant ideology at a level much more profound than Joan or Cade ever achieves. Segregated by generic restrictions, the plebeian characters in the first tetralogy can rebel against their oppression, but they can never finally transcend the conventions of comic representation that keep them in their social place and mark their separation from the serious historical world of their betters. In the second tetralogy, by contrast, these distinctions break down. Although *Richard II* is constructed as a tragedy (and designated as a tragedy on the title pages of the Quartos), the comic scenes that occupy most of its fifth act are performed not by plebeian clowns but by the Duke and Duchess of York and the King of England.[36] In the Henry IV plays, even the dramatic structure that shapes the historical action becomes comic, and the future king who is the play's protagonist acts the comic part of madcap and speaks the plebeian language of colloquial prose. Falstaff acts the king in Eastcheap, and Prince Harry acts the clown. Both

---

[36]For a discussion of the comic degradation of noble characters in these scenes, see Chapter 3.

step out of the places dictated by the doubly determined decorum of social and dramatic convention.[37] Destabilizing dramatic representations by an increasing metadramatic self-consciousness, the last three plays in the second tetralogy exploit the subversive potential implicit in the very act of theatrical performance to expose the limitations of historical writing.

— II —

Adapting written historiographic narratives designed to justify hereditary privilege for oral performance by common players who made their living by stepping out of their hereditary roles to impersonate kings and nobles, Shakespeare's history plays were situated at the margins of opposed discourses. Generic hybrids, they straddled the boundaries that divided past from present, writing from speech, fact from fiction, and nobles from commoners.[38] Written at a time when a new sense of temporality made the past seem alien and irrecoverable, they mediated between the absent past of historical representation and the embodied presence of theatrical speech. Translating the univocal historical writing that obscured contradictions into the polyphonic theatrical scripts that projected them into dramatic conflict, they enacted, by their very form, the tensions and struggles that shaped the heterogeneous, changing world in which they were produced. Speaking with a variety of voices, ranging from elevated literary verse to slangy colloquial prose, they constituted an arena for ideological contest. Their sources came from a historiographic tradition predisposed to justify hereditary privilege, but the plays were written for a new com-

[37]Their displacement may very well have been literal as well as symbolic. In the light of Robert Weimann's suggestion that different positions on the Elizabethan stage were associated with different modes of speech, action, and social rank as well as different relations between actors and theater audiences, Hal's movement from the historical court of Henry IV to the Boar's Head Tavern can also be seen as a movement from the elevated *locus* of theatrical representation to the *platea* of plebeian theatrical performance. See *Shakespeare and the Popular Tradition*, pp. 73–85, 224–26 and "Bifold Authority," pp. 409–10.

[38]For a brilliant Marxist analysis of the interaction between popular and learned culture in Shakespeare's theater, see Walter Cohen, *Drama of a Nation: Public Theater in Renaissance England and Spain* (Ithaca: Cornell University Press, 1985).

mercial theater where socially heterogeneous audiences were assigned their places not by the prerogatives of hereditary status, but simply by the price each person paid for admission. Celebrating the heroic struggles of kings and noblemen and recording their patriarchal genealogies, Renaissance historians provided a rationale for the social hierarchy of their own time. "Mingling Kings and clownes" and making "greatness" much too "familiar," the theater was often perceived as subverting it.[39]

Reading Renaissance historiography, one is hard put to remember that over 95 percent of the population in Shakespeare's England fell below the ranks of the gentry.[40] Like the status system that prescribed elaborate gradations of rank between and among the major and minor nobility but simply ignored the vast majority of the population, Renaissance historians told the story of an elite minority. Ignoring the common details of ordinary life, Shakespeare's historical sources recorded the political and military contests of kings and noblemen. By the fifteenth century, the period in which most of Shakespeare's historical drama is set, wars were fought by immense armies.[41] Nonetheless, the common men who served in those armies remained nameless in the historical accounts, and the conflicts remained focused in the persons of their leaders.

[39]The first quotation comes from Sidney's "Defense," p. 49, the second from Sir Henry Wotton's description of *All is True* (probably Shakespeare's *Henry VIII*), quoted in Chambers, 2:419–20: "The King's players had a new play, called *All Is True*, representing some principal pieces of the reign of Henry VIII, which was set forth with many extraordinary circumstances of pomp and majesty, even to the matting of the stage; the Knights of the Order, with their Georges and garters, the Guards with their embroidered coats, and the like: sufficient in truth within a while to make greatness very familiar, if not ridiculous." Many critics in recent years have explored the subversive implications of theatrical role-playing in the Renaissance, but see especially Louis Adrian Montrose, "The Purpose of Playing: Reflections on a Shakespearean Anthropology," *Helios* n.s. 7.2 (1980), 51–74; Franco Moretti, "'A Huge Eclipse': Tragic Form and the Deconsecration of Sovereignty," *Genre* 15 (1982), 7–40; and Stephen Orgel, "Making Greatness Familiar," in *The Power of Forms in the English Renaissance*, ed. Stephen Greenblatt (Norman, Okla.: Pilgrim Books, 1982), pp. 41–48.

[40]Peter Laslett, *The World We Have Lost*, 2d ed. (New York: Charles Scribner's Sons, 1971), p. 27.

[41]Maurice Keen, *Chivalry* (New Haven: Yale University Press, 1984), pp. 239–40.

Single combat between highborn men was the style of warfare required by chivalric tradition. As Stephen Greenblatt explains,

A heroic encounter is a struggle for honor and must conform to the code which requires that the combatants be of roughly equal station. This requirement . . . [originates] in the symbolic economics of appropriation suggested by the Church of England hymn: "Conquering Kings their titles take/ From the foes they captive make." . . . [Peasants, having] no titles to seize, . . . can yield up no titles to adorn the victor's monument. Indeed, in the economy of honor they are not simply a cipher but a deficit, since even a defeat at the hands of a prince threatens to confer upon them some of the prince's store of honor, while what remains of the victorious prince's store can be tarnished by the unworthy encounter.[42]

Shakespeare plays out the conflict between the pragmatic requirements of actual warfare and the demands of chivalric tradition in his representation of the Battle of Shrewsbury in *1 Henry IV*. In the rebels' dialogue before the battle (IV.i), Worcester worries about the absence of Northumberland and his troops, while Hotspur argues that his father's absence "lends a lustre and more great opinion, / A larger dare to our great enterprise, / Than if the Earl were here." Numbers mean nothing to Hotspur. Vernon anxiously reports that Glendower, like Northumberland, will not be there with his army, that the Earl of Westmerland is marching to support the king with seven thousand soldiers, and that the king's forces number thirty thousand. Hotspur gallantly replies, "Forty let it be! / My father and Glendower being both away, / The powers of us may serve so great a day."

True to chivalric tradition (but not to the chronicle accounts of the battle), Hotspur and Hal offer to settle the conflict between Henry IV and the rebels in single combat. Worcester and Vernon, less honorable and more pragmatic, deceive Hotspur to ensure that the Battle of Shrewsbury will be fought (just as Holinshed reported it had been fought) by the two armies. Shakespeare contrives his account of the battle, however, to culminate in the single combat between the two Harrys, re-

[42]"Murdering Peasants," pp. 10–11. Greenblatt also cites the encounter between Hotspur and Hal at the Battle of Shrewsbury.

casting the political and military struggle between rival factions to stage it as a chivalric contest for honor. Just before they fight, Hotspur tells Hal, "would to God / Thy name in arms were now as great as mine"; and Hal replies, "I'll make a greater ere I part from thee" (V.iv.69–71). In the bright light of Hal's triumph, the thirty thousand men who constitute the pragmatic basis for the victory of the king's forces fade into the background, represented only by Falstaff's solitary account of the fate of his pitiful ragamuffins: "There's not three of my hundred and fifty left alive, and they are for the town's end, to beg during life" (V.iii.36–38).

It is significant, I believe, that Falstaff's ragamuffins, like the common soldiers in the two armies, are represented only by numbers. Enumerating but not naming his troops, Falstaff follows the practice of Renaissance historians. Moreover, in *2 Henry IV*, when we actually see Falstaff recruiting, the poor countrymen he recruits are fictitious characters, invented by Shakespeare. The recourse to fiction is necessary because common soldiers had no place in the historiographic record.[43]

Shakespeare's most compelling representation of the historical imperatives that excluded the common soldiers comes in the fourth act of *Henry V*. In an invented scene on the night before the Battle of Agincourt, both Shakespeare and his protagonist king resort to theatrical fiction, attempting to incorporate the common soldiers in their great historical project. Both end, however, by succumbing to the historical imperatives that erase the names and efface the existence of the common soldiers. To represent the common soldiers in the English army, Shakespeare invents the characters of John Bates, Alexander Court, and Michael Williams, endowing them with names and vivid dramatic voices that complain of the cold and express their fears

---

[43]Cf. Sir Philip Sidney's letter to his brother Robert, 18 October 1580, in *The Prose Works of Sir Philip Sidney*, ed. Albert Feuillerat (Cambridge: Cambridge University Press, 1968), 3:131. The recognition that common people are absent from the historiographic record seems to lie behind Sidney's comment that a historian who wishes to include the common people in his stories must take on the role of a poet: he "makes himself . . . a Poet in painting forth the effects, the motions, the whisperings of the people, which though in disputation one might say were true, yet who will marke them well shall finde them taste of a poeticall vaine, and in that kinde are gallantly to be marked, for though perchance they were not so, yet it is enough they might be so."

of the coming battle. In this same scene, Shakespeare's Henry also resorts to theatrical fiction, disguising himself in a borrowed cloak and posing as a common soldier named "Harry le Roy" to mingle with his men and hear their misgivings about the war.

The scene has no precedent in Shakespeare's historical sources; instead it draws on the theatrical tradition of the king in disguise, often employed in late sixteenth-century English history plays, in which a popular motif was the interaction between a disguised king and fictional commoners.[44] It is only as actors that kings can mingle with common people and only by resorting to theatrical fiction that playwrights can incorporate plebeian characters and plebeian life in their stories. The fictiveness of the scene on the night before Agincourt is necessitated by the exclusions of Renaissance historiography; its theatricality invokes a dramatic tradition that transgressed the boundaries dividing subject from king in a hierarchical society.[45] Only by moving beyond the boundaries of historiographic discourse into the liberties of theatrical invention can Shakespeare find a place for the common soldiers in his historical drama.

On the morning of the battle, Henry resumes his royal role and the blank verse that bespeaks it. The common soldiers, so vividly present the night before, have melted into an anonymous crowd that listens silently on stage, marked only by the stage direction at the beginning of the scene, "*Enter . . . Erpingham with all his host.*" Playwright and king, however, continue their effort to enlist the common soldiers in their great

[44]Anne Barton, "The King Disguised: Shakespeare's *Henry V* and the Comical History," in *The Triple Bond: Plays, Mainly Shakespearean, in Performance*, ed. Joseph G. Price (University Park: Pennsylvania State University Press, 1975), pp. 93–96. The plays Barton describes are *George a Greene, the Pinner of Wakefield, Fair Em, The True Chronicle History of King Leir*, Peele's *Edward I*, and Thomas Heywood's *The First Part of King Edward IV*.

[45]As Barton points out, it also invokes an even older folk tradition recorded in medieval ballads that described meetings between commoner and king: "the wish-dream of a peasantry harried and perplexed by a new . . . impersonal bureaucracy against which the ordinary man seemed to have no redress" (p. 97). In these ballads, as in Dekker's *Shoemaker's Holiday*, king and subjects discover that they share the same values, and the king redresses their grievances. Barton argues, however, that Shakespeare invokes this tradition only in order to discredit it, using "Henry's disguise to summon up the memory of a wistful, naive attitude toward history and the relationship of subject and king which this play rejects as attractive but untrue: a nostalgic but false romanticism" (p. 99).

history-making enterprise. Shakespeare invents a rousing speech in which Henry addresses his troops as a "band of brothers," promising them everlasting fame and the gentle status that will ensure their place in history:

> ... Crispin Crispian shall ne'er go by,
> From this day to the ending of the world,
> But we in it shall be remembered—
> We few, we happy few, we band of brothers;
> For he to-day that sheds his blood with me
> Shall be my brother; be he ne'er so vile,
> This day shall gentle his condition.
>
> (IV.iii.57–63)

But despite Henry's efforts to incorporate the soldiers in his historical project, the written historiographic record finally keeps them out. Once the battle is over, Shakespeare and Henry both turn from dramatic fiction to historical record for an authoritative account of the casualties. Abandoning theatrical invention, Shakespeare turns to Holinshed; and Henry, rather than relying on his own observation of the battle, turns to a document supplied him by a herald. Speaking with the voice of history, playwright and king recite the words of the written records that obliterated the names of the common soldiers who died, just as the battle had snuffed out their lives.

Holinshed's account of the casualties, carefully distinguishing between the gentlemen "of name" and the "meaner sort," reads as follows:

There were slaine in all of the French part to the number of ten thousand men, whereof were princes and noble men bearing baners one hundred twentie and six; to these of knights, esquiers, and gentlemen, so manie as made up the number of eight thousand and foure hundred ... of the meaner sort, not past sixteene hundred. Amongst those of the nobilitie that were slaine, these were the chéefest, Charles lord de la Breth high constable of France, Iaques of Chatilion lord of Dampier admerall of France, the lord Rambures master of the crossebowes, sir Guischard Dolphin great master of France, Iohn duke of Alanson, Anthonie duke of Brabant brother to the duke of Burgognie, Edward duke of Bar, the earle of Nevers an other brother to the duke of Burgognie, with the erles of Marle, Vaudemont, Beaumont, Grandprée, Roussie, Fauconberge, Fois and Lestrake, beside a great number of lords and barons of name.

Of Englishmen, there died at this battell, Edward duke Yorke, the earle of Suffolke, sir Richard Kikelie, and Davie Gamme esquier, and of all other not above five and twentie persons, as some doo report.[46]

Henry quotes almost verbatim from Holinshed when he reads from the herald's report the names and titles of French noblemen who were killed:

> Charles Delabreth, High Constable of France,
> Jacques of Chatillion, Admiral of France,
> The master of the cross-bows, Lord Rambures,
> Great Master of France, the brave Sir Guichard Dolphin,
> John Duke of Alanson, Anthony Duke of Brabant,
> The brother to the Duke of Burgundy,
> And Edward Duke of Bar; of lusty earls,
> Grandpré and Roussi, Faulconbridge and Foix,
> Beaumont and Marle, Vaudemont and Lestrake.
>
> (IV.viii.92–100)

Still following Holinshed's account and still reading from the herald's note, Henry next recites the list of English dead, again giving the full names and titles of the noblemen who were killed, but when he comes to the common soldiers, all he can find is a body count:

> Edward the Duke of York, the Earl of Suffolk,
> Sir Richard Ketly, Davy Gam, esquire;
> None else of name; and of all other men
> But five and twenty.
>
> (IV.viii.103–6)

Lost to history as well as to life, the five and twenty dead English "brothers," brought to life by Shakespeare's theatrical invention, have become the "others" of Holinshed's historical record.

Reading from the official tally, Henry can report only the number of the common soldiers who were killed fighting for him, even though he can supply both names and titles for the French nobles who died on the other side. The fictional

---

[46]Holinshed, 3:83.

scene before the battle and Henry's fictional exhortation to his army expose the real dependency that fifteenth- and sixteenth-century monarchs had on the common soldiers who fought in their wars. The ideologically motivated exclusions of historical writing, which Shakespeare found in Holinshed's text and reproduced in the herald's report, repress that dependency, reducing the soldiers to anonymous enumeration and recording only the names of aristocrats. Shakespeare reproduces Holinshed's exclusions, but he also marks them: the aristocratic names and titles and the plebeian numbers in the herald's report are Holinshed's, but the poignantly resonant phrase "none else of name" is Shakespeare's, emphasizing that the common English soldiers, unlike the nobles who died in both the armies, have no names in the historical record.[47]

It is appropriate that a herald presents Henry with the written document that excludes the names of the common soldiers. Medieval heralds did in fact perform such functions on medieval battlefields, identifying the gentlemen who fell by reading their coats of arms. Moreover, heraldry was closely associated not only with the historically rationalized status system that distinguished gentlemen from commoners but also with naming itself. Heraldic devices often played on the family names of their bearers—a luce for Sir Richard Lucy, butlers' cups for Sir John le Botiler, and so on—a practice that Shakespeare parodies in 2 *Henry VI* when Jack Cade attempts to establish a genealogy that will entitle him to the throne:

*Cade.* My father was a Mortimer—
*Dick.* [*Aside.*] He was an honest man, and a good bricklayer.
*Cade.* My mother a Plantagenet—
*Dick.* [*Aside.*] I knew her well, she was a midwife.
*Cade.* My wife descended of the Lacies—
*Dick.* [*Aside*] She was indeed a pedlar's daughter, and sold many laces. (IV.ii.39–45)

[47]Cf. the beginning of *Much Ado About Nothing*, written at about the same time as *Henry V* (both plays were marked "to be staied" in the *Stationers' Register*, 4 August 1600). In response to Leonato's question, "How many gentlemen have you lost in this action?" a messenger replies, "But few of any sort, and none of name."

A famous medieval treatise on heraldry, *De insigniis et armis,* made the connection explicit, stating "that men were as free to take arms . . . as they were to take names."[48] The same exclusions governed both.

Without property or status to bequeath, commoners had no place in the genealogically constructed historical records that were designed to trace the transmission of property and status from one generation to the next. The same connection between namelessness and lack of property and status can be seen in *Richard II,* when the newly deposed king, deprived of his throne and detached from the genealogical chain of hereditary status, complains that he has lost his name along with his crown: "I have no name, no title, / No, not that name was given me at the font, / But 'tis usurp'd" (IV.i.255–57).[49]

In Shakespeare's own time it was the College of Heralds which established the genealogies that distinguished the gentle from the mean and rationalized new wealth in terms of hereditary status. As Maurice Keen points out, heraldic devices began in the twelfth century as insignia for identifying warriors encased in armor but quickly became "infused with powerful overtones of pride of lineage," marking the hereditary ownership of land as well as "esteem for martial achievement."[50] Increasingly detached from its original military function, by Shake-

---

[48]Keen, p. 130.

[49]Richard's complaint, of course, is hyperbolic, and it is not finally vindicated, for it denies the power of history. Bullingbrook usurps Richard's hereditary throne, but he never becomes Richard's legitimate heir: possession alone is not sufficient to establish entitlement. Richard's name and his bloodily contested historical legacy will both play important roles in the troubled history of his Lancastrian successors. This contested relationship between the power of present possession and the authority of historical entitlement underlies all Shakespeare's history plays except for *Henry VIII,* not only the rebellions against Henry IV and the conflict between France and England in *King John* but also the entire contention between Lancaster and York. It first surfaces in *1 Henry VI* when Richard Plantagenet, deprived of his ancestral titles and possessions by his father's execution for treason, is subjected to Somerset's taunts in the Temple Garden that he is a mere "yeoman." Warwick answers the attack by an appeal to history: reciting the names and titles of Plantagenet's grandfather and great-grandfather, he concludes, "Spring crestless yeomen from so deep a root?" (*1 Henry VI*: II.iv.81–85). In the following scene, the appeal to history is reinforced by Mortimer's detailed account of Plantagenet's royal genealogy, a narrative that begins with Richard's deposition (II.v.63–86).

[50]Keen, p. 132.

speare's time the heraldic crest that symbolized a family's status was rooted in new wealth as well as old blood and inherited property. It was also rooted in writing. Heralds had become historians, keepers of genealogical records, and they had also become monitors of the status system. The interrupted narrative of Cade's bogus genealogy subverts the learned tradition at the same time that it subverts the genealogical myths, both discursive rationalizations for elite privilege. Dick's puns invoke the body to subvert the word, invoke the base to subvert the elite.

Wealth and property formed the basis for status, but titles and historical records were required to verify it. Whatever their wealth, people without genealogies were still commoners, and not all gentlemen owned vast estates. A rich, landowning yeoman or a prosperous merchant was not a gentleman until he obtained a title,[51] and titles and genealogies could be purchased even when land was lacking. A member of the learned professions, for instance, could acquire a genealogy and coat of arms by virtue of his literacy.[52] Harrison's *Description of England* (1587) explicitly states,

> Whosoever studieth the laws of this realm, whoso abideth in the university giving his mind to his book. . . . can live without manual labor, and thereto is able and will bear the port, charge and countenance of a gentleman, he shall for money have a coat and arms bestowed upon him by the heralds (who in the charter of the same . . . pretend antiquity and service and many gay things), and thereunto being made so good cheap, be called master, which is the title that men give to esquires and gentlemen, and reputed for a gentleman ever after.[53]

For the new gentry that Harrison describes, gentility was doubly implicated in writing: it was based on the learning that permitted the educated to buy their titles and legitimated by the genealogies that were written to justify the titles they bought. Although the discourse of heraldry was based on the principle of heredity, it was the payments of the new gentry that enriched the heralds; and the heralds tended—in theory as

---

[51]Laslett, p. 29.
[52]Laslett, p. 33.
[53]William Harrison, *The Description of England*, ed. Georges Edelen (Ithaca: Cornell University Press, 1968), pp. 113–14.

well as in practice—to support their claims to nobility. The herald Sir John Ferne argued in *Blazon of Gentrie* (1586) that the new gentry, whose titles were based on personal virtue, better deserved to be called noble than those whose claims rested only on heredity. In *Catalogue of Honor* (1610), Thomas Milles, also a herald, argued that the basis of nobility was not blood but upbringing and education and that in schools children of lower birth, "in the same studies, strive with noblemen's children . . . with greater profit and praise."[54]

A mark and basis for social position, the literacy that enabled the new gentry to buy their way into the status system served, like the titles they acquired, to distinguish them from the great masses of their countrymen (and from even more of the women) who could neither read nor write.[55] A similarly unequal division marked off the province of historiography. Written by, about,

[54]Mervyn James, "English Politics and the Concept of Honour, 1485–1642," in *Society, Politics and Culture: Studies in Early Modern England* (New York: Cambridge University Press, 1986), pp. 382–83. Shakespeare's own family provides an excellent illustration of the uneasy relationship between new money and heraldic legitimation. As Samuel Schoenbaum reports, Shakespeare's father had first approached the College of Heralds some time after he became bailiff of Stratford in 1568, then let the matter drop when his financial reverses made the heralds' fees prohibitively expensive. The application was successfully brought to conclusion over twenty years later, abetted, no doubt, by the money William Shakespeare had earned writing for the stage. Nonetheless, the arms were granted in the first instance to Shakespeare's father, not only because he was the living head of the family but also because, as a former bailiff, his social position was higher than that of his playwright son. The writer of a 1602 document that attacked the validity of the newly-granted Shakespeare arms contemptuously labeled a sketch of them "Shakespear ye Player by Garter." On the other hand, among the trades and crafts Ferne considered qualified for coat armor were clothing manufacture, architecture, and "the art and skill of plays, practised in Theaters, and exposed to the spectacle of multitudes." See Schoenbaum's *William Shakespeare: A Compact Documentary Life* (New York: Oxford University Press, 1978), pp. 227–32, and James, p. 382.

[55]See David Cressy, *Literacy and the Social Order: Reading and Writing in Tudor and Stuart England* (Cambridge: Cambridge University Press, 1980). Here again Shakespeare himself makes a good case in point; although his literacy enabled him to earn the money that finally purchased John Shakespeare's coat of arms, it is very likely that both of his parents were illiterate. See M. C. Bradbrook, *Shakespeare: The Poet in His World* (London: Methuen, 1978), p. 10. Even Samuel Schoenbaum, who is unwilling to accept the general scholarly consensus, admits, "not a single autograph by [John Shakespeare] is extant" and that all the documents that required his signature are authorized with various marks (*A Compact Documentary Life*, pp. 37–38).

and for a privileged elite, Renaissance historiographic texts excluded the unlettered masses who constituted the majority of the population. The theater, by contrast, was accessible to the illiterate as well as to the learned. Adapting historical writing for oral theatrical performance, Shakespeare transgressed the socially significant boundary between writing and speech, but vestiges of this boundary survive in his texts, distinguishing the invented colloquial dialogues between commoners from the transcriptions of historical reports recited in the elevated language of his kings and noblemen. Shakespeare transcribes Holinshed's prose into the blank verse that assimilates his noble historical characters into the written, heroic tradition.[56] For his fictional characters, he invents a colloquial prose that associates them with the oral culture of the Elizabethan present. When Henry V reads in formal verse from the herald's list, the common soldiers disappear.[57] They are present only in the prose of the dialogue that Shakespeare invented for oral performance on his stage.

Theatrical creations, Shakespeare's commoners live in the Elizabethan present rather than the medieval past of his historical kings and noblemen. The Athenian gentry in *Midsummer Night's Dream* have names like Demetrius and Lysander, Hermia and Helena, Egeus and Philostrate. The noblest characters of all, Theseus and Hippolyta, are also the most firmly located in the classical past, being based on characters in Greek legends. By contrast, Bottom, Flute, Starveling, and Snout are creatures of the Elizabethan present. Analogues to this practice can be found in the plays of Shakespeare's predecessors, from Mak and Gyll in the *Second Shepherds' Play* to Rafe, Robin, and Dick in John Lyly's *Gallathea*, recognizable English characters who

[56]It is worth noting that Surrey's incomplete translation of Vergil's *Aeneid* (ca. 1538) was both the first example of English blank verse and the first English translation of the great Latin epic (Hyder Rollins and Herschel Baker, *The Renaissance in England* [Boston: D. C. Heath, 1954], p. 517).

[57]Not only its blank verse but also its structure as a list identifies the herald's report with writing as opposed to speech. As Walter Ong points out, "Normally in oral utterance nouns are not free-floating as in lists, but are embedded in sentences: rarely do we hear an oral recitation of simply a string of nouns—unless they are being read off a printed list." *Orality and Literacy: The Technologizing of the Word* (London: Methuen, 1982), p. 123.

interrupt the mythological action as they attempt to cope with the harsh, economic vicissitudes of recognizable contemporary worlds.

The restrictive protocols of historical writing excluded the nameless and illiterate masses who had no place in the council-chambers and battlefields where history was made and the genealogies and chronicles where it was recorded. They belong instead to the present world of oral theatrical performance. Both the status distinctions that separated the elite from the common and the new sense of anachronism that distinguished between past and present were closely implicated in the distinction between the written and the oral. The concept of anachronism that was transforming historical consciousness in Shakespeare's time was closely associated with the invention of printing and the proliferation of written texts. So long as events are transmitted in oral tradition, they are subject to a continual process of revision, removing inconsistencies and discrepancies, introducing unwitting anachronisms, and reshaping the past to suit the interests of each generation of storytellers. Once committed to writing, however, older accounts survive into the future to reveal the differences between past and present. The anachronistic paraphernalia of ordinary sixteenth-century life with which Shakespeare surrounds his lower-class characters bespeaks their affinity with the immediate theatrical occasion, their separation from the textualized world of the historical past.

The character who poses the greatest challenge to that separation is Falstaff, the degraded knight who insists on the prerogatives that belong to Sir John but goes by the anonymous, plebeian name of Jack and belongs to the plebeian, theatrical, anachronistically modern world of the Boar's Head Tavern that Shakespeare opposes to the historical action in the Henry IV plays.[58] Like the chameleon players of the antitheatrical tracts, Falstaff resists confinement to any single, defined place in the

[58]On the liminality of Falstaff's social position, see Michael Bristol, *Carnival and Theater*, p. 205. As Bristol points out, "Falstaff is socially as well as ethically ambivalent. He is Sir John, but prefers to name himself Jack, the most versatile and familiar name for every nameless hero of plebeian culture." On Falstaff's anachronism, see Weimann, *Shakespeare and the Popular Tradition*, p. 244. On Falstaff as clown, see David Wiles, *Shakespeare's Clown: Actor and Text in the Elizabethan Playhouse* (Cambridge: Cambridge University Press, 1987), pp. 116–35.

social hierarchy and thus threatens to destabilize the entire hierarchical order. Playing the roles of king and prince in the Boar's Head Tavern, Falstaff subverts the hierarchy not simply because of the subversive things he says but also because it is Falstaff who is saying them. When a person of lesser rank plays a king, the connection between culturally ascribed status and personal identity is necessarily exposed as arbitrary and mutable. Retaining the titles (king, prince) that authorized the powerful but changing their referents (fat Jack Falstaff, a common player), theatrical performance was always potentially subversive.

The most purely theatrical character in the *Henriad*, Falstaff is also the most subversive. The prince plays even more roles than Falstaff does, but from his first soliloquy, we know that no matter how long we have to wait, we will finally see the sunlike majesty that marks the mirror of all Christian kings and that beneath the roles there is a single, historically defined and historically responsible character. Falstaff, by contrast, exemplifies the many ways in which theatrical performance could subvert the historical record. A fictional character, he interrupts, retards, and parodies the historical action with his own theatrical plots and schemes, like the mock interview between king and prince at the Boar's Head Tavern that proleptically parodies the real one in the following scene, or the feigned death at the Battle of Shrewsbury that mimics Hotspur's true one. His language is equally subversive, equally opposed to the language of history. The elevated blank verse of Shakespeare's historical characters reproduces the ideological mystifications of the official historical record, but Falstaff's witty, irreverent prose constantly threatens to expose them. Not only the language that marks his status as a base, comic character, Falstaff's prose is also the emblem of his freedom, his origin in the disorderly theatrical world of unpredictable present speech, and his separation from the written discourse of official history, which is always already known, not only because the events have already occurred but because their interpretation has been determined in the very act of historiographic production.

Although plays were subject to censorship, the control of printed material, and of histories in particular, appears to have been much more stringent and effective. Histories of the recent past were especially risky, but even accounts of older times could be considered dangerous if they impugned the authority of church or state.[59] Renaissance beliefs that the past contained useful lessons and instructive analogues for the present made history valuable, but they also made it dangerous. A description of Richard II's inadequacies as a ruler could be taken to apply to Queen Elizabeth, as in the case of John Hayward's history, *The First Part of the Life and Raigne of King Henrie IIII*. The book was burned and Hayward was imprisoned for three years.[60] A comparison with Shakespeare's play of *Richard II* is instructive. Although Essex's followers sponsored its performance on the eve of their rebellion, neither the playwright nor the players were punished. They were, in fact, invited to play at court within a few days of Essex's trial.[61]

Players, like licensed fools, enjoyed a measure of freedom that could not be tolerated in the discourse of the powerful or in the empowered and empowering discourse of written historiography.[62] Moreover, the censorship of plays was more difficult and less effective than that of texts written for publication.

[59]On the censorship of historical writing, see F. Smith Fussner, *The Historical Revolution: English Historical Writing and Thought 1580–1640* (London: Routledge and Kegan Paul, 1962), pp. 37–41.

[60]On Hayward's history and his prosecution, see Lily B. Campbell, *Shakespeare's "Histories": Mirrors of Elizabethan Policy* (San Marino, Calif.: Huntington Library, 1968), pp. 182–92; Annabel Patterson, *Censorship and Interpretation: The Conditions of Writing and Reading in Early Modern England* (Madison: University of Wisconsin Press, 1984), pp. 44–48; and Margaret Dowling, "Sir John Hayward's Trouble over His *Life of Henry IV*," *The Library*, 4th ser. 11 (1931), 212–24.

[61]Paul Yachnin makes this point in "The Powerless Theater," forthcoming in *English Literary Renaissance*.

[62]I am indebted to Paul Yachnin for the connection between the relative powerlessness of plays and their freedom. On the comparison between players and licensed fools, see Philip Finkelpearl, "'The Comedians' Liberty:' Censorship of the Jacobean Stage Reconsidered," *English Literary Renaissance* 16 (1986), 123–38, especially p. 135. See also Christopher Hill, "Censorship and English Literature," in *Writing and Revolution in Seventeenth Century England* in *The Collected Essays of Christopher Hill* (Amherst: University of Massachusetts Press, 1985), 1:32–72. Hill makes the following points that are relevant to my argument: (1) Printed books were perceived as more dangerous and subjected to more stringent censorship than manuscript materials; (2) Books of history, particularly histories of English kings, were especially dangerous and subject to especially rigorous censorship (among other examples, he cites Holinshed as a case in point); (3) Despite censorship, subversive views did find expression on the stage.

It varied with the political and religious climate, the severity of officials, and the intercession, for or against the plays, of powerful persons. As E. K. Chambers points out, "the activities of the Master of the Revels did not [always] prevent the players from overstepping the boundaries of what . . . the government would tolerate. . . . Up to a point the players had a fairly free hand even with contemporary events."[63] Moreover, theatrical performance, by its very nature, defies comprehensive censorial control. The 1581 patent that assigned responsibility for the censorship of plays to the Master of the Revels required the players "to present and recite [their plays] before our said servant, or his sufficient deputy" before performing them in public; but the normal practice appears to have been to submit the written text of a play for censorship; objectionable material added in performance could only be censored after the fact. The possibilities for subversion were limited only by the actors' boldness and imagination: not only improvised speech, but gesture, expression, costume, intonation and stage-business could, as Chambers points out, "fill with malicious intention a scene which read harmlessly enough in the privacy of the censor's study."[64]

The blank verse into which Shakespeare transcribed the official historical record was designed for *recitation*, for speech that reproduced writing. It required reasonably faithful reproduction on stage; the metrical structure of the lines not only militated against improvisation but also tended to predetermine by its

---

[63]*The Elizabethan Stage*, 1:322. On the censorship of plays, see Chambers, pp. 318–28; Clare, 169–83; and Gerald Eades Bentley, *The Profession of Dramatist in Shakespeare's Time, 1590–1642* (Princeton: Princeton University Press, 1971), pp. 145–196. See also Andrew Cairncross's introduction to the Arden edition of *2 Henry VI*, pp. xv–xix. Cairncross makes the point that "the degree of theatrical censorship varied with the political and religious atmosphere of the time."

[64]See Bentley's account in *The Profession of Dramatist*, pp. 164–65, of the case of Jonson's *Magnetic Lady*, in which playwright and censor were both exonerated from blame because the offending lines had not been present in the original manuscript that the censor read but were added by the players in performance. See also Hamlet's warning to the players, "let those that play your clowns speak no more than is set down for them" (III.ii.38–40) and his last-minute revision of *The Murther of Gonzago* (II.ii.541–42: "a speech of some dozen lines, or sixteen lines, which I would set down and insert in't") to give the play a dangerous topical relevance.

own music the tonal coloring of the actor's speech. Prose exerts less control on its speaker, and it is also more difficult to memorize exactly.[65] Falstaff's prose, with its seemingly inexhaustible capacity for wordplay and improvisation, vividly exemplifies this spontaneity and uncontrollability. It directly opposes the rigidity of official language and defies the regulation of prior restraint to which written texts were always subject in an age of censorship.

Falstaff's irrepressible, irreverent wit epitomizes the unruliness of present oral speech, which, unlike a written text, can never be fully subjugated to official censorship and authoritative control. Every aspect of Falstaff's characterization, his language, no less than his actions, makes him a threat to the historiographic project. Opportunistic, self-willed, and dangerously charming—both to the future king and to the audience—Falstaff threatens to decenter the historical plot and demystify the historical record. It is significant, I believe, that in the comic world of *The Merry Wives of Windsor*, Falstaff can be included in the final feast, even though he has devoted all his energies for five acts to seducing the Windsor wives and swindling their husbands. In the historical world of the *Henriad*, he must be banished and finally killed.

Fluellen's comparison of Henry V to the hero he insists upon calling "Alexander the Pig" (IV.vii.24–50) makes the connection. A parodic representation of the humanist historians who ran-

---

[65]This difficulty must have been even greater in Shakespeare's time than it is now. As Gerald Eades Bentley points out in *The Profession of Player in Shakespeare's Time: 1590–1642* (Princeton: Princeton University Press, 1984), p. 82, "Not only were most companies producing scores of new plays, but in the earlier years of the period, 1590–1610, rarely was a play given consecutive performances. . . . Under such conditions, a letter-perfect rendition must have been unheard of." On the recognition that verse is an aid to memory, see Sidney's *Defense of Poesy*, pp. 33–34. Sidney says that the fact that "verse far exceeds prose in the knitting up of the memory" is "a thing . . . known to all men," evidenced by the fact that anyone who "ever was scholar" will remember "even to his old age" some of the verses of "Virgil, Horace, or Cato which in his youth he learned" and that in all the arts "from grammar to logic, mathematics, physic, and the rest, the rules chiefly necessary to be borne away are compiled in verses." "The reason," Sidney says, "is manifest": "The words . . . being so set as one cannot be lost, but the whole work fails, which, accusing itself, calls the remembrance back to itself and so most strongly confirms it. Besides, one word so (as it were) begetting another, as be it in rhyme or measured verse, by the former a man shall have a near guess to the follower."

sacked classical texts to find models for modern princes, Fluellen finds fishy analogies wherever he looks. He is struck by the fact that "there is a river in Macedon" and likewise "a river at Monmouth" and that "there is salmons in both," but his final proof that Henry V belongs in the tradition of heroic history exemplified by Alexander the Great is Henry's repudiation of Falstaff:

> If you mark Alexander's life well, Harry of Monmouth's life is come after it indifferent well; for there is figures in all things . . . as Alexander kill'd his friend Clytus, being in his ales and his cups; so also Harry Monmouth, being in his right wits and his good judgments, turn'd away the fat knight with the great belly doublet. He was full of jests, and gipes, and knaveries, and mocks—I have forgot his name. (IV.vii.26–50)[66]

What the historian forgets is as significant as what he remembers. In this case, the forgetting marks a site of danger, the place where the historical name of Sir John Oldcastle was erased.[67] The epilogue to 2 *Henry IV* emphatically states that "Oldcastle died [a] martyr, and this is not the man," anxiously attempting to contain the disorderly theatrical energy that Fal-

[66]In addition to the general parody of humanist historiography, Shakespeare may have been thinking more specifically of Francis Meres's *Palladis Tamia: Wits Treasury* (1598), which included "A Comparative Discourse of Our English Poets with the Greeke, Latine, and Italian Poets." The "Discourse," along with dozens of other not terribly illuminating comparisons between English writers and classical precedents, celebrates Shakespeare's early plays in a famous, if fatuous, comparison: "As Plautus and Seneca are accounted the best for comedy and tragedy among the Latins, so Shakespeare among the English is the most excellent in both kinds for the stage" (quoted in Smith, *Elizabethan Critical Essays*, 2:317–18).

[67]Cf. Harry Levin, "Shakespeare's Nomenclature," in *Shakespeare and the Revolution of the Times: Perspectives and Commentaries* (New York: Oxford University Press, 1976), p. 76: "Mistress Page cannot hit upon Falstaff's name, and even the conscientious Fluellen has forgotten it. Would they have remembered Oldcastle, we wonder?" Levin's allusion to Mistress Page recalls the doubled name of Ford's pseudonym in *Merry Wives*. The Folio version is "Broome," but the Quarto version is "Brooke," the family name of the sixteenth-century descendants of Oldcastle who probably brought the pressure that caused both of the names to be changed. For a detailed account of the matter, see the Arden edition of *The Merry Wives of Windsor*, ed. H. J. Oliver (London: Methuen, 1971), pp. lii–lviii.

staff represented in Shakespeare's world as well as his stage.[68] Erasing the name of Oldcastle, Shakespeare severs the connection between his disreputable theatrical creation and its original historical namesake in order to evade censorship and prosecution. Named for the real historical Oldcastle, the character would have real historical consequences for the players in the enmity of Oldcastle's present descendants. Dehistoricized by the name of Falstaff, he acquires the impotence (fall-staff) of fiction, but he also acquires its license.

The fact that it is Fluellen who does the forgetting is also significant. Because Fluellen is a historian, he can tell that Alexander's historical friend was called Cleitus, but he cannot recall the unhistorical name of Falstaff, even though he vividly remembers his physical appearance (the great-belly doublet) and theatrical performance (the jests, gipes, knaveries, and mocks). Like the anonymous soldiers killed at the Battle of Agincourt, Falstaff has no place in the historical record. Fully versed in the "disciplines of war," Fluellen is equally expert in the protocols that governed the discourse of Renaissance historiography. The transhistorical system of analogies that found "figures in all things" defines Henry's historical significance by likening him to Alexander. The exclusive protocols of Renaissance historiography determine the price Henry must pay to take his place in the historical record. Jack Falstaff is turned away on the new king's coronation day and never allowed on stage in *Henry V*.

As soon as he enters the textualized domain of official history, Henry must banish "plump Jack" and with him "all the world" (*1 Henry IV*: II.iv.479–80) of messy, corporeal theatrical life. "Make less thy body hence," he commands (*2 Henry IV*: V.v.52), rejecting the embodied physical life that Falstaff's corpulence exuberantly presents on Shakespeare's stage. To assume his historical role as Henry V, the new king must banish his own

[68]For accounts of the renaming of Oldcastle as Falstaff, see the Arden edition of *2 Henry IV*, ed. A. R. Humphreys (London: Methuen, 1966), pp. xv–xx, and the Variorum edition of *1 Henry IV*, ed. Samuel Burdett Hemingway (Philadelphia: Lippincott, 1936), pp. 447–56. Even the new name caused anxiety— and for the same reasons. See the Arden edition of *1 Henry IV*, ed. A. R. Humphreys (London: Methuen, 1967), pp. xvii–xviii for seventeenth-century protests against the use of the name of the historical Sir John Falstaffe, who was in his own time "a noble valiant souldier" and "a *Martial man* of merit."

former self along with the fat knight.[69] Entering the "reality" of history, he disclaims his own former life with Falstaff in the fictional, contemporary world of the Boar's Head Tavern as a mere dream: "I have long dreamt of such a kind of man . . . but being awak'd, I do despise my dream" (2 *Henry IV*: V.v.49–51). Inscribed and circumscribed by his coronation in the discourse of history, Henry V can no longer see beyond its limits. "I know thee not, old man," he says to Falstaff at the beginning of the banishment speech, and the historical king who appears in *Henry V* never has any contact with the low comic characters who were his constant companions in the two parts of *Henry IV* or admits that he ever knew them.

When Fluellen reports (III.vi) that one of the Duke of Exeter's men "is like to be executed for robbing a church, one Bardolph, if your majesty know the man. His face is all bubukles, and whelks, and knobs, and flames a'fire," the king does not admit that he knows the man. All Henry says is, "We would have all such offenders so cut off," ignoring the vivid corporeality of Fluellen's description and his own previous acquaintance with Bardolph, disposing of the whole messy issue (and of Bardolph's life) by consigning him to the abstract category of "such offenders."[70] Having entered history, Henry V reveals no knowledge of anything that was not included in the historical record, like the disreputable theatrical creations who surrounded Prince Hal in the *Henry IV* plays and the identity of the church robber (who, like the twenty-five common English

[69]In a sense, he must also banish Shakespeare's theater audience. Marjorie Garber makes this point in "'What's Past Is Prologue': Temporality and Prophecy in Shakespeare's History Plays," in *Renaissance Genres: Essays on Theory, History, and Interpretation*, ed. Barbara Kiefer Lewalski (Cambridge: Harvard University Press, 1986), p. 330. As Garber points out, the "I know you all" of Hal's soliloquy at the end of the second scene of 1 *Henry IV*, uttered on an empty stage, implicates the audience. "I . . . will a while uphold / The unyok'd humor of your idleness" refers not only to the disorderly doings of the characters at the Boar's Head Tavern but also to the idle, potentially disorderly audience in Shakespeare's theater. Once Hal enters history, he will have to banish both.

[70]As Anne Barton points out ("The King Disguised," p. 105), Henry's "sudden use here of the first person plural of majesty, occurring as it does in a scene where even the French herald Montjoy is addressed by Henry as 'I,' constitutes the real answer to Fluellen's question. As a twin-natured being, the king is stripped not only of personal friends but also of a private past."

soldiers killed at Agincourt, was mentioned, but not named, in the chronicles).

Like the chorus, the king (who often speaks with the same voice as the chorus), can see his life only in heroic, historic terms. The chorus repeatedly insists on the inadequacy of theatrical representation: the "unworthy scaffold" (Pro.10), the "vile and ragged foils (right ill-dispos'd, in brawl ridiculous)" that will "disgrace . . . the name of Agincourt" (IV.Cho.49–52). The history-making king seems subject to the chorus's repressions. He seems to have forgotten his personal, theatrical history in the *Henry IV* plays: although his former companions still speak of him, he never mentions their names. In the same way, the chorus at the beginning of each act advertises the historical business to come, but never acknowledges the existence of the comic scenes that increasingly intrude to interrupt and retard the progress of the historical plot and parody the heroic action (two in act II, three in act III, and so on).[71]

At the beginning of act II, for instance, the chorus tells us how "all the youth of England are on fire" to follow "the mirror of all Christian kings" to France and promises to take us first to Southampton and then to France. In the scene that follows, however, we are taken not to Southampton but to London, where we see Pistol and Nym quarreling over Nell Quickly and hear of Falstaff's illness, his heart, like Nell's language, "fracted" (II.i.124) by his separation from the king. The promised scene at Southampton follows, depicting the exposure of the three traitors, motivated, as the chorus said they would be, by French bribery (not by the Yorkist claim to Henry's throne) and ending with Henry's rousing couplet, delivered in the triumphant idiom of the chorus:

[71]Not all of those comic scenes deal with commoners. In act III, scene iv, for instance, Shakespeare shows the French Princess Katherine taking a lesson in English, a lesson devoted entirely to the names for the parts of the body. Although Katherine is a princess, she too was marginalized in Shakespeare's historical sources, reduced to a term in the peace treaty that Henry negotiated with her father. Like the commoners, she provides a fictional comic interlude in the historical action, and like them she speaks in a language that marks her exclusion from the discourse of English patriarchal authority and associates her with the embodied life that eluded historiographic narration. For a fuller account of Katherine's role, see Chapter 4.

> Cheerly to sea! The signs of war advance!
> No king of England, if not king of France!

But we don't go to France, at least not yet. Another London scene intrudes, where we hear the Hostess mangle the king's English in a poignant account of Falstaff's death[72] and Pistol's antiheroic echo to Henry's glorious, patriotic rhetoric:

> Let us to France, like horse-leeches, my boys,
> To suck, to suck, the very blood to suck!
>
> (II.iii.55–56)

From this point on, Shakespeare keeps obtruding the unhistorical characters who challenge the heroic story until the king finally confronts them in that theatrical scene on the night before the Battle of Agincourt when he disguises himself as a common soldier for whom he invents the name Harry le Roy. The invented name is significant: it looks backward to the youthful "Harry" who mingled with the fictional lowlifes in the Boar's Head Tavern, and it looks forward to the historical title that Henry V hopes to win in France; it bespeaks Henry's double role as theatrical player and history-making king even as it conceals his identity. In this scene, the theatrical interlude that the player king Harry le Roy and the common player William Shakespeare invented for the night before the great, historical climax of the play, Henry and the audience are forced to hear an eloquent challenge to the official version of events and a powerful case against war itself, that is, against the king's entire historical enterprise. The character who makes the case is a theatrical creation, a common soldier for whom William Shakespeare invented the name of Williams.

Williams initiates his argument with a curious image: If the king's "cause be not good," he says,

> the King himself hath a heavy reckoning to make, when all those
> legs, and arms, and heads, chopp'd off in a battle, shall join

---

[72]The placement of the account of Falstaff's death is suggestive: if Falstaff must be banished before Henry can become king, it also seems that he must die before Henry can confirm his kingship at Agincourt ("No king of England, if not king of France").

together at the latter day and cry all, "We died at such a place"—
some swearing, some crying for a surgeon, some upon their wives
left poor behind them, some upon the debts they owe, some upon
their children rawly left." (IV.i.134–41)

Unlike the other fictional commoners in the Henriad, Williams
is allowed to speak standard English. Not for him the regional
dialects of Fluellen, Jamy, and Macmorris, the stagy absurdities
of Pistol's language, or the wonderful malapropisms by which
Nell Quickly announces her illiteracy—linguistic deformities
that bespeak their exclusion from the dominant official discourse
of the King's English. But Williams does not really speak for
himself, and he speaks with great difficulty. Recalling the nameless soldiers killed in the battle and the suffering wives and
children left behind in England and excluded from the historical
action, Williams gives voice to the forgotten casualties of Henry's great historical enterprise. Preposterously attributing that
voice to the legs and arms and heads chopped off (*dismembered*)
in battle but still swearing and crying, he re-members the
speechless, embodied life that was forgotten by the historical
record.

*Henry V* is not the only play in which Shakespeare associates
a character who shares his own name with inarticulate, humble
life obliterated by the elite textualized world of his betters. In
*As You Like It* (V.i), the country swain William, who can barely
speak, let alone read or write, loses his sweetheart to the courtier
Touchstone, who cites Ovid (III.iii.8), quarrels "in print, by the
book" (V.iv.90), and declares that he would prefer a "poetical"
love to an "honest" one (III.iii.16–29). In *2 Henry IV*, Shakespeare interrupts the historical action with invented scenes set
in Gloucestershire, full of local color and homely details that
evoke the texture of real country life. We hear talk of pippins
and leathercoats, shoeing and plough-irons, young capons and
short-legged hens, John Doit of Staffordshire and Will Squele,
a Cotswold man.[73] "William," in fact, appears to be the most
popular name in this neighborhood. Like the graffiti sprayed
on our own city walls at night and in secrecy, it marks the
neighborhood with the name of an invisible owner and stakes

[73]Cf. the discussion of the Gloucestershire scenes in Chapter 3, section V.

his claim to it. Davy's dishonest friend is "William Visor of Woncote" (V.i.38). "William" is the three-times repeated name of Shallow's cook (V.i.10, 16, 28). And almost the first thing we hear in Gloucestershire is Shallow's inquiry about his cousin, a young student at Oxford, who may or may not be a good scholar (III.ii.9–11). Like William Visor and William cook, this character never appears on stage. His name is William Silence.

Finally, there is that other schoolboy William, the one we meet in *Merry Wives of Windsor*, the inhabitant of another country village rich with the closely observed details of daily life: the contents of Mistress Ford's laundry basket and the list of Mistress Quickly's household chores (washing, wringing, brewing, baking, scouring, dressing meat and drink, and making the beds: I.iv.96–97). In a scene with no clear relevance to the main action, young William Page is brought on stage to take a lesson in Latin grammar (IV.i). Worried that the boy "profits nothing in the world at his book," his mother asks his tutor, Parson Evans, to quiz his pupil on the grammar of the learned, written language. Here, as in *Henry V*, Shakespeare parodies classical learning by making its purveyor a Welshman who "makes fritters of English" (V.v.143), and here too he opposes the written ancient language with present speech that invokes the disorderly demands of embodied life.[74] He opposes it, in fact, with what is quite literally a vulgar (or mother) tongue, for an illiterate woman keeps interrupting William's lesson, misconstruing the Latin words he recites because their spoken sounds remind her of English bawdry. Asked to recite the "genitive case," William responds "*Genetivo, horum, harum, horum*," but Mistress Quickly interrupts, "Vengeance of Jinny's case! Fie on her! Never name her, child, if she be a whore." Disrupting an inept male discourse of written learning with comical invocations of disreputable, embodied female life, her comments serve a parodic

---

[74]See Patricia Parker, *Literary Fat Ladies: Rhetoric, Gender, Property* (London: Methuen, 1987), pp. 27–41, for a suggestive discussion of the ways this scene opposes "humanism (with its pedagogical economy of men and boys)" to "an extravagantly errant female speech, the female in question being that seemingly irrepressible producer of malapropisms, Mistress Quickly." For the sociopolitical dimensions of this opposition, see Allon White, "'The Dismal Sacred Word': Academic Language and the Social Reproduction of Seriousness," *Literature/Teaching/Politics* 2 (1983), 4–15.

function very much like those of the fictional comic scenes that interrupt the historical action in the Henry IV plays and *Henry V*. Shakespeare uses the illiterate, common woman to parody the discourse of written historical learning and to invoke the disorderly common life that transgresses the social and linguistic protocols dividing the nameable from the nameless.

I have digressed to discuss these other Williams because I believe they help to show what issues are at stake in the Williams scenes in *Henry V*. The last time we see Williams is at the end of the Battle of Agincourt, when the king stages an encounter between him and Fluellen, suggesting an attempt to negotiate an alliance between the textualized world of the historical past represented by Fluellen's constant citations of classical precedents and the embodied speech of plebeian oral culture represented by Williams' invocation of the dismembered bodies of the common soldiers and the wives and children they left behind. But the attempted negotiation ends on an ambiguous note. The king presents Williams with a gift of money, thus seeming to pay tribute to the subversive plebeian voice that threatened to discredit his great historical project,[75] but when Fluellen offers Williams a "silling" (IV.viii.71), Williams refuses to take it. Fluellen reiterates his offer, but their dialogue is interrupted by the arrival of the herald who enters with the document from which Henry reads Holinshed's list of the noblemen who died in the battle. After this, Williams never speaks again.

Williams is the only character in *Henry V* who ever manages to confront the king with a challenge to the official version of events. Accepting the challenge and attempting to satisfy Williams with a gift of gold crowns, Henry attempts to come to terms with (in fact, to re-appropriate) the embodied human life

[75]Or perhaps to buy it, or buy it off. Presenting Williams with a *gift* of money, Henry mystifies their relationship in terms of the older code of feudal service and noble largesse, a code that had been radically transformed even by Henry's time by the use of mercenary armies. Essex's contemporary campaign in Ireland, compared in the chorus to act V to Henry's French invasion, also relied on mercenaries. See Keen, *Chivalry*, chap. 12, "Chivalry and War"; and Cohen, *Drama of a Nation*, p. 140. For the suggestion that Henry is trying to buy Williams off, see Marilyn L. Williamson, "The Episode with Williams in *Henry V*," *SEL* 9 (1969), 280: "The point of argument between Henry and Williams is the question of whether Henry might ransom himself to the French. . . . Though Henry does not pay off that quarrel, he does fulfill Williams's prophecy about him in small by stopping their quarrel with payment."

he sacrificed to take his place in history. In act V, he woos the French princess, not only as a victorious king but also as a plain man. The mythical figure of the great rhetorician described at the beginning of the play—"when he speaks, the air, a charter'd libertine, is still, and the mute wonder lurketh in men's ears, to steal his sweet and honeyed sentences" (I.i.47–50)—gives way to the inarticulate human wooer depicted in act V. Henry plans a human, corporeal future with the French princess he insists upon calling by the English colloquial name of Kate. Their triumphant union will be embodied in a triumphant son: "Shall not thou and I, between Saint Denis and Saint George, compound a boy, half French, half English, that shall go to Constantinople and take the Turk by the beard?" (V.ii.206–09). In this scene Henry plans a victory over time that will be won on the battlefield of his own face: "The elder I wax, the better I shall appear. My comfort is that old age, that ill layer-up of beauty, can do no more spoil upon my face" (V.ii.229–31).

For the wooing scene, Shakespeare went not to the historical chronicles but to an old play, *The Famous Victories of Henry the Fifth*. With the final chorus, however, he returns to the historical record to refute Henry's confident expectations of long, human life. The chorus interrupts before Henry can even marry Kate, predicting Henry's early death and limiting the action to the military and political. Announcing Henry's historically ordained destiny, the unanswerable chorus denies his human aspiration for long life, just as the force of history has eradicated all the characters who speak for common humanity: Falstaff banished to die of a broken heart, Bardolph executed for a minor theft, and Williams silenced by the entrance of the herald with the written historical document. The document, like the chorus, represents the closure of the historical record. Silenced Williams, like his predecessor William Silence and his maker William Shakespeare, marks its exclusions.

# Index

*Library of Congress Cataloging-in-publication Data*

Rackin, Phyllis.
    Stages of history : Shakespeare's English chronicles / Phyllis
Rackin.
        p.    cm.
    Includes bibliographical references and index.
    ISBN 0-8014-2430-5 (cloth : alkaline paper). —ISBN 0-8014-9698-5
(paper : alkaline paper)
    1. Shakespeare, William, 1564-1616—Histories.   2. Historical
drama, English—History and criticism.   3. Great Britain—
History—1066-1687—Historiography.   4. Great Britain in
literature.   I. Title.
PR2982.R34
822.3'3—dc20                                            90-55196